52 WEEKS

• THROUGH THE •

BIBLE

A YEAR-LONG BIBLE STUDY

JOHN MACARTHUR

HarperChristian Resources

52 Weeks Through the Bible

Published in Grand Rapids, Michigan, by HarperChristian Resources. HarperChristian Resources is a registered trademark of HarperCollins Christian Publishing, Inc.

Requests for information should be sent to customercare@harpercollins.com.

ISBN 978-0-310-16910-9 (softcover)
ISBN 978-0-310-16911-6 (ebook)

Material used in the introduction to each week, the reflections, and the study questions are adapted from the MacArthur Bible Studies published by HarperChristian Resources. Material used in the introduction to the Old Testament, introduction to the New Testament, and content related to the Song of Songs is adapted from *The MacArthur Study Bible*, copyright © 2004 by Thomas Nelson, and *The MacArthur Bible Commentary*, by John MacArthur, copyright © 2005 Thomas Nelson Publishers.

Information included in the callouts adapted from *The MacArthur Study Bible*, copyright © 2004 by Thomas Nelson, and *The MacArthur Bible Commentary*, by John MacArthur, copyright © 2005 Thomas Nelson Publishers.

Image of the tabernacle (week 2) taken from *The MacArthur Study Bible*, copyright © 2004 by Thomas Nelson. Images of Solomon's Temple (week 10) and Herod's Temple (week 38) generated by InsideOut Creative Arts (www.insideoutcreativearts.com).

All maps were created based on information found in *The MacArthur Study Bible*, copyright © 2004 by Thomas Nelson; *The MacArthur Bible Commentary*, by John MacArthur, copyright © 2005 Thomas Nelson Publishers; and *Nelson's Complete Book of Bible Maps and Charts*, third edition, © 1996 by Thomas Nelson.

First Printing November 2024 / Printed in the United States of America

CONTENTS

THE OLD TESTAMENT

THE NEW TESTAMENT

THE OLD TESTAMENT

"Ezra opened the book in the sight of all the people. . . . They read distinctly from the book, in the Law of God; and they gave the sense, and helped them to understand the reading" (Nehemiah 8:5, 8). Although this momentous renewal of interest in Scripture occurred more than 2,400 years ago, this has been the primary need of every subsequent generation: to read and understand the Bible and thereby know the blessing of God (see Revelation 1:3).

This is the goal of *52 Weeks Through the Bible*—to lead you day by day through selected passages of Scripture over the course of the next year, provide you with an overview of the content you are reading, give you a few reflections on what you have read, and then prompt you to respond with study questions—all with the goal of helping you to truly know and understand the Word of God. You will spend roughly the first half of the year (Weeks 1–27) in the Old Testament, reading approximately two to six selected chapters of the Bible each day (with the exception being the books of 1 and 2 Chronicles, which have content that is covered in other books—including 1 and 2 Samuel and 1 and 2 Kings).

The Old Testament can be broken into five sections. The first five books (Genesis–Deuteronomy) form a literary unit called the Pentateuch, meaning "five scrolls." The five books of the Pentateuch were written as an unbroken unity in content and historical sequence, with each succeeding book beginning where the last left off. The Pentateuch begins with God's creation of the universe (Genesis 1:1), relates the story of Abraham and the patriarchs, covers the exodus of the Hebrews from Egypt, and ends with Moses' speeches to the people before they enter Canaan, which God had promised to give to them. Moses is traditionally held to be the author the Pentateuch (see Exodus 17:14; 24:4; Numbers 33:1–2; Deuteronomy 31:9), and thus another title for the collection is "The Books of Moses."

The next section of the Old Testament (Joshua–Esther) is known as the historical books. These twelve books begin with the rise of Israel in conquering the land of Canaan under the leadership of Joshua. This is followed by a period in which the people of Israel were ruled over first by judges (enduring many foreign invasions) and then by kings (Saul, David, and Solomon). This is followed by a period of decline in which the nation was divided into two separate kingdoms: Israel in the north and Judah in the south. The kingdom of Israel then comes to an end with the invasion of Assyria, with its people generally assimilated into the foreign empire's culture. Judah comes to an end with the invasion of Babylon, though its people are preserved in exile from their homeland. Eventually, under the Persians, the Jewish exiles are allowed to return in waves to Jerusalem, ending the post-exilic period.

The next section of the Old Testament (Job–Song of Songs) is known as the wisdom books. These five books portray a wide range of life circumstances from a divine perspective. Some are theological in purpose, probing the deeper meaning of life (Job and Ecclesiastes); others expose the more obvious practicalities of life (Proverbs and Song of Songs); and one book (Psalms) is comprised of a collection of sacred songs or poems that were used in worship.

The final two sections of the Old Testament are known as the major prophets (Isaiah–Daniel) and minor prophets (Hosea–Malachi). This division is made according to the relative lengths of the books, with the major prophets generally being longer and the minor prophets being shorter. (Lamentations is included among the major prophets because of its connection with Jeremiah.) The writing prophets appeared during the period of the divided kingdom in Israel's history, generally warning the people of God's judgments if they did not turn from their idolatry and sin, and continued through the post-exilic period. The period of the writing prophets ended about 400 years before the coming of Christ.

As you go through this Bible study over the course of the next year, remember that even with the wealth of books, apps, and resources available today, the Bible remains the only source of divine revelation and power that can sustain you in your walk with Christ. The Bible is the *source* of God's truth (see John 17:17). It is the *source* of God's blessing when it is obeyed (see Luke 11:28). It is the *source* of your victory over Satan when you wield it as a weapon (see Ephesians 6:17). It is the *source* of spiritual growth in your life (see 1 Peter 2:2). It is the *source* of your power as a follower of Christ (see Romans 1:16). It is also the *source* of God's guidance on how you should live (see Psalm 119:105).

The Bible is important for you as a follower of Christ because it contains God's mind and will for your life. It is *infallible* in its totality (see Psalm 19:7). It is *inerrant* in its parts (see Proverbs 30:5–6). It is *complete* (see Revelation 22:18–19), *authoritative*, and *final* (see Psalm 119:89). It is totally *sufficient* for your needs (see 2 Timothy 3:16–17). The Bible will accomplish what it *promises* (see Isaiah 55:11) and will provide the *assurance of your salvation* when you obey its commands (see John 8:14).

The psalmist wrote, "Blessed is the man who walks not in the counsel of the ungodly, nor stands in the path of sinners, nor sits in the seat of the scornful; but his delight is in the law of the Lord, and in His law he meditates day and night. He shall be like a tree planted by the rivers of water, that brings forth its fruit in its season, whose leaf also shall not wither; and whatever he does shall prosper" (Psalm 1:1–3). This is the goal of *52 Weeks Through the Bible*—to help you delight in the Word of God as you meditate on its truths, apply its teachings to your life, and allow its wisdom to transform every aspect of your being. In this way, you will experience a blessed and fruitful life as you journey with God.

WEEK 1

GOD ALWAYS KEEPS HIS PROMISES

GENESIS 1–36

DAILY READINGS: **1** | Genesis 1–4 **2** | Genesis 6–9 **3** | Genesis 10–11 **4** | Genesis 12–16 **5** | Genesis 17–22 **6** | Genesis 23–27 **7** | Genesis 28–33

Every story, like every life, has a beginning. So it is no surprise the Bible begins the story of mankind at the very beginning, before there was life of any kind and the world had just been shaped. Yet even then there was one life—God, who is Life. We see Him issuing commands from heaven while also hovering over the waters of the newly formed planet earth.

God's last act of creation was to pick up some soil and fashion man (Adam), as a sculptor might mold clay. He breathed life into man's nostrils and then formed the female (Eve) from the male. God planted a garden using the plants and life forms He had already created and placed the man and his wife there. Finally, He gave the man a task. Adam spent his first day of life getting to know God's creation and bestowing names on all the animals.

God had told Adam that he could eat from any tree in the garden except the tree of knowledge of good and evil. At this time, there was no death in the world—all God's creation was at peace. But everything changed when Adam and Eve disobeyed God. The animals became hostile to them and to one another. Thorns and thistles sprang up where once only edible plants had grown. Worst of all, suffering and death entered the world.

Adam and Eve were forced to leave the garden. Soon after, their first son, Cain, was born, followed by Abel. The Scripture suggests that God had explained to Adam and his family how to enter His presence with proper sacrifices, with God Himself making the first animal sacrifice in the garden. So when Cain brought an offering of fruits and vegetables, it was rejected by God, while the sacrifice of an animal offered by his brother, Abel, was accepted. This made Cain angry, and he murdered his brother.

Time passed, but the condition of mankind did not improve. Roughly 1,500 years after creation, the wickedness on earth was so great that God decided to send a flood in judgment. Only one righteous man, Noah, was found to become a second Adam. The flood lasted for forty days. After the waters receded, God promised to never again send a flood to destroy mankind. It was then up to Noah and his family to reestablish the human race, repopulating the planet and building towns, villages, and cities.

All of mankind, at this point, spoke one language—probably the language that Adam spoke with God in the garden of Eden. Having one common language made it possible for mankind to unite together in carrying out great projects. But this changed when the people gathered together to build a great city, with a tower reaching into the heavens, to bring glory to themselves. Man was still intent on becoming a god unto himself, excluding the lordship of the Creator. So the Lord confused mankind's language, making it more difficult for humanity to join together in an effort to become "like God."

Many years later, one of Noah's descendants, a man named Abram, was living in the city of Ur. He was seventy-five years old when God told him to travel to a distant land that would be revealed to him. Abram was to leave his family and friends behind—with the exception of his wife, Sarai, and his nephew, Lot—and head to a place with a different culture and in which he knew no one. Abram obeyed the word of the Lord and eventually arrived in the land of Canaan, which by that time had been settled by the descendants of Ham (a son of Noah). God then made a promise to Abram that in spite of his old age, He would make him into a great nation. God made it clear this promise would come through a son of miraculous birth—a child born through the union of Abram and his wife, Sarai.

But as the years passed, Sarai doubted God's promise. Even worse, she convinced her husband to *act* on her doubts, giving her handmaid Hagar to him. Sarai's scheme did lead to a birth, as Hagar bore a son named Ishmael. But God rejected Ishmael as the son of promise, and Sarai's plan led to tension and division in the family. When God's promised son was finally born to Abram and Sarai—who by then were renamed Abraham and Sarah—she called him Isaac, which means "he laughs." But one person's laughter proved to be the source of another's jealousy, and Ishmael started to mock Isaac's status. This led Sarah—who had persuaded Abraham to have the child with Hagar—to call for them to be cast out.

God provided for Hagar and Ishmael, but His covenant continued through the line of Isaac. However, when Isaac was older—between the ages of fourteen and twenty-one—God told Abraham to put Isaac to death as a sacrifice to Him. How would God's promise come to pass if Isaac died so young? The command made no sense to Abraham, but he trusted God and obeyed. When God saw that Abraham was faithful even in carrying out this instruction, He provided a sacrificial ram and spared Isaac's life.

Isaac married a woman named Rebekah, who bore him twin sons: Esau and Jacob. Esau, being the eldest (if only by seconds or minutes), was given his family's birthright. But Esau foolishly traded it to his younger brother for a bowl of stew, and then Jacob schemed with his mother to deceive his father into giving him the blessing of that birthright. Esau was angry and vowed to kill Jacob, so Jacob fled to live with his mother's brother, Laban, for a time.

Jacob fell in love with Rachel, Laban's younger daughter, and agreed to work for seven years for her hand in marriage. But when the wedding arrived, Laban substituted her older sister, Leah, forcing Jacob to work another seven years to gain Rachel's hand. This led to tensions in Jacob's family, which only increased when children began to arrive. After many years, family friction grew to the point where Jacob and Laban could no longer live together. So Jacob headed back toward Bethel and his homeland.

Esau learned of his arrival and rode out to meet him with 400 men. In desperation, Jacob called on the Lord—and God arrived, in the form of a man who wrestled with him throughout the night. As the new day broke, the Lord gave Jacob a limp but also a blessing and a new name. Emboldened, Jacob went out the next day (with gifts) to meet Esau. The two brothers embraced and were reconciled.

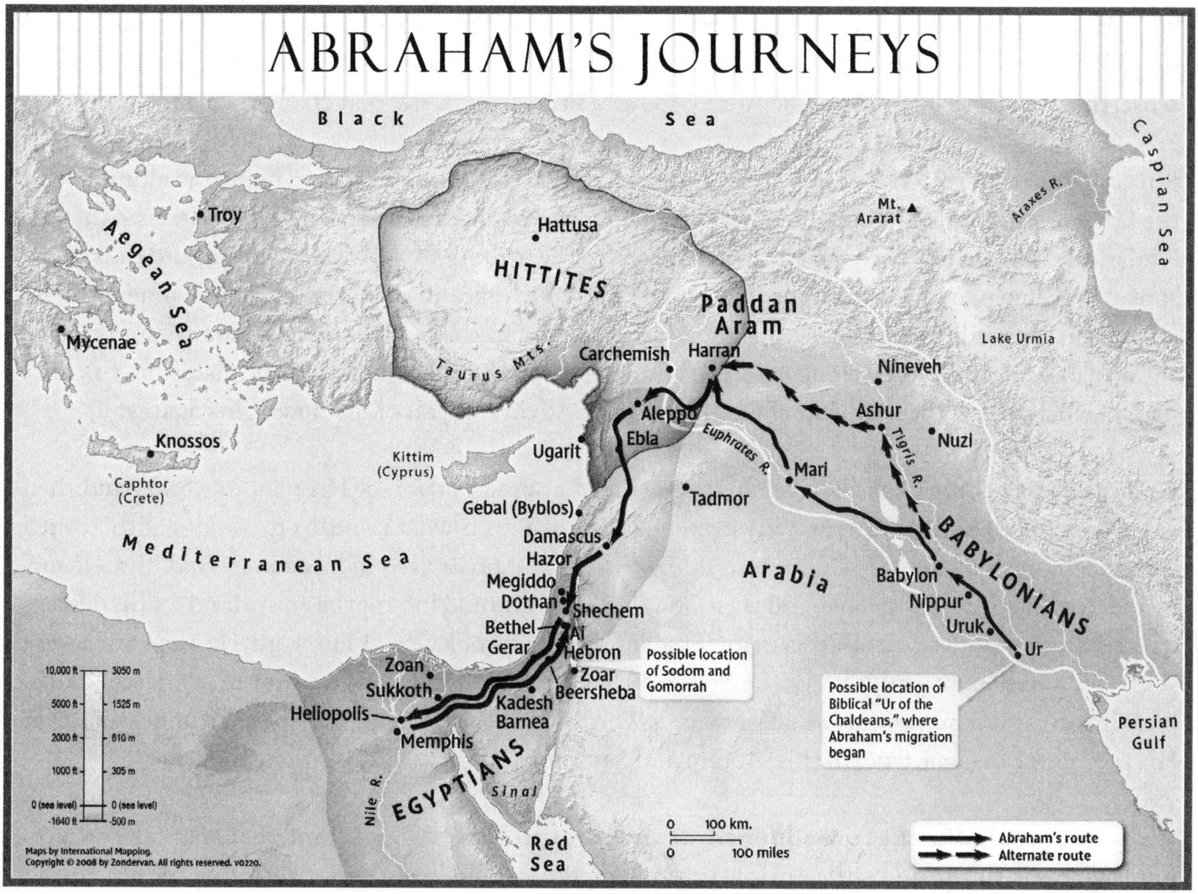

REFLECTIONS

God loves His creation. One of the striking things we discover in the opening chapter of Genesis is God's love toward all creation. This becomes a theme throughout Scripture, culminating in the costly sacrifice God's own Son would make on the cross. We find God's Spirit hovering above the waters of creation before the earth was even shaped (see Genesis 1:2), and His presence is similar to that of a mother hen guarding her chicks. God spoke to His creatures as they were created, and His words were all blessing: "Be fruitful and multiply" (verses 22, 28). God the Creator also concluded each day by stepping back and assessing His own work—and each day He declared that "it was good" (verses 3, 10, 12, 18, 21, 25, 31). Clearly, God was pleased by the work of His hands and loved His entire creation.

Mankind is unique in all of creation. Genesis underscores that mankind is different from the rest of creation. We share the same original material with the rest of creation, as God used the dust of the earth to create us (see Genesis 2:7). However, the Lord did more than merely speak a command when He created Adam: He fashioned the dust with His own hands and breathed life directly into him. Only human beings are created in the *image* of God. This in itself is a deep subject for consideration. In an intellectual sense, Adam and Eve were like God in that they could exercise reason and understanding. In a moral sense, they were like God because they were good and sinless (of course, that changed when they sinned.)

Sin results in separation. Adam's sin separated him from God. He had enjoyed daily communion with the Lord, talking with Him like close friends, but sin ruined that for Adam and all his descendants. As Paul would later write, "Through one man sin entered the world, and death through sin, and thus death spread to all men, because all sinned" (Romans 5:12). This face-to-face communion will never be restored this side of heaven. Sin also separated mankind from the rest of creation. Adam's sin brought suffering and death to everything, and everything began to rebel against man's headship, just as man had rebelled against the headship of God. Because of Adam's sin, all of life now fights against us.

God calls His people to walk in faith. God revealed a small portion of His plan to Abram and then asked him to respond by walking away from all he knew. This is what it means to walk in faith: to step into the unknown with only God's word to depend on. Abram arrived in Canaan to find himself surrounded with unfriendly people, and then God told him he would inherit the entire land for his descendants. Circumstances made this seem impossible, yet Abram took God at His word. He was seventy-five years old and had no children, yet he believed that God was going to give him many descendants. Walking in faith requires that we accept God's Word at face value, even when it seems impossible that His promises can come true. In this, Abram and Sarai provide us with a great role model.

We can never predict the consequences of sin. Sarai probably did not think that her plan concerning Hagar was sinful, and she certainly never thought it would bring about suffering for her family.

Abram may well have understood this, yet he did not stop to count the cost of disobedience. There are times when we persuade ourselves that "this one little bit" of sinful behavior won't hurt "just this once." However, this single act of disobedience in Abram and Sarai's case led to countless deaths and acts of persecution that have continued to this present day. Humans are specialists at self-justification. We can always excuse and condone the "little sins" we commit. However, we should keep in mind that we cannot predict what consequences each "one little sin" may produce—such as how many innocent people may suffer, how long the ripples may continue, or even what price we may pay.

God calls us to costly obedience. Abraham was tested by God's command to sacrifice his son. Yet this was not a random test; God's purpose was to prove the strength of Abraham's faith. He also wanted to present to the world a picture of His plan to sacrifice His own Son on the cross. God will sometimes ask us to obey Him in ways that are costly. The principle He wants us to learn is that faith-filled obedience is more valuable than anything this world has to offer. The other side to this principle is that costly obedience leads to eternal riches. Abraham's obedience brought a priceless blessing to the entire world, showing mankind just how much God was willing to do to redeem us. Jesus was willing to obey at any cost, and we must follow His example.

> By FAITH Abraham, when he was tested, offered up Isaac . . . he who had received the PROMISES offered up his only BEGOTTEN SON.
>
> HEBREWS 11:17

God's purposes are not furthered by our schemes. God intended from the beginning for Esau to be subservient to Jacob. He promised it before the boys were born and would have accomplished it without plots from Isaac's family. We saw the same principle in the life of Abraham: he had God's promise of an heir through Sarah, yet he allowed his fears (and his wife's schemes) to override his faith in God's word. In each case, the schemes of men led to bad consequences. Jacob's schemes alienated him from his twin brother and led to his being deceived by others. Abraham's involvement with Hagar led to a deep-seated enmity between people groups. God accomplishes what He promises. This does not mean that we are not involved in those promises, but our involvement requires obedience, not scheming. Our involvement may sometimes require no effort at all on our part—except for placing our faith in God's provision.

God uses us despite our failures. Jacob had many weaknesses and shortcomings, and from a human perspective he was not the sort of man that most people would trust. But God was still able to use him in mighty ways, and he is listed among the heroes of the faith. "The LORD does not see as man sees; for man looks at the outward appearance, but the LORD looks at the heart" (1 Samuel 16:7). The Lord looked on the heart of Jacob and found a man who ultimately longed for His blessing and intimacy. When we have a relationship with our Creator, He instills within us character traits that are pleasing to Him. Through His Spirit, He develops those things in us, making us more like Christ as we grow. This process may not always be pleasant, but in the end we will reflect the image of His Son.

STUDY QUESTIONS

1. How does Genesis 1:1–2:2 emphasize God's gentleness and love toward creation? What does this suggest about His view of you?

2. What was the nature of God's curse in Genesis 3:17–19? In what ways have you seen this curse carried out in your own life? Give some real examples.

3. What exactly was mankind doing in Genesis 11:1–9 that was displeasing to God? Why were they doing these things? Why was God not pleased?

4. If you had been Abram, knowing that you and your wife were both growing old, how would you have viewed God's promise that you would have a son (see Genesis 15:1–6)?

5. How did Sarai's solution to the problem of her childlessness show lack of faith in her thinking? How did it reveal her shortsightedness in God's larger plans (see Genesis 16:1–4)?

6. Put yourself in Abraham's place. How would you have reacted if God commanded you to sacrifice your child (see Genesis 22:1–19)? What would you have done?

7. Why might Esau have been so willing to sell his birthright? Whose sin is worse in your opinion: Jacob's or Esau's (see Genesis 25:27–34)?

8. Why did God give Jacob a limp during the wrestling match (see Genesis 32:24–32)? How did Jacob's limp serve as a reminder of his weakness and need to depend on God?

WEEK 2

GOD DELIVERS US FROM BONDAGE

GENESIS 37 – EXODUS 40

DAILY READINGS:	**8** | Genesis 37–41	**9** | Genesis 42–45	**10** | Exodus 1–3
11 | Exodus 7–11	**12** | Exodus 14–17	**13** | Exodus 19–20	**14** | Exodus 32–35

Jacob, having moved his family from Shechem to Bethel, took delight in the sons his beloved wife, Rachel, had borne him late in life. But Jacob's ten older sons came to resent his playing favorites with Joseph and Benjamin, and ultimately they took it out on Joseph. First, they attempted to murder him; then they sold him into slavery and told their father he was dead.

Joseph was purchased by the captain of the guard in Pharaoh's kingdom: a man named Potiphar. At this time Egypt was the most influential world power and a place of great luxury and technology. By contrast, Joseph's family had been nomadic shepherds for several generations, living in tents. Joseph was entering a nation that spoke a different language, operated under different cultural norms, and served foreign gods. Now that Joseph was also a slave, his status in Egypt was about as low as it could sink.

During Joseph's enslavement, the "wheel of fortune" swung him violently from a position of favor (in Potiphar's house), to a position of subjugation (falsely accused and imprisoned), then back up again (serving the warden) . . . only to be dashed down once more (forgotten by Pharaoh's chief butler after he returned to the royal household). But then one day, Pharaoh had a troubling dream that none of his wise men could interpret. The butler finally remembered Joseph, who had accurately interpreted his dream while they were both in prison.

Pharaoh sent for Joseph, and the Lord gave him the interpretation: there would be seven years of plenty in the land followed by seven years of drought that would threaten all peoples in the known world. In a remarkable reversal of circumstances, after thirteen years as a slave and a prisoner, Joseph was elevated to second in command of Egypt and tasked with preparing the nation for what was ahead.

Due to Joseph's wise management during the years of abundance, the inhabitants of the region had food when the famine came. As soon as people in other lands heard this, they traveled to Egypt to secure grain. This is how Joseph's brothers ended up before their long-lost brother—but they failed to recognize him. After a series of tests convinced Joseph that his brothers' hearts had truly changed, they were reconciled, and he provided the entire family with a new home in the richest part of Egypt.

As the famine came to an end, so did Jacob's time on earth. In his last recorded act in Genesis, he gathered his twelve sons and pronounced a blessing—specific prophecies—on each one. Although Jacob was now blind, he saw each son with accurate vision, and his blessings reflected the sovereignty of the Lord God at work. While Joseph's life was filled with seemingly arbitrary events that were out of his control, they were never out of God's control. The Lord had a large-scale plan for His chosen nation, and that plan included using the evil plans of Joseph's brothers to advance His plan for good in Joseph's life.

According to Exodus, the Israelites stayed in Egypt after Joseph died. Over time, their growing numbers worried the king. So the Egyptians made the Hebrews their slaves, and they remained slaves for more than 400 years—until God's appointed time to bring Abraham's descendants back to Canaan.

God selected a Hebrew man to lead them: Moses, whom the Lord had saved as a baby from Pharaoh's murderous plot and brought into the king's own house to be raised in the royal Egyptian court.

Decades later, God called Moses out of self-imposed exile (and comfort zone), and Moses returned to Egypt to fulfill his assignment. The Lord told Moses that He would deliberately harden Pharaoh's heart. God would use Pharaoh's stubbornness to show forth His glory and, in the end, redeem His people from bondage.

The Lord sent nine plagues on the land of Egypt—each more drastic than the one before it—yet Pharaoh did not relent. God then commanded His people to prepare for a calamitous event. Just as He had spared Israel from the other plagues, so He would spare them from this final one. However, to protect themselves, they were required to sprinkle the blood of a sacrificed lamb on the doorposts of their houses. God's destroying angel did not look on individuals but on this blood. He entered every house that was not sprinkled with the blood of the Passover lamb, slaying the firstborn. That very night, Pharaoh allowed the Israelites to leave Egypt.

During their travels toward the "promised land" of Canaan, God's people witnessed His power and faithfulness in many ways. He went with them in a pillar of cloud by day and a pillar of fire by night. He provided food and water and delivered the Israelites from the most deadly army on earth by granting them safe passage through the Red Sea. He met with Moses face to face, giving him the Ten Commandments. Yet the people constantly grumbled against God and Moses.

The Lord gave Moses strict instructions concerning the construction of a portable tabernacle to use for worship during their wilderness travels, the details of which accentuated the gulf separating a sinful people from their holy God. The Lord not only endowed certain individuals with skills to create a dwelling place for Him of exceeding quality, but He had also already given the Israelites great riches from the Egyptians that could be used for the raw materials. The fact that something so exquisite could be constructed while the people lived in the wilderness testifies to the supernatural enablement they received from God.

When the work was finished, God's glory filled the tabernacle, confirming for Moses and the people that the work had been properly done, and that He would remain with them.

THE TEN COMMANDMENTS

(BASED ON EXODUS 20:1–17)

1. You shall have no other gods before the Lord.
2. You shall not make any idols for yourself.
3. You shall not take the name of the Lord in vain.
4. Remember the Sabbath day and keep it holy.
5. Honor your father and your mother.
6. You shall not murder.
7. You shall not commit adultery.
8. You shall not steal.
9. You shall not give false testimony.
10. You shall not covet.

REFLECTIONS

God uses trials to prepare us for greater tasks. God permitted Joseph to endure trials to strengthen his faith and teach him practical lessons that he would need later. Joseph had no idea that he would one day rule over all Egypt—second in command to only Pharaoh himself—and he could not have prepared himself with the skills that would be required for him to assume that role. Only the Lord knew those things, and He used disappointments, setbacks, slavery, and imprisonment to train Joseph for the future. We may never become world leaders in this life, but the Lord's plans for our future are still important in the eternal scheme. He is preparing each of us now to be ready for that great role of leadership, and He uses every circumstance in our lives for that preparation—including suffering and hardship.

God is in control of all our circumstances. This is the overarching theme of Genesis. The Lord told Abraham, many years before Joseph was born, that his descendants would go into Egypt for 400 years (see Genesis 15:13–14). It was His plan from the beginning that Joseph should lead his family into Egypt, and the trials he endured there were part of that plan. Joseph did not sit rejoicing at the bottom of the pit, thrilled that God was sending him to Egypt to fulfill His prophecy to Abraham. Yet he could recognize the Lord was completely sovereign over all things in his life. In the same way, God has promised that He will always be faithful to us as His children: "And we know that all things work together for good to those who love God, to those who are the called according to His purpose" (Romans 8:28).

God will empower us for what calls us to do. Moses suffered from some form of speech defect. He may have stuttered, as traditional Jewish writers have suggested, or he may simply have felt he was not eloquent. Whatever the cause, he was convinced he could not fulfill the assignment God was calling him to perform. Yet God promised Moses, at each objection, that He would overcome his shortcomings. The Lord may sometimes call us to do tasks that seem beyond our ability, but we must remember that we are not the ones who are at work but the Holy Spirit within us. God can use even our weaknesses to bring about His glory, and He will never call us to do something that we cannot do without His help.

We are to live in expectation of Jesus' immediate return. The Israelites were commanded to eat the Passover feast dressed in an unusual fashion: with sandals and walking tunic and staff, ready to leap up and march at a moment's notice. This proved necessary that night, as Pharaoh drove them out of Egypt in the middle hours of darkness. Jesus likewise promised that He would return to take His people home—whisking us to heaven just as He suddenly carried His people out of Egypt. We are called to live expectantly, ever ready for the sudden and glorious appearing of Jesus Christ. "It is like a man going to a far country, who left his house and gave authority to his servants, and to each his work, and commanded the doorkeeper to watch. Watch therefore, for you do not know when the master of the house is coming—in the evening, at midnight, at the crowing of the rooster, or in the morning—lest, coming suddenly, he find you sleeping. And what I say to you, I say to all: Watch!" (Mark 13:34–37).

We walk by faith, not by sight. The Egyptian army was feared around the world and equipped with the latest technologies and best training. The Israelites, on the other hand, were newly released slaves with no military experience or chariots. It is no wonder they were frightened when they saw the dust cloud of Pharaoh's army bearing down on them. But the greatest army on earth is no match for the power of God. He led the Egyptians into the Red Sea and then plucked off the wheels of their chariots as simply as one snaps a toothpick. He then led His people through the sea on dry ground. They did not even get their feet wet! Our tendency is to believe the evidence of our senses. But the Lord God calls us to "walk by faith, not by sight" (2 Corinthians 5:7), and to rely fully on His unlimited power and faithfulness.

God's Law is summarized by the two greatest commandments. A man once asked Jesus what was the greatest commandment in the law. Jesus answered, "'You shall love the LORD your God with all your heart, with all your soul, and with all your mind.' . . . And the second is like it: 'You shall love your neighbor as yourself.' On these two commandments hang all the Law and the Prophets" (Matthew 22:36–40). The Ten Commandments fall into these two categories. Some of them spell out what it means to love God with all our hearts, souls, and minds, while others give practical ways of loving our neighbors as ourselves. These two principles summarize what it means to live a godly life.

God wants us to draw closer to Him. Moses made an audacious request when he asked to see God's glory. In fact, the Lord was already showing His presence among His people. Yet Moses yearned to know *more* about God—and the Lord was pleased to grant him as much as he was able to bear. In the same way, God has already revealed much of His glory to us today by redeeming us from sin and making His presence freely available to us. Yet there is much more to know! We can deepen our understanding of His character through diligently reading and studying the Bible and by humbly asking Him to teach us more about Himself. As we draw near to God, we find that He draws near to us (see James 4:8).

THE TABERNACLE

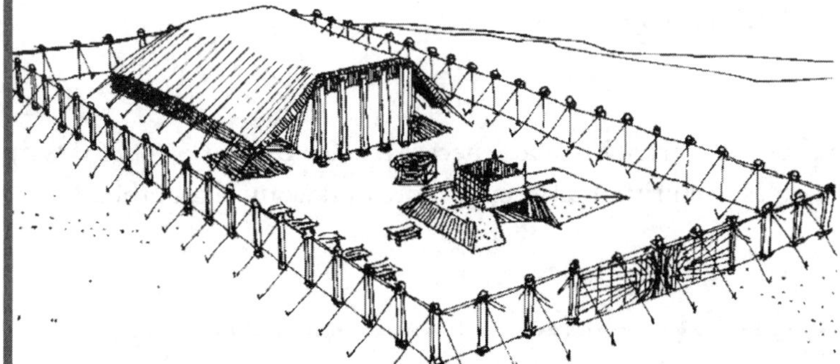

The tabernacle was to provide a place where God might dwell among His people. The term *tabernacle* sometimes refers to the tent, including the Holy Place and Most Holy Place, which was covered with embroidered curtains. But in other places it refers to the entire complex, including the curtained court in which the tent stood.

STUDY QUESTIONS

1. It was God's plan for Joseph to go into Egypt (see Genesis 37:12–36). What are some ways in which God was leading the events in Joseph's life behind the scenes?

2. Why did God allow Joseph to suffer mistreatment first at the hands of his brothers and then in Potiphar's household when he had done nothing to deserve it (see Genesis 37:19–36; 39:6–20)?

3. How had God prepared Joseph to become second-in-command in Egypt when Pharaoh gave him that role (see Genesis 41:37–45)? Provide a few specific examples.

4. Why do you think God sent such a horrific drought and famine on the world (see Genesis 41:53–57)? What were His purposes—and what were His provisions?

5. What was required on Joseph's part to be reconciled with his brothers when they came to Egypt? What was required on his brothers' part (see Genesis 45:1–15)?

6. Turning to the book of Exodus, if you had been in Moses' position, how would you have responded to God's command to lead the Israelites out of Egypt (see Exodus 3:7–10)?

7. Why did Pharaoh persistently refuse to release the Israelites from their bondage in Egypt (see Exodus 8:29–32; 9:7, 12, 35; 10:20; 11:10 14:1–6)?

8. Why were the roles of all who built the tabernacle equally necessary (see Exodus 35:4–35)? Why do people sometimes think some roles in spiritual service are more important than others?

WEEK 3

GOD INSTRUCTS US ON HOW TO LIVE

LEVITICUS 1 – NUMBERS 36

READING PLAN: **15** | Leviticus 1-5 **16** | Leviticus 8-10 **17** | Leviticus 6; 23 **18** | Numbers 10-14 **19** | Numbers 15-17 **20** | Numbers 20-21 **21** | Numbers 22-25

The exodus from Egypt occurred c. 1445 BC, and the tabernacle was finished one year later. Leviticus picks up the record at this point, while Israel is camped at Mount Sinai. Until now, the Israelites had never had a central place of worship. But with the tabernacle now complete, structured sacrifices, feasts, and established roles for the priesthood were required, as well as instruction for the people about purity in ritual settings and everyday life.

The Israelites had been slaves for centuries in Egypt—the land of a seemingly infinite number of gods—and so their concept of worship and godly living was severely distorted. The purpose of the Levitical laws was thus not to restrict the Israelites or curtail their freedoms but to help them live in holiness, set apart from the pagan and immoral practices of the peoples around them. This included Egypt, the country from which the Lord had freed them, and Canaan, the new homeland the Lord was giving them.

The first codified set of sacrifices that God gave for worshiping Him symbolized the worshiper's desire to be purged of sin. Three of these were voluntary: the burnt, grain, and

OFFERINGS

(FROM LEVITICUS 1-7)

Burnt: Given to atone for sin and signify complete consecration to God.

Grain: Given to signify a person's thanksgiving and homage to God.

Peace: Given to express peace and fellowship between offerer and God.

Sin: Given to atone for sins committed unknowingly where restitution was not possible.

Trespass: Given to atone for sins committed unknowingly where restitution was possible.

peace offerings; while the last two were compulsory: sin and trespass offerings. These requirements were followed by further regulations for how the priests should carry out the sacrifices.

Leviticus 8 describes a critical moment: the consecration of the new nation's priests. Moses gathered the entire congregation of Israel to serve as witnesses. He then physically and spiritually cleansed and anointed Aaron and his sons through a series of rituals, sanctifying them for priestly service. Unfortunately, the initiation of the sacrificial system did not unfold as planned. Two of Aaron's sons died the first time they ministered because they did not follow God's regulations.

The lives of God's people—from sacrifices and criminal codes to diet, clothing, cooking, sexual practices, and even dealing with diseases—were ordered by God to teach Israel they were to live differently from everyone else. While there were practical benefits to these laws, God was primarily training His people in holiness. He wanted them to look different, act different, and even eat different because He was their God. His people had to learn to live His way—in everything.

God also gave instructions for various feasts and holy days (such as the Day of Atonement and Passover) and celebrations of rest and freedom (such as the weekly Sabbath and the year of Jubilee). The goal was both worship and remembrance so that God's people, and the generations to come, would not forget His faithfulness.

A month later, when the record in Numbers begins, God's people were still camped at Mount Sinai. One particular miracle had been taking place daily for the entire year that the Israelites had been traveling in the wilderness: each morning and evening, the Lord rained down a tasty, wafer-like substance called manna. It was so nourishing that the people needed nothing else to eat. They did not have to go out and hunt for it either; the Lord delivered the manna right to their doorsteps! Best of all, there was always more than enough for everybody, so no one ever went hungry.

There was so much of God's love in the manna that it is hard to believe that anyone would complain about it. But the people did, recalling the variety of foods they had enjoyed in Egypt (while conveniently forgetting their slave labor) and grumbling about their meatless diet. Moses was fed up with their constant complaining. God was displeased as well. The Lord did send them meat, but their lust for it came at a terrible price in the form of a plague.

In spite of the people's complaints and missteps, the Lord faithfully continued to lead them to the banks of the Jordan River, the border of the Promised Land. He was about to give them this land flowing with milk and honey. But first Moses sent twelve men, one from each tribe of Israel, to spy out the region and plan a military strategy. Those twelve men all saw the same things: giants, walled cities, and immense grapes. Ten of them determined that Israel could never conquer the land, while two of them were convinced that, with God's power, they could take it. Sadly, the negative report of the ten spies prevailed, leading the people to lose faith in God and, in their despair, refusing to enter Canaan. Due to this rebellion, the Lord sentenced all the adults (except Caleb and Joshua, the two faithful spies) to die in the wilderness, and the Israelites were forced to wander in the wilderness for many more years.

When the people found themselves without water at Meribah, they complained once more. The Lord resolved the problem just as He had years before at Rephidim: by instructing Moses to speak to the rock. But Moses lost his temper with the people and failed to follow God's exact command—and the consequence caused him grief. Moses would be prohibited from bringing the people into the Promised Land.

As the "Exodus generation" of the Israelites died out, the next generation grew to adulthood. The Israelites had recently destroyed several Canaanite armies, and the Lord's power was so abundantly evident that the nations of Canaan were afraid of them. One of those nations was Moab, whose people were descended from Lot. In spite the Lord's promise years earlier that Lot's descendants would enjoy an inheritance in the land of Canaan, the leaders of Moab were afraid Israel would destroy them.

One Moabite leader, Balak, decided that if he couldn't defeat the Israelites with physical force, he would fight them spiritually. He hired a pagan prophet named Balaam to help in this effort. Balaam taught the Moabites to seduce God's people through pagan practices. The Israelites fell into sexual immorality, and God sent a plague in judgment. After the plague was lifted, a second numbering of the people took place as they prepared to inherit the Promised Land. Numbers ends with the Israelites poised on the eastern side of the Jordan River across from Jericho. The conquest was about to begin . . .

REFLECTIONS

Sin is serious. Imagine being a child in the time of Moses. You see your father lead a lamb or bull to the entrance of the tabernacle. After a conversation with the priests, your father places his hand on the animal's head and then cuts its throat. The message would be clear: sin is serious. Sin leads to death, because God is utterly righteous and perfectly just. And sin can only be covered over with blood.

Choose contentment. God led His people into a region devoid of food and water to demonstrate He would provide for their needs. He rained manna on them twice a day and provided water miraculously. But the people grew tired of these provisions and grumbled about not having any meat in their diet. This demonstrates a key principle: we can choose whether or not to be content (see Philippians 4:11).

Grumbling has a negative effect on others. The Israelites constantly complained during the exodus from Egypt. Even though God demonstrated His grace and power to them again and again, they continuously accused Him of treachery. It is a natural human response to complain when things go wrong, but when we do so, we are actually saying that we do not trust the Lord's sovereignty. Instead, as Paul wrote, we should choose to "do all things without complaining and disputing" (Philippians 2:14).

STUDY QUESTIONS

1. How did the sacrificial system emphasize the holiness of God and the high cost of Israel's sin (see Leviticus 1–5)? When have you been confronted by the seriousness of sin?

2. How would you describe the events that took place on the Day of Atonement? What role did the scapegoat play in the Day of Atonement ceremonies (see Leviticus 16:1–34)?

3. What was the purpose of the feasts of the Lord? How many of these feasts are described in Leviticus 23:1–44? Why did God want His people to celebrate them?

4. Why were the Israelites not content with the manna that God mercifully provided to them in the wilderness (see Numbers 11:4–6)? What is needed to find contentment?

5. What led Miriam and Aaron to rebel against Moses—and how did God respond to it? How did their attitude differ from Moses' attitude (see Numbers 12:1–16)?

6. Why did the ten spies say the Israelites could not defeat their enemies (see Numbers 13:17–29)? Why did Joshua and Caleb say they *could* defeat them (see Numbers 13:30; 14:6–9)?

7. Why was Balaam unable to curse Israel (see Numbers 22:1–6)? How did Balaam ultimately earn the money that Balak paid him to curse them (see Numbers 25:1–3)?

8. What does God reveal about His character through the story of Balaam (see Numbers 22:4–24:25)? What do we learn of human nature?

WEEK 4

GOD IS ALWAYS FAITHFUL

DEUTERONOMY 1-34

READING PLAN: **22** | Deuteronomy 1-4 **23** | Deuteronomy 5-9 **24** | Deuteronomy 12-16 **25** | Deuteronomy 26-27 **26** | Deuteronomy 28-29 **27** | Deuteronomy 30-32 **28** | Deuteronomy 33-34

Shortly after their exodus from Egypt, the Israelites had followed God's visible presence to the land He had reserved for them—a land flowing with milk and honey. Yet in spite of the miracles they had witnessed God perform, they refused to enter their new home. They were afraid of the Canaanites, a warlike people who occupied the Promised Land at the time.

In rejecting God's plan, the Israelites rejected God Himself. As a result, God commanded them to wander as nomads in the wilderness for forty years, during which time the generation that had rejected God died. Under Moses' guidance, the new generation of Israelites prepared for when God would once again present the land promised to them.

As part of this preparation, Moses, in the last few weeks of his life, committed a series of speeches to writing and gave them to the priests and elders. Deuteronomy records these explanations from Moses about the Law and its implications for the new generation as they prepared to enter the Promised Land. These words bring into focus all that was revealed in Genesis to Numbers, thus completing the five-part literary unit known as the Pentateuch.

Like Leviticus, the events of Deuteronomy take place in one location, in the span of about one month's time. Now, however, the Israelites were camped east of the Jordan River, across from Jericho.

Moses could have taken many tacks in these final words to the people of Israel. Yet he chose to begin with their recent history. Specifically, he began with their moment of greatest transgression and shame: their refusal to obey God's command to go in and possess the land He had promised to Abraham, Isaac, and Jacob. Moses wanted to burn that moment into the people's collective memory—not to punish them but so they would avoid repeating the same sinful pattern in the future. He also desired to warn the people about the future dangers they would face in the land of Canaan, foremost of which was idolatry, and called for them to focus on obeying God's commands.

Moses' second address in Deuteronomy stretches from the end of chapter 4 through chapter 28. He gave the Israelites a clear understanding of their covenant with God. This included several commands and methods designed to help parents teach their children what it meant to live in covenant with God.

Moses' initial instruction for worshiping God was perhaps most shocking: the Israelites were to utterly destroy all the false places of worship throughout Canaan when they possessed the land. This was a reminder that God's people were to have no connection with pagan practices. In the instructions to the future kings of Israel, each was required to literally handwrite a copy of the law—and to read it all the days of their life. Why? So they would learn to fear the Lord.

Moses also prophesied about a future Prophet, whom we know as the Messiah, Jesus Christ. According to Moses, this Prophet would speak with God's voice and display the same power and authority that God displayed at Mount Horeb (Sinai), when the Israelites shook with fear.

Through Moses, God further prescribed a powerful ceremony to be carried out as soon as the Israelites crossed the Jordan River. They were to set up huge stones, paint them white, and write on them all the words of the law, which likely meant the entire book of Deuteronomy. Only when this was done were the people to build an altar, make sacrifices to God, and celebrate together.

In the conclusion of Moses' second address to the Israelites, he detailed all the blessings the people would receive if they remained faithful to God as they inhabited Canaan. He also laid out the curses they would incur if they rebelled as their ancestors had. To dramatically demonstrate this, God commanded that representatives of Israel's twelve tribes climb two mountains within their new homeland. One group would shout the blessings; the other group would shout the curses.

THE SPEECHES OF MOSES

First Address: A Historical Prologue	Deuteronomy 1:3–4:43
Second Address: Stipulations of the Sinaitic Covenant	Deuteronomy 4:44–28:68
Third Address: Another Covenant	Deuteronomy 29:1–30:20

Moses' third and final address reaffirmed the covenant between God and the generation of Israel entering the land. It differed from the others in that it was written in the form of a song.

Even as Moses called that generation to covenant faithfulness, he understood they would not uphold their part of the agreement. Future generations would turn away from God, repeating the sins of the past. Yet in spite of Israel's coming rebellion, Moses still looked toward the future with hope. He counted on the time when God would establish yet *another* covenant with His people—a new covenant marked not by physical circumcision but by circumcision of the heart.

One of Moses' final tasks was passing the torch of leadership to Joshua. Moses' personal assistant and leader of Israel's armies during the wilderness years would bring God's people to their new home. Finally, having led the Israelites for more than forty years—and after a lifespan of 120 years—God gave Moses a view of the Promised Land from Mount Nebo and then called His faithful servant home.

The final two chapters of Deuteronomy were likely written by Joshua, as they record the events immediately before and after Moses' death. These chapters reinforce the primary themes that Moses had covered: God is always faithful to His chosen ones, He is sovereign, and He alone is God.

The Lord went to incredible lengths to stress to His people the critical importance of personal holiness at the very beginning of their journey to the Promised Land. Moses, at the end of his life, called that same people to reject the mistakes they had made in their history and choose a better future—one of *life* rather than *death*, and *blessing* rather than *curse*.

REFLECTIONS

Trust and obey. Much of what Moses communicated to the Israelites can be boiled down to one central idea: *trust in the Lord.* The previous generation had failed to make this choice to trust God because they were terrified of the strength of the Canaanites. So Moses was setting this same choice before this generation. He was also reminding them *why* they could trust God: because of His character.

Choose blessings over curses. Moses' words in Deuteronomy 28 are filled with stark contrasts. The first fourteen verses describe the blessings Israel would receive if they remained faithful to God. The remaining fifty-four verses describe the curses that would fall on them if they were unfaithful to Him. People today have been presented with the same options. Those who obey the Lord will be blessed, while those who disregard His truths will suffer the consequences of disobedience, both in this life and for all eternity. Blessing for obedience and cursing for rebellion is a truth that flows from God's justice.

God is faithful. Moses began Deuteronomy by detailing the failure of Israel's past generation when they refused to obey God and enter the Promised Land. He ended with a song that highlighted the same theme. In both cases, Moses pointedly called the Israelites' attention to God's faithfulness. Despite their repeated transgressions, God had been faithful to them. He is *always* faithful to His chosen ones.

STUDY QUESTIONS

1. Why was it important for Moses to recount the Israelite people's history to them? What did Moses say had caused Israel to rebel against God (see Deuteronomy 1:26–46)?

2. How had God shown His faithfulness to His people when it came to helping them overcome threats from the nations around them? (Cite a few examples from Deuteronomy 2–3.)

3. What did God identify to His people as being the greatest commandment? What were the Israelites to never forget (see Deuteronomy 6:1–12)?

4. Moses prophesied about Jesus in Deuteronomy 18:15–22. How might the promise of a coming Messiah have helped guard the Israelites from falling into old, sinful patterns?

5. What purpose did the stones and the altar described in Deuteronomy 27:1–10 serve? What were some of the key principles in the covenant that Moses described in Deuteronomy 29?

6. How did Moses assure the people in Deuteronomy 31 that God would be with Joshua as their new leader? How do you think the people reacted when Moses gave them this news?

7. What key themes are present throughout Moses' blessings over Israel in Deuteronomy 33? How many leaders are mentioned in this particular blessing?

8. How is Moses' death described in Deuteronomy 34? What do the closing words of the book say about the legacy that Moses left behind to the people of Israel?

WEEK 5

GOD LEADS US TO VICTORY

JOSHUA 1-24

READING PLAN: **29** | Joshua 1-2 **30** | Joshua 3-4 **31** | Joshua 5-6
32 | Joshua 7-8 **33** | Joshua 9-10 **34** | Joshua 11-12 **35** | Joshua 23-24

The years of Israel's wandering were nearly over. The Israelites and their leader, Joshua—whom Moses had trained—were now poised on the plains of Moab, east of the Jordan River, preparing to finally enter into the land God had promised them and take possession of it. The first stronghold standing in their way was the city of Jericho. Joshua, seeking information about its inhabitants and defenses ahead of the battle, sent in two spies.

The city of Jericho was surrounded by two massive walls that were six and twelve feet thick. Small, simple houses had been built between them, often with windows that opened through the city walls. Such houses were typically inhabited by the city's poor—and worse. Their location near the city gates, for instance, was perfect for carrying on the business of prostitution. The constant flow of people entering and leaving Jericho was good for business, especially since it was easy to enter and exit such a house unnoticed.

This element of anonymity was useful for Joshua's spies, who hid in the house of a prostitute named Rahab. She recognized the God of Israel would deliver Canaan into their hands and made up her mind to make *their* God *her* God. In exchange for risking her life to help the two men escape the city through her window, she asked them to spare her life and the lives of her family.

Upon the spies' return to camp, the people were commanded to sanctify themselves in preparation to cross the Jordan. Joshua had been present on that fateful day, decades earlier, when the Israelites had also stood on the doorstep of Canaan—and rebelled. God had told them to move forward, but their faith had faltered. As a result, God decreed no one of that generation would enter the Promised Land.

As the Israelites surveyed the Jordan River once again, they vowed not to make the same mistake. "All that you command us we will do," they said, "and wherever you send us we will go" (Joshua 1:16).

The priests carried the sacred ark of the covenant to the river's swollen banks. The ark represented the very presence of the Lord with His people and visually indicated that He was leading them. When the priests stepped into the water, it was suddenly (and miraculously) cut off. All Israel followed, crossing over on dry ground while God held back the Jordan. The Lord was reiterating for His people that He would remove any obstacle that stood between them and their inheritance in Canaan.

Off in the distance stood Jericho. In addition to its fortress-like walls, the city was built on a tall mound of land and surrounded by an earthen embankment. To attack it, an enemy had to charge uphill, climb over the embankment, and try to breach Jericho's two main gates—all while being shot at from the walls above. How were the Israelites to take such a city? They had the presence of almighty God. He gave the Israelites an incredible victory there. The people marched around Jericho seven times, the priests blew the trumpets, and the walls fell down.

Except for Rahab and her family, God had instructed the Israelites to take away nothing whatsoever from Jericho after its fall. Everything was to be destroyed as a sacrifice to Him as part of the victory. But one man disregarded God's command: Achan took a souvenir and some treasures for himself.

Soon after the Jericho battle, Joshua prepared his army to attack Ai. Joshua's spies advised him to send only a few thousand men. Had Joshua consulted the Lord prior to making his strategic plans, God would certainly have told him there was sin in the camp that needed to be dealt with first. Going into battle with only a few thousand men proved to be a gross miscalculation. The spies thought there were "few" inhabitants in Ai, but in truth there were some 12,000 people there. There were far too many for Israel's small force to take without the hand of the Lord protecting them.

When Joshua learned of the sin within Israel, he repented, Achan was put to death, and his family and their possessions were destroyed. God then delivered Ai into Israel's hands in a second battle.

Word spread that Israel's God was fighting on their behalf. Most of the cities of Canaan responded by attacking Israel in hopes of defeating her before the Lord intervened. One city, however, adopted a different approach. The people of Gibeon, recognizing they could not win if they remained enemies, determined to make peace with the Israelites. But instead of asking for peace directly, they resorted to subterfuge by pretending they lived far away and posed no threat to God's people. The leaders of Israel were deceived by this ruse and signed a covenant in God's name to live at peace with Gibeon.

Meanwhile, the king of Jerusalem formed an alliance with four other kings, and they desperately sought a way to defeat Israel. When they learned of Gibeon's peace covenant, they realized their best course was to attack Israel's friends rather than Israel itself. Gibeon pleaded with Joshua for help. Israel's armies, already exhausted from an all-night uphill march, arrived at the scene of battle to face not one, but *five*, enemy armies. Yet the Lord commanded Joshua to not give in to fear.

God honored Israel's covenant, refusing to allow the Canaanite kings to defeat the Gibeonites. The Lord first sent deadly hailstones on the enemy. He then caused the sun to stand still, making the earth pause on its axis for a period of hours, so that His people would have the victory. Through these momentous events, Israel's omnipotent God proved there was nothing He wouldn't do for the sake of His people—even to the point of *not* moving heaven and earth on their behalf.

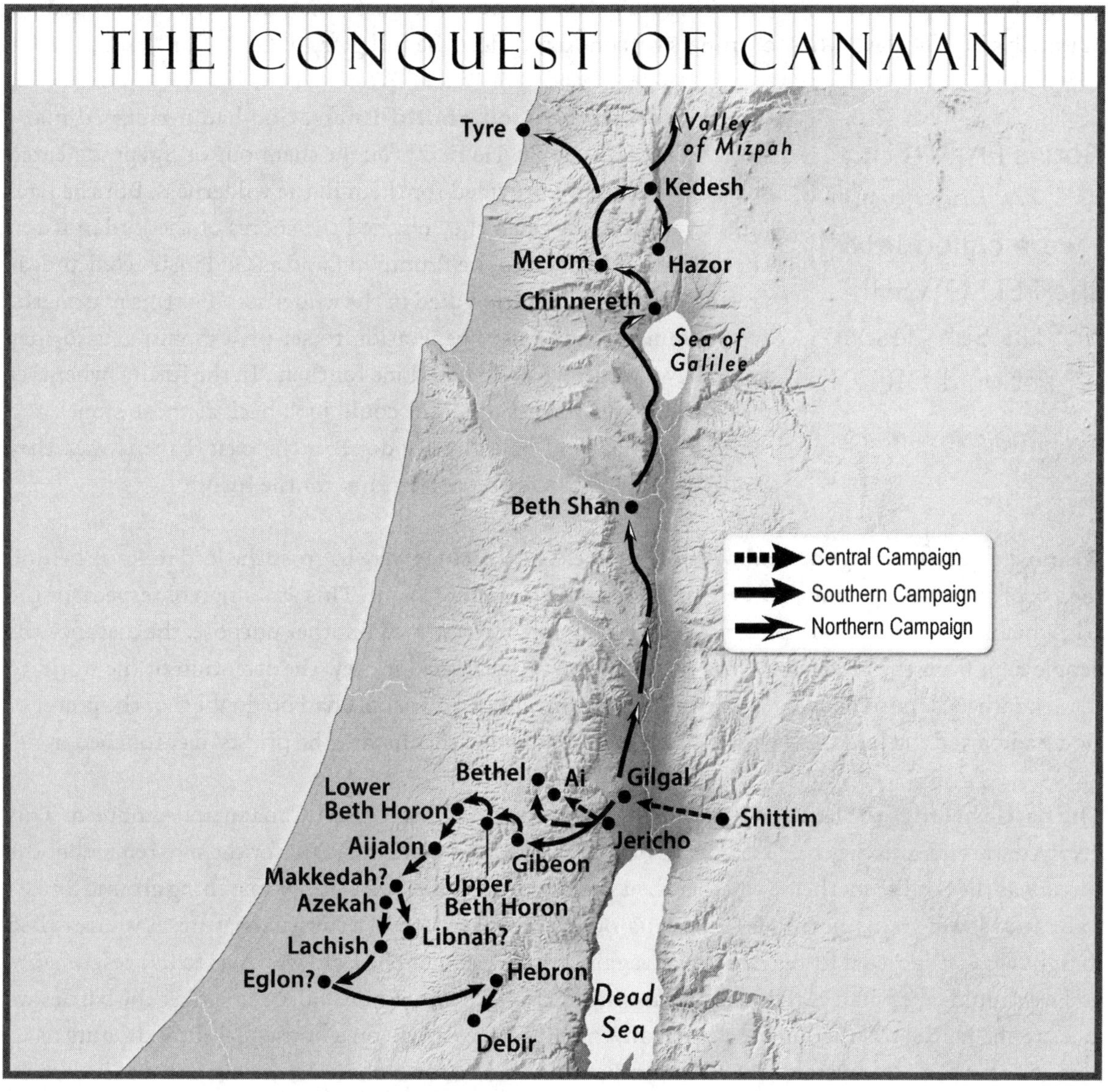

REFLECTIONS

God transforms sinners into saints. Rahab was not obeying God's commands for a righteous life, so it was an act of grace for Him to save her from the judgment that fell on Jericho. However, He did more than just that—He also transformed Rahab into a woman of God and placed her in the lineage of Christ. Our salvation is merely the first step in God's amazing work of redemption. When we repent of our sins and embrace God's grace through faith in Jesus Christ, we receive the inestimable gift of eternal life and also the gift of the Holy Spirit. The Spirit immediately begins the work of transformation in our lives, gradually making us more like Jesus Christ. This ultimate act of transformation exceeds even that done in Rahab's life, for the lowliest of sinners will one day reflect the full glory of God's Son, Jesus!

God is FAITHFUL, by whom you were called into the FELLOWSHIP of His Son, Jesus Christ our LORD.

1 CORINTHIANS 1:9

We are to remember God's faithfulness. God had performed many miracles for His people. He had brought them out of Egypt, defeated Pharaoh's army, and provided for them in the wilderness. But the Israelites had lost heart when they reached the shores of the Jordan River. They refused to cross into the Promised Land as God instructed and, as a result, an entire generation died in the wilderness. For this reason, the Lord commanded the next generation to set up a monument so they would never forget what He had done for them. In the future, whenever they faced powerful enemies, they could look back at those stones and remember what God had already done in the past. In this way, they would have courage to also trust in Him for the future.

We must treat the things of God with reverence. The Israelites were to cross the Jordan River behind the ark of the covenant, but they were to keep a great distance from it. This was a sign of respect for the ark, which symbolized God's presence with His people. Yet it served another purpose: the distance the people kept from the ark enabled the entire nation to see it, and it drew the attention of the world to the ark rather than to them. By remaining 1,000 yards back, the people had no doubt that the power of God had parted the Jordan River, because the water divided the instant the priests' feet touched it.

The battle belongs to the Lord. God commanded the Israelites to enter Canaan and subdue it. This involved warfare, and they needed to learn how to fight. But it was important for them to remember the battle was the Lord's, not theirs, whether their part involved taking up arms or marching around a city's walls and blowing rams' horns. As Christians, our warfare is mostly of a spiritual nature, as we are called to fight against spiritual forces rather than against other people. The Lord wants us to live responsibly, and we should take whatever actions we can within His will. But we must also remember the battles we face are the Lord's, whether or not there is anything that we can do on a human level. God wants us to place our faith in His sovereignty and remember that the outcome of our lives is entirely in His hands.

God cannot be deceived. Achan understood the Lord's command not to touch any of the treasures in Jericho, but he believed that he could take just a few items without any consequences. He then buried those items in the ground beneath his tent—an excellent hiding place if ever there was one. Achan and his family actually did succeed in hiding their sin from other people. It would appear that nobody outside of Achan's family was aware of the stolen property, and Joshua confidently led the army into battle in the belief that all was well. Yet the Lord knew what Achan had done, and He was not willing to overlook the transgression. All sin, no matter how small in the world's eyes, is an abhorrent offense in the eyes of God. It is easy to hide our sins from other people, but we can never hide them from God. He calls His people to purify their lives from all sins and confess them openly before Him.

God can move heaven and earth to accomplish His purposes. Or, more specifically to the events in Joshua, the Lord can cause the earth and heavens *not* to move. For the sun to stand still "in the midst of heaven" (Joshua 10:13), the earth would have needed to stop revolving on its axis—and evidently this is exactly what God did for the Israelites on that day. He literally caused the earth to stop for a period of hours so His people would have victory in battle. The Lord went beyond even this earthshaking miracle when He moved heaven itself to send His Son to earth as a man. He temporarily set aside the laws of biology and caused a virgin to become pregnant with the Son of God. Beyond even this, He permitted His Holy One to take on the sin of humankind, caused the One who is Life to taste death, and subjected the Creator to the whims of those He had created. He did all of this so we might be reconciled with Him.

We are to be strong and of good courage. The command not to fear appears frequently in the book of Joshua—usually at times when there was genuine cause for the people to be afraid. For instance, when the armies from the north gathered against the Israelites, the Lord said to Joshua, "Do not be afraid because of them, for tomorrow about this time I will deliver all of them slain before Israel" (Joshua 11:6). We are likewise commanded to resist fear, which reveals that fear is something we can master. This is done by shifting our focus away from the situation and instead focusing on the Lord who redeems us. He is completely faithful to save His people. After all, if He was willing to make the sun stand still for Israel's army, He will be willing to intervene in our lives as well.

CITIES OF REFUGE (JOSHUA 20:1-9)

Moses had named six cities in Israel as refuge centers. A person who inadvertently killed another could flee to the nearest of these for protection. Three cities lay west of the Jordan River, and three lay to the east, each reachable in a day for those in its area. Authorities at the refuge protected the slayer and escorted him to a trial. If found innocent, he was guarded at the refuge until the death of the current high priest, and then could return home. If found guilty of murder, he suffered appropriate punishment.

STUDY QUESTIONS

1. Why did the spies hide in the house of a prostitute when they entered the city of Jericho? In what ways would this have been a strategic move (see Joshua 2:1–7)?

2. In what ways was God's hand guiding the events in Rahab's life when she chose to hide the spies? What was His purpose for her (see Joshua 2:8–21; 6:22–23)?

3. Why did the Lord command the people to pile up stones rather than build an ornate shrine to Him (see Joshua 4:1–9)? What does this suggest about the focus of our own memorials?

4. Why did the Lord instruct the people to carry the ark with them when they marched around Jericho? What was God saying about who was fighting the battle (see Joshua 6:1–21)?

5. Why did God command Achan's entire family to be put to death (see Joshua 7:1–26)? What does this severe punishment reveal about God's view of disobedience?

6. Why did the people of Gibeon use deception to make peace with Israel? Why did God honor Israel's covenant with them anyway (see Joshua 9:1–26)?

7. What does it say about Joshua's faith that he commanded the sun to stand still (see Joshua 10:12–14)? Why do you think God honored this bold request?

8. What did Joshua command the people to do in his "farewell address" given in Joshua 23:2–16? What choice did he given them in Joshua 24:14–15?

WEEK 6

GOD JUDGES OUR SINS

JUDGES 1–21

READING PLAN: **36** | Judges 1–3 **37** | Judges 4–5 **38** | Judges 6–8
39 | Judges 10–12 **40** | Judges 13–14 **41** | Judges 15–16 **42** | Judges 17–18

The people of Israel entered the Promised Land with great joy. They witnessed the power of their God at work through incredible miracles such as the parting of the Jordan River and the sun standing still, as well as through miraculous victories over their enemies. There could be no doubt the sovereign Lord was fighting on their behalf. Yet He still commanded the people to be *involved*. They needed to walk in obedience to His commands.

One of those commands had been to drive out the people of Canaan and tear down their pagan altars. The Israelites had started strong in this mission, settling into the Promised Land and moving from victory to victory. But after Joshua's death, the people began drifting away not only from this command but also from worship of the Lord.

The author of the book of Judges, which the Jewish Talmud identifies as the prophet Samuel, described seven of these cycles. Over the course of about 450 years, a distinct sequence repeatedly occurred: (1) Israel would depart from God; (2) as judgment, God would permit military defeat and subjugation; (3) in response, Israel would pray for deliverance;

(4) God would faithfully raise up leaders to shake off the oppressors; and then (5) the people would forget God's mercy and faithfulness and depart from Him again.

As part of the "deliverance" phase, the Lord appointed a succession of individuals called *judges*—fourteen in total—to lead the nation to victory over its enemies and back toward obedience to Him. The first three judges were Othniel, Ehud, and Shamgar.

After the death of Ehud, the people again fell into sin. So God allowed Jabin, the king of Hazor, to lead a powerful coalition army to fight against them. Jabin's army was equipped with a huge force of chariots—iron chariots. Iron was a relatively new invention, used for swords and armor, and it was vastly superior to the bronze it replaced. Israel did not have any iron weapons or armor and certainly no iron-clad chariots. Outclassed and outnumbered, God's people were oppressed by Jabin for twenty years.

The northern tribes of Israel were being led at this time by a judge named Deborah. She was a woman of wisdom and prudence. The fighting men of Israel were led by a man named Barak. One day, according to the Lord's command, Deborah called for Barak to deploy 10,000 men against Sisera, the commander of Jabin's army. God had promised Barak victory, but instead of obeying, Barak bargained, perhaps thinking of how underequipped his men were against Sisera's iron chariots. His counteroffer to Deborah was, "If you will go with me, then I will go" (Judges 4:8).

The army of Israel did route Sisera's forces, but their leader escaped, and the Lord brought Sisera's death by the hand of a woman name Jael. Had Barak not balked at the Lord's word, God would have delivered Sisera into his hands. Instead, to his disgrace, his victory was ascribed to a woman.

In the life of Gideon, the fifth judge, we see another of God's chosen men hesitant to take the lead. Gideon was evidently from a wealthy family and had lived his life tending crops and herds. Israel's enemies at that time, the Midianites, were raiding the land and plundering God's people, causing such devastation that food was scarce and the people lived in fear for their lives.

We meet Gideon as he was trying to thresh wheat in secret, hoping his enemies would not swoop in and kill him as he did. We then read that God came to Gideon in human form and greeted him as a man of valor. At first glance this seems incongruous, as Gideon was trying to avoid any open confrontation! But God had great plans for Gideon and saw beyond his timidity. The first assignment that He gave to Gideon was to cleanse his own house of idolatry. Gideon was instructed to tear down the altar of Baal and build an altar to the Lord. Only then could he lead God's people against the Midianites.

It took time for Gideon to live up to the badge of honor God had given him, and he continued to demonstrate his fear by putting the Lord's promises to the test. But eventually God used Gideon to route the Midianite army. Unfortunately, after this great victory, Gideon made a gold ephod (a sleeveless garment worn by the priests) that led the people into idolatry.

Gideon was followed by the judges Tola, Jair, Jephthah, Ibzan, Elon, and Abdon. At this point, the Philistines were the nation's overlords. The Philistines were a wealthy and powerful civilization whose armies were feared. Rather than imposing harsh punishments or enslavement, they ruled by economic means, imposing taxes and laws. The Israelites were kept on a leash, but it was a golden leash. They experienced a measure of comfort and economic wealth during this time—it was an easy yoke to bear.

However, this was part of the problem: the Israelites were becoming too comfortable under the dominion of their heathen neighbors. They were slipping into a state of spiritual lethargy, embracing the practices of the world around them, and were in danger of becoming just one more pagan nation in the land of Canaan. God would not tolerate such apostasy, so He raised up yet another judge. However, this time God would use His judge to stir up trouble between Israel and the Philistines in order to awaken His people to the grave danger they were in.

This was the calling of Samson, a man raised as a Nazirite—one who took a vow to abstain from wine, avoid dead bodies, and never cut his hair. Samson was called to a life of purity, and during his time as a judge, his God-given strength enabled him to secure many victories over the Philistines. Yet Samson did not live up to His calling as a Nazirite and engaged in many sinful pursuits. Ultimately, the Spirit of God left him after his final choice to betray his Nazirite vows, though the Lord did give him one last victory over his enemies, during which time Samson pulled down the pillars of a pagan temple and killed 3,000 Philistines.

Samson was the twelfth judge and the final one who is mentioned in the book of Judges. (Two other judges, Eli and Samuel, are mentioned in the book of 1 Samuel.) The remaining chapters of Judges after Samson's death vividly demonstrate how deep sin can become when people throw off the authority of God. The results of Israel's choices served as a tragic conclusion to a bleak period of Israelite history.

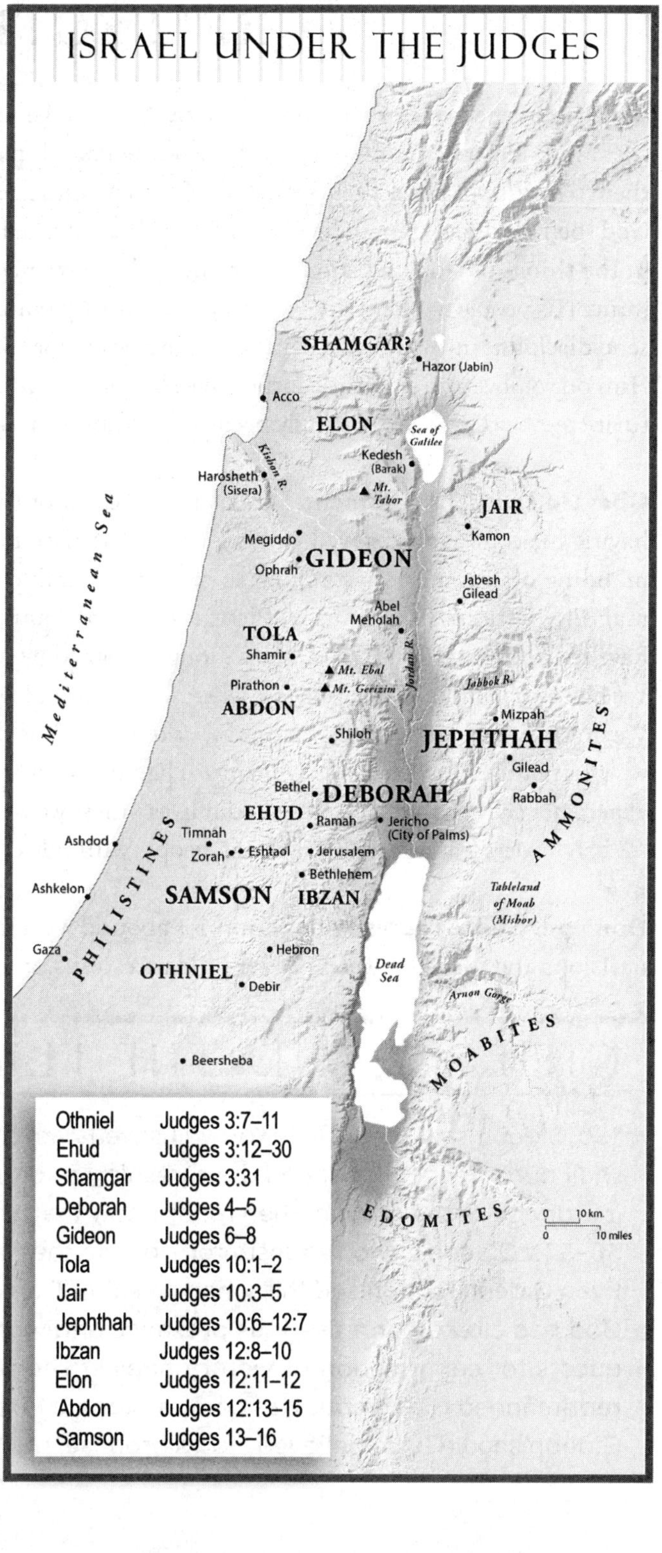

REFLECTIONS

Stay out of the cycle of sin. Judges relates how the Israelites disobeyed God's commands, which led them into idolatry. God responded by sending hardship on the people as a form of discipline, urging them to return to Him. This oppression from enemies and other calamities forced Israel to repent, and God then graciously sent judges to lead them back to obedience. But after a time, the people lost interest in the things of God and soon began the cycle all over again! This cycle was not pleasing to God. He wants His people to obey Him willingly and worship Him voluntarily with their whole hearts. God will send discipline into our lives to make us purer and more like Christ, but His deep desire is for us to obey Him out of love and gratitude rather than by the compulsion of hardship. It is a mark of spiritual maturity to obey God's Word simply because we know that it pleases and glorifies the Father.

Obey God without argument. Barak was the leader of Israel's military. As such, he was accustomed to having his commands obeyed without argument. (After all, a good soldier never talks back to a commanding officer.) So it is startling to read that Barak countermanded the direct orders of his Commanding Officer—God Himself. Picture a general commanding a soldier to move into battle only to have the soldier respond, "I will go as long as you come with me." The soldier's career would be short. Yet how much more audacious is it when we try to find ways around simple obedience to God's Word! We do this when we obey only partway, or tell ourselves that we will begin to obey tomorrow, or when we ignore the Holy Spirit's promptings. The Lord wants us to eagerly obey His Word—and we cannot experience the Lord's full blessing in our lives unless we willingly obey His commands. As Deborah sang, "When leaders lead in Israel, when the people willingly offer themselves, bless the LORD!" (Judges 5:2).

Don't put God to the test. The Scriptures abound with men and women who were faced with difficult decisions and turned to the Lord for guidance. Jesus urged His disciples to seek the Father's will in all

GIDEON AND THE FLEECE (JUDGES 6:36-40)

"So Gideon said to God, 'If You will save Israel by my hand as You havae said—look, I shall put a fleece of wool on the threshing floor; if there is dew on the fleece only, and it is dry on all the ground, then I shall know that You will save Israel by my hand" (verses 36–37). Gideon's two requests for signs in the fleece should be viewed as weak faith. Even Gideon recognized this when he said, "Do not be angry with me" (verse 39), since God had already promised His presence and victory. But they were also legitimate requests for confirmation of victory against seemingly impossible odds. God nowhere reprimanded Gideon but was compassionate in giving what his inadequacy requested. Gideon should have believed God's promise, but he needed bolstering, so God gave it.

things, teaching them to pray, "Your will be done on earth as it is in heaven" (Matthew 6:10). Today, Christians receive the indwelling of the Holy Spirit, whose role, in part, is to guide us into all truth (see John 16:13). There is no need to "test" God in order to receive His direction. Actually, it is important to recognize in Gideon's story that he was not really seeking guidance by putting out his fleeces. The Lord had already told him exactly what to do. The issue was that Gideon feared the Lord would not keep His promises, so he sought verification of God's faithfulness. But God had already proven Himself faithful in Israel's history—parting the Jordan River, bringing down the walls of Jericho, providing one victory after another—and Gideon should have rested in faith that the Lord would keep His word once again.

Seek to remain effective for God. It is surprising to read about Samson, so plagued with fleshly indulgence, and realize the Spirit of God continued to use him in mighty ways. Samson spent much of his life consorting with the enemies of his people. He indulged in wine in spite of his vow to refrain from it. He married a Canaanite woman, which was expressly forbidden of God's people. Samson even hired prostitutes and carried on an immoral relationship with Delilah. Yet still, the Lord used him to begin the overthrow of the Philistines! However, the sad truth is that Samson's effectiveness was greatly limited by his sin. Instead of being both a political leader and a spiritual example in Israel, he was a moral failure who accomplished far less than his potential. The Lord did use Samson to accomplish a small part of His plan, but his sinful habits prevented him from accomplishing so much more. In the same way, God does not abandon us when we sin, but our sinful habits can severely interfere with our effectiveness in His service. Our sin grieves the Holy Spirit and quenches His power in our lives. When we walk in ungodliness, we risk ending in tragedy, just as Samson did.

> ABSTAIN from fleshly LUSTS which war against the SOUL.
>
> 1 PETER 2:11

Do not quench the Spirit of God. Samson believed his great strength came from some magical effect of never cutting his hair. He did not understand that his power came from the Spirit of God, who had chosen to indwell him. So it was that when Samson unintentionally permitted Delilah to cut his hair, he was effectively repudiating his Nazirite vow and declaring the God of Israel was not his Lord. His life was ruled by his passions. The same Holy Spirit who empowered Samson indwells every follower of Christ. The Holy Spirit, of course, is not an impersonal force but a divine Person who, as the third member of the Trinity, is coequal and consubstantial with the Father and the Son. The Bible teaches that the Spirit has all of the attributes of personality and deity, including intellect, emotions, volition, eternality, omnipresence, omniscience, omnipotence, and truthfulness. The Spirit also sanctifies, instructs, illuminates, and empowers us for spiritual service. He enables us to be obedient to the truth. When we walk in accord with the Word of God, which the Holy Spirit inspired, we walk according to the Spirit and thereby exhibit the fruit of the Spirit. On the flip side, when we gratify the desires of our sinful nature (as Samson did), we quench the Spirit and exhibit the fruit of the flesh (see Galatians 5:16–25).

STUDY QUESTIONS

1. Why did God command the Israelites to not make any covenants with the Canaanites and to tear down their altars? What resulted from their failure to obey (see Judges 2:1–6)?

2. How might the Israelites have justified their failure to drive out the people of Canaan? In what ways do Christians today sometimes justify their disobedience and worldliness?

3. What was wrong with Barak's request to have Deborah join him? How might the outcome of the battle been different if Barak had fully obeyed God's command (see Judges 4:4–10)?

4. Why did Gideon ask for miraculous signs from God? What did this reveal about his faith? What does this reveal about God's character (see Judges 6:14–21, 36–40)?

5. Why did the Lord command Gideon to destroy his father's pagan altar? Why was this important for him to do first before fighting the Midianites (see Judges 6:25–32)?

6. How would you characterize Samson's character based on what you read in Judges 14–15? What were his greatest strengths? What were his greatest weaknesses?

7. What did Samson ultimately reveal to Delilah about how to enslave him (see Judges 16:1–17)? What do you think led him to that point—and why could he not foresee what would happen?

8. Why did God continue to use Samson through so many years of disobedience? Why did the Holy Spirit leave Samson when he cut his hair (see Judges 16:18–21)?

WEEK 7

GOD IS OUR SOVEREIGN KING

RUTH 1 – 1 SAMUEL 17

READING PLAN:	**43** | Ruth 1–4	**44** | 1 Samuel 1–3	**45** | 1 Samuel 4–6
46 | 1 Samuel 7–8	**47** | 1 Samuel 9–12	**48** | 1 Samuel 13–15	**49** | 1 Samuel 16–17

The beautiful drama of Ruth is a true account that bridges the time from the judges to Israel's monarchy. It is the story of a Moabitess who arrived in Bethlehem as a foreigner, became a maidservant, devoted herself to the God of Israel, married wealthy Boaz (who became Ruth's kinsman redeemer), and was an important link in the physical lineage of Christ.

The people of Israel had been living in the Promised Land for several generations when the land of Judah experienced a famine that was severe enough for a man named Elimelech to move his wife and two sons to the land of Moab. The Moabites were the perennial enemy of Israel, yet Elimelech married his sons to Moabite women.

Many years later, Elimelech's widow, Naomi, returned to Judah, accompanied by Ruth. The future looked bleak for both women. Naomi's sons had died, Ruth's late husband had not produced a son, and they had lost the family property through poverty.

The women arrived in Judah during the barley harvest. The law of Moses required farmers to leave behind portions of grain for the poor to glean for food. However, it did not require farmers to feed the gleaners or pay them any special attention—to do that would be to go above the call of duty. It is in this setting that we meet Boaz, and he met Ruth. The Lord was already working to bring these two together through His divine sovereignty—literally a match made in heaven. Through their descendants, God would bring about the human birth of His Son, Jesus Christ.

As 1 Samuel begins, Israel was at another low point. But God would raise up a prophet/judge to lead them, prepared for a lifetime of faithful service by his parents—notably his mother, Hannah. In the grief of her barrenness, she had dedicated her firstborn son to the Lord. When that child, Samuel, was born and reached the age of two or three, Hannah fulfilled her vow and brought him to Shiloh, where he grew up ministering to the Lord before Eli, a judge and high priest. Eli's two sons, who also served as priests, were wicked, and they were causing the Lord's name to be profaned in Israel. Because Eli did little to stop them, God determined his house would forfeit the priesthood. Samuel's first assignment as a young prophet was to deliver this horrible news to the man he loved as a father.

Beyond Eli's failure to discipline his sons, he led the entire nation into error. The Israelites, thinking they could use the ark of the covenant as a lucky charm that would ensure victory over their enemies, rashly decided to remove the ark from the temple at Shiloh and take it with them into battle. When they lost not only the battle but also the ark to the Philistines, Eli died of shock, and the people acted as if they had lost their God. The Lord used this event to punish them for their sin and display His greatness over Dagon, the Philistine god. The Lord proved how ridiculous it was for the Israelites to think that He resided in a box or that they could manipulate Him into giving them victory.

Twenty years later, the people were finally ready to return to the Lord. While they were gathered publicly to repent of their idolatry, the Lord gave them a tremendous victory over the Philistines. He also revealed that Samuel would be the one taking over Eli's judgeship. God would work powerfully throughout Samuel's days as Israel's final judge.

In time, though, the people looked around at the neighboring nations of Canaan, saw that everybody else had a king, and decided they wanted one of their own. Samuel was deeply grieved and must have felt as though his life of faithful service had been in vain. But as the Lord gently reminded Samuel, those who reject Him will also reject His servants.

The Lord warned the people of the servitude that would come with a kingship, knowing they would not be happy with their choice. Still, they insisted, and eventually God acquiesced. The young man the Lord selected for the job was Saul. Outwardly, he had the perfect qualifications for a king. But his heart was not turned toward the Lord.

After Saul had a military victory against the Ammonites, the people came to Gilgal to crown him as king. Saul rode the wave of success into his next battle against the Philistines. At first things went well, but when the battle grew fierce, Saul's army deserted. This would prove to be his big test. Would he submit to the Lord as the true King of Israel? Or would he take that authority upon himself?

Saul decided to usurp the authority of God's chosen priests. In a subsequent battle, he kept the choice plunder for himself, against the Lord's command. Saul excused his disobedience as simple expedience, but in both cases, he only obeyed in part. His life was characterized by decisions like these, where he set his own will above God's. Consequently, the Lord rejected Saul as king and called on Samuel to anoint the new king from among Jesse's seven sons.

Although one of these sons, David, was just a youth, he had already developed godly character and learned many skills that would become useful as the Lord called him from shepherding animals to shepherding His people. David's first engagement was against Goliath. For forty days, this Philistine giant of a man came before the Israelites morning and evening, taunting them and challenging them to fight him. As a result, the Israelites "were dismayed and greatly afraid" (1 Samuel 17:11).

David undoubtedly also felt fear when saw Goliath, but he knew he was going in the strength of the Lord. God gave him the victory through a well-placed stone from his slingshot. Once the Israelites saw how God had honored David's obedience, they shook off their own fear and went into battle. David's obedience bred courage in those around him. Yet the episode revealed the Holy Spirit had truly left Saul and was now with David. From that point on, Israel's victories would be under David's leadership.

REFLECTIONS

God's salvation is available to all. God had forbidden the Moabites from entering the congregation of Israel, but Ruth forsook the gods of Moab and embraced the God of Israel. In that moment, she went from being an outsider with no hope of entering God's presence to being included in the human line of Jesus. Likewise, any sinner who embraces salvation through Christ is transformed from death into life.

Jesus is our Kinsman Redeemer. Ruth was doomed to poverty. Her only hope lay with a stranger who had little to gain from a marriage to her. Yet Boaz took upon himself the full responsibility of caring for his relatives. Boaz provides us with a picture of Christ in His role as our Redeemer. We were without hope, but Jesus took upon Himself the full responsibility of caring for us and is preparing a place for us as His bride for all eternity. He did this voluntarily—even to the point of willingly dying on the cross.

God is pleased by a willing heart. Samuel was no older than fourteen when he heard the Lord call his name. He did not lie in bed and ignore what he heard but ran to Eli's side. When God ultimately gave him some bad news for Eli, his heart quaked at the thought of delivering such a message to the man who was like a father to him, yet he did so in obedience to the Lord—and he delivered it in full.

Courage is found by trusting in God's sovereignty. When David confronted Goliath, he did not just charge across the valley and hope things would work out. Blind action in the face of fear is folly. David was courageous because he knew two things: he would be king over Israel, and the Lord would not be mocked. Fear grows when we focus our eyes on the things of this world. The Israelite army was terrified because they were busy looking at Goliath and his terrible weapons. David, however, scorned those material weapons. He understood that worldly weapons are powerless against the Lord God.

STUDY QUESTIONS

1. Skim through Ruth 1–2 and look for behind-the-scenes evidence of God's sovereign hand. How did He work out all the details for Naomi and Ruth?

2. What did it cost Boaz to become the kinsman redeemer for Ruth and Naomi (see Ruth 4:1–12)? What did Ruth gain? What did Naomi gain?

3. Why did Peninnah abuse Hannah about her childlessness? What did this reveal about her character? What did it reveal about their home life (see 1 Samuel 1:1–11)?

4. Why do you think God sent such a devastating judgment against Eli? What had he done wrong (see 1 Samuel 2:27–33; 4:4–18)?

5. Why didn't the Lord simply defeat the Philistines miraculously without any fighting on the part of the Israelites (see 1 Samuel 7:5–13)?

6. Why did the Israelites want a king (see 1 Samuel 8:19–20)? Why were they unsatisfied with the judges that God had given them?

7. What qualities did David possess that prepared him to become king? How did those qualities differ from the qualities that Saul possessed (see 1 Samuel 16:4–23)?

8. What motivated David to face Goliath? Why was his response to the threat so different from Saul's response (see 1 Samuel 17:34–37)?

WEEK 8

GOD REWARDS A FAITHFUL HEART

1 SAMUEL 18 – 2 SAMUEL 10

READING PLAN: **50** | 1 Samuel 18–21 **51** | 1 Samuel 22–26 **52** | 1 Samuel 27–31 **53** | 2 Samuel 1–3 **54** | 2 Samuel 4–5 **55** | 2 Samuel 6–8 **56** | 2 Samuel 9–10

The events in 1 and 2 Samuel span about 135 years of history, between the birth of Samuel and the last words of David. During those years, Israel was transformed from a loosely knit group of tribes under judges to a nation under the reign of a centralized monarchy.

As the events of 1 Samuel 18 unfold, Saul, who was slowly going mad, was still on the throne, even though David had been anointed as God's chosen ruler. Saul, ever jealous of David's popularity, set about getting rid of him. Meanwhile, David valiantly and faithfully served Saul as a soldier. He was also the only person who could soothe Saul when an evil spirit persecuted him. Yet nothing David did alleviated the king's hatred. Saul eventually drove him out of his court, forcing David to go on the run and hide anywhere he could find.

Jonathan stepped into this deadly situation. He was Saul's son, which meant David was his main rival to the throne. Yet Jonathan understood the Lord had chosen David to be Israel's king. So instead of joining in his father's attempts to eliminate David, he opted to remain loyal to his closest friend, even risking his life to help David ascend the throne.

One day, when David and his men were hiding from Saul in a cave, the Lord delivered Saul into his hands. David was given the perfect opportunity to finally end all the madness by simply ending Saul's life. If *anyone* had the right to slay his attacker, it was David, the legitimate king of Israel. But he refused to do any harm to Saul because he was intent on respecting the one whom God had anointed as king.

Samuel, Israel's last judge and one of God's great prophets, had warned the people about the consequences of exchanging the Lord for a human monarchy. Sadly, Samuel's words of warning were fulfilled. By the end of Saul's life, Israel was being decimated by their enemies, Saul's ego had placed his own pride above Israel's well-being, and, in one of his final acts, he chose to completely turn his back on God and seek out a witch for guidance. In short, Israel got exactly the king that they had wanted.

DAVID'S TRIUMPHS
(FROM 2 SAMUEL)

Becomes the king of Judah (2:4)

Becomes the king of Israel (5:3)

Conquers the city of Jerusalem (5:7)

Returns the ark of the covenant (6:12)

Receives covenant from the Lord (7:16)

Defeats Philistines, Moab, Ammon, and Syria (8:1-2:10 16, 19)

Tragically, Saul died in battle against the Philistines, and all of his sons died with him—except for one, named Ishbosheth. As the book of 2 Samuel opens, God has just called David to go to Hebron, where he would be anointed king over Judah. But Saul's sole survivor felt the throne was his by birthright, leading to division in the nation, with each faction placing their allegiance behind a different successor to the throne.

Abner, the general of Ishbosheth's army, initially sided against David, and then made his own play for the throne. Yet God sovereignly used him to convince the people who had sided with Ishbosheth that God's chosen king over all Israel was David. Ishbosheth was defeated, and the tribes then came to Hebron to declare David their king. After this, David conquered the city of Jerusalem and defeated the remainder of the Philistines.

Once David was established as Israel's sole ruler, he decided the time was right to bring the ark of the covenant—the ornate chest containing the tablets of the Law and other sacred objects—back to Jerusalem. The ark was the symbol of God's presence among His people. The Philistines had captured it in battle many years earlier, but when God swept disease and death through their cities, they hastily placed it on an oxcart and sent it away. It ended up in the town of Kirjath Jearim, where it had remained ever since.

God had given strict instructions to His people about not only *how* to move the ark but also *who* was supposed to move it. Yet David disobeyed these directives, leading to the death of one man. Fearing more calamity might come, David left the ark in the home of a man called Obed-Edom the Gittite. But three months later, reports came to David that the Lord had blessed the household where the ark resided. David quickly recognized that God also desired to bless His people, and so the ark was then brought to Jerusalem with gladness. This time, the people carried it in the correct manner, bearing it on the shoulders of the Levites rather than trundling it along in an oxcart like the Philistines had done.

David, settling into his kingship, issued a search for any remaining descendants of Saul—not to have them killed but to show kindness to them and thus keep the oath of friendship he had made with

Jonathan. When Jonathan's son Mephibosheth was located, David showed him compassion . . . and went far beyond, even to the point of showering gifts and honor on him.

David's rule would prove to be primarily characterized by conflict and warfare. The Israelites had many enemies who persisted in trying to conquer them—and some even wanted to wipe them off the map. The Philistines, whose land lay to the west on the coast of the Mediterranean Sea, were one of their most dangerous enemies. David would spend the majority of his reign trying to overthrow their tyranny while dealing with other foreign enemies and rebellions from the Israelites themselves. Yet in spite of this opposition to his rule, he never lost sight of the fact that all his blessings had come from God.

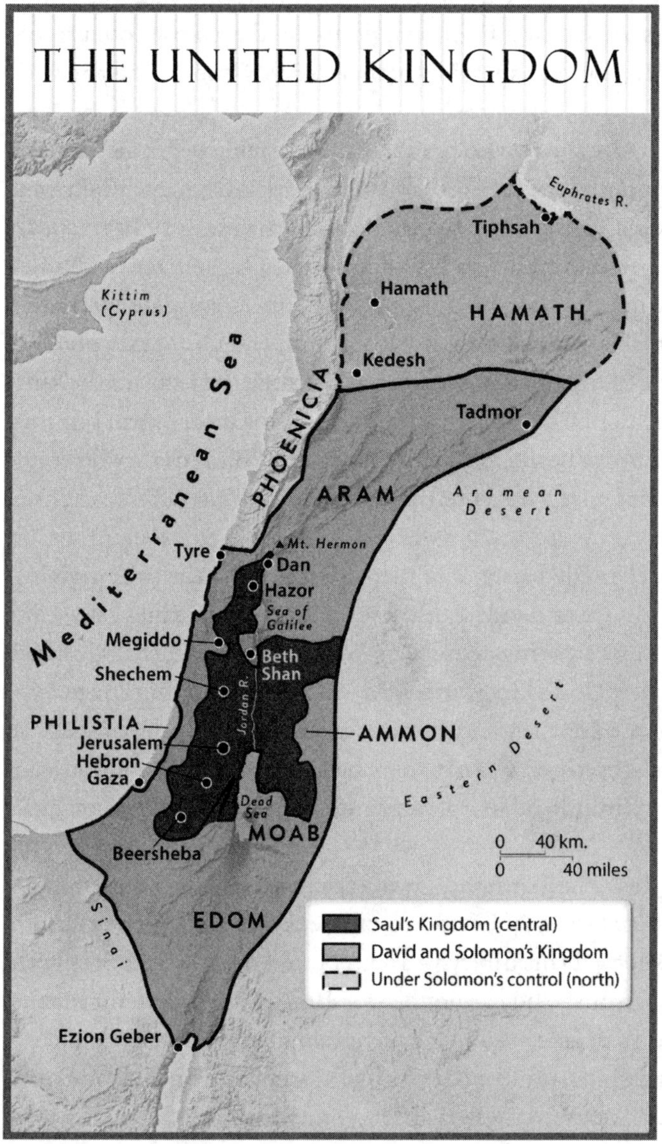

David was called "a man after [God's] own heart" (1 Samuel 13:14), and the Lord made many promises to him concerning his life and the future of his kingdom. One of these promises came after David, sensing it was not right for him to be living in a grand palace while God dwelt in a portable tent, devised a plan to build a temple—a permanent dwelling for the Almighty where the people could worship God. Although the Lord would not allow him to construct the temple, He promised that David's son would build it, and this promise was soon fulfilled in Solomon. However, God went even further in this promise to David.

The Lord told David that the Israelites would be "planted" in the Promised Land—no longer moving about from place to place and continually being harassed by enemies. Furthermore, God said to David, "I will set up your seed after you, who will come from your body, and I will establish his kingdom. He shall build a house for My name, and I will establish the throne of his kingdom forever" (2 Samuel 7:12–13). This promise would be fulfilled in the short term through David's son Solomon. However, it also was (and will be) fulfilled in the long-term (eternal) sense through Jesus, whose human ancestry is traced through the seed of David.

REFLECTIONS

Devotion to God outweighs the riches of the world. In the world's eyes, Jonathan was heir to the throne, and the army was at his command to protect that inheritance. His father, in fact, was actively working to remove Jonathan's sole "rival" to the throne. All that Jonathan needed to do was cooperate with Saul's plan to kill David, and his inheritance would have been (in Saul's thinking) fully secure. But Jonathan understood that the earth's kingdoms will all pass away and only love shall remain—and he invested his future in his love for David. He was willing to sacrifice all the honors that were rightfully his by birth and even risk his life to help David ascend the throne that might have been his own. Christians are likewise called to choose faithfulness to God over their own desires and even over their families: "But seek first the kingdom of God and His righteousness" (Matthew 6:33). We seek God *first.*

I say to you, LOVE your enemies, BLESS those who curse you, do GOOD to those who hate you.

MATTHEW 5:44

We are not to revile those who persecute us. In spite of David's service to Saul, he lived under the threat of murder and was frequently betrayed by his own people. If ever there were a person who had a right to speak harshly to his persecutor, it was David. But when he confronted Saul—even after sparing his life—he did not revile his enemy. He respected Saul's position as king and bowed before him. David did not pretend that Saul was not sinning against him, but he spoke the truth to the king in a humble fashion. This can be a hard lesson for us to learn, but it is important if we are to be like Christ. As Jesus said, "Bless those who curse you, and pray for those who spitefully use you" (Luke 6:28).

Division is the devil's tool. The nation of Israel divided after Saul died, with some of the people giving their allegiance to Ishbosheth. Satan's goal is always to divide God's people, because he knows if we are busy contending against one another, we won't be fighting against his forces. He knows that a united body of believers is a powerful force for advancing God's kingdom on earth. The Lord wants His people to function as one body, to focus on serving one another, and to care for one another as members of that body. As Paul wrote, "Now I plead with you, brethren . . . that there be no divisions among you, but that you be perfectly joined together in the same mind and in the same judgment" (1 Corinthians 1:10).

God is to be worshiped in His prescribed way. The Lord had given strict instructions on who was allowed to move the ark, appointing a particular family of Levites to oversee the ark's transportation. When David first tried to move the ark, he disobeyed this directive and replaced the Levite priests with political leaders of Israel. The results were disastrous. God cannot be worshiped using whatever means we deem most appealing or acceptable. As God's people, we must not worship simply by external conformity to religious rituals. Rather, we must worship based on the truth of God's Word and with a Spirit that longs to obey His commands. If the proper heart attitude is absent, our worship is false.

It is good to pour out our worship to God. David danced before the Lord when the ark was brought back to the city of Jerusalem, leaping and whirling in an open expression of joy. He was the king of Israel, one of the most powerful leaders in the world, and his position certainly required times of sober dignity. Yet he was also the leader of God's people, and it was in that capacity that he led them in a joyful demonstration of their love for God. David and the Israelite people had good reason for joy, just as we—as believers in Christ—have good reason for joy. We should emulate David's example, expressing our joy to God in blissful praise and worship. As the apostle Paul later wrote to the believers in Ephesus, "Be filled with the Spirit, speaking to one another in psalms and hymns and spiritual songs, singing and making melody in your heart to the Lord" (Ephesians 5:18–19).

God's promises are fulfilled in Christ. God swore that He would establish David's throne and kingdom forever, not just for the lifetimes of men. As we have seen, the Lord had made covenants with others before David—such as with Noah and Abraham—but those promises were only partially brought to completion during the lives of the patriarchs. Jesus is the complete fulfillment of God's promises and covenants. All human history has been leading up to God's final redemption of Adam's descendants—the eternal kingdom of God established and ruled over by His Son, Jesus Christ. Jesus is both Son of God and Son of Man, and His human ancestry is traced from the seed of David. Although David did see God's promises come to pass during his own lifetime, the final fulfillment will come in eternity through Christ.

We must fulfill our promises. David and Jonathan loved each another like brothers. They had sworn an oath of friendship, with David promising Jonathan that he would always show kindness to his family. So when David learned that Mephibosheth, a son of Jonathan, was living in the house of "Machir the son of Ammiel" (2 Samuel 9:4), he went beyond what was merely expected of him and deliberately showed compassion to Jonathan's son. In this David was imitating the character of God, who always keeps His promises. As God's people, we too should take care to fulfill our word, whether it is given as a solemn oath (as in marriage vows) or a simple promise. In fact, according to James, it is much better for us not to give our word at all than to give it and not keep it (see James 5:12).

THE DAVIDIC COVENANT

(FROM 2 SAMUEL 7:10–16)

1. God will appoint a place for His people.
2. God will arrange for the permanence of His people.
3. God will prevent oppression from His people's enemies.
4. God will set up the Davidic dynasty (house of David).
5. God will establish the Davidic kingdom.
6. God will ensure the certainty of the Davidic throne.

STUDY QUESTIONS

1. Why was Saul trying to kill David? Why did Jonathan choose to defend him (see 1 Samuel 18:1–16; 19:1–10)? How have you seen jealousy affect your life?

2. Why did David decide not to kill Saul when he was in the cave (see 1 Samuel 24:1–7)? What does this show about his understanding of God's control over Israel?

3. Why did Saul feel that he needed to consult a witch (see 1 Samuel 28:3–25)? What would it have taken at this point to restore his relationship with the Lord?

4. What caused Abner to shift his allegiance to David? What was the root cause of the rift that developed between Ishbosheth and Abner (see 2 Samuel 3:6–11)?

5. Compare the two attempts at moving the ark in 2 Samuel 6:1–19. What was done differently in each attempt? What remained the same?

6. How do the promises God made to David connect to Christ (see 2 Samuel 7:1–17)? What elements of the promises were specifically referring to Jesus?

7. What does David's prayer reveal about his attitude toward God's blessings (see 2 Samuel 7:18–29)? What does it reveal about his character?

8. What motivated David to honor Mephibosheth (see 2 Samuel 9:1–7)? If you had been in David's place, how do you think you would have acted?

WEEK 9

GOD RESTORES US WHEN WE FALL

2 SAMUEL 11 – 1 KINGS 4

READING PLAN: **57** | 2 Samuel 11–12 **58** | 2 Samuel 13–15 **59** | 2 Samuel 16–19 **60** | 2 Samuel 20–22 **61** | 2 Samuel 23–24 **62** | 1 Kings 1–2 **63** | 1 Kings 3–4

David was Israel's second king, but he was the first king to follow after God's own heart. Yet he was also a king who fell into a season of sin. His downward spiral began when he decided to stay at home in his palace when the Israelites went to war against the Ammonites.

We are not told why David chose not to be involved in the fighting, but at least in some measure he was shirking his responsibilities, as in those days the king was responsible to lead his army into battle. This self-indulgence led to lust and sexual immorality with a woman, named Bathsheba, who was not his wife. He then further erred by trying to hide his guilt—and, ultimately, this sin led to the murder of Bathsheba's husband.

Time passed (probably a year or so), and David married Bathsheba, who bore him a son. However, David had not yet repented of his sins. God, not content to pretend that nothing wrong had been done, sent the prophet Nathan to confront the king.

David finally did repent when he was brought face-to-face with his sin as God viewed it. The Law demanded that he should be put to death for both adultery and murder, but God commuted that sentence—though the child of David and Bathsheba died. (A second son was born to them shortly after, whom they named Solomon.) Nevertheless, the temporal results of David's sins were not removed. David's family, and the nation, suffered for his transgressions. Nathan also brought a prophecy that the sword would never depart from David's household. This soon began to unfold.

David had numerous wives and concubines who bore him many sons. This fostered jealousies and strife, especially as David's sons began vying for their father's throne. David's firstborn son was Amnon, whose mother was Ahinoam. By rights, Amnon was the successor to David's throne, but another son of David named Absalom had other ideas. Absalom was born to Maacah, herself the daughter of a king, and he evidently felt himself better qualified to take his father's place.

At one point, Amnon acted on an unhealthy desire for his half sister, Tamar, and raped her. This gave his rival, Absalom (the full brother of Tamar), an excuse to murder him—and the seeds of revolution were sown. Absalom killed his brother, then fled Jerusalem and went to live with his grandfather, the king of Geshur. He lived there for three years. All the while, David mourned for him and yearned to see him again. Joab, the commander of Israel's army, eventually intervened (using a tactic similar to Nathan's confrontation) and persuaded the king to send word to Absalom to return to Jerusalem.

However, once Absalom returned, David refused to see him. Perhaps he was torn between fatherly love and his guilt over not executing justice after Amnon's murder. Whatever David's motives, Absalom had to content himself by living in Jerusalem without access to his father. In this, however, he was anything but content. Absalom took matters into his own hands—getting Joab's attention by setting his field on fire. Joab soon intervened, and the relationship between David and Absalom was restored.

Yet there was much more that Absalom desired. He lusted for power and would not be satisfied until he had killed his father and taken his throne. Through his political tactics and charisma, Absalom was able to win so many of the people's hearts that David was forced to flee Jerusalem. But God had determined for Absalom's revolt to be defeated, and He controlled all the intrigues among the usurper's counselors. Ultimately, Absalom brought about a course of events that ended in his own death.

When David was restored to the throne, both loyal friends and former enemies swore their allegiance to him. David desired to regain his rule without unnecessary bloodshed, so he offered forgiveness to his enemies and rewards to those who had been faithful. Yet seeds of discontent still stirred across the land. So it was that when a quarrel erupted between the tribes of Israel and Judah, it provided a spark for another uprising against David, led by a man named Sheba. This revolt also failed.

David, toward the end of his life, composed a song to praise the Lord for His blessings. He then declared an oracle—a record of direct speech from God—communicating the Lord's standard for His ideal king. David confessed his house had not always ruled over the people in righteousness. Yet David rightly believed the Lord would be faithful to His promise of future hope through his seed. This eternal King, the coming Messiah, would establish a kingdom of righteousness and peace forever.

The book of 1 Kings begins with the final years of David's reign. By this time, David was seventy years old and plagued with circulatory problems. The news of David's failing health soon prompted Adonijah, David's fourth son, to assert his claim to the throne.

However, the prophet Nathan knew that Adonijah was not God's choice for Israel's next ruler. This distinction would fall to Solomon, the second son born to David and Bathsheba. Nathan's intervention prompted David to formally recognize Solomon as his successor. When David summoned Solomon to impart some final words to him, he not only encouraged his son to be courageous and faithful to the Lord but also charged him with tying up some loose ends from his reign.

Solomon began his reign on good footing. He asked God to give him wisdom to shepherd His people, and the Lord not only gave him wisdom but also riches and power. Solomon made his wisdom and justice accessible to all types of people in his kingdom. When he discerned the truth in a case between two prostitutes, Israel was in awe and willing to submit to his rule because of this wisdom from God.

REFLECTIONS

God calls us to confess our sins. David slipped into a spiral of sin, beginning with self-indulgence and leading to his adultery with Bathsheba. His immediate concern seemed to be that people would find out what he had done, and this misdirected fear led him to attempt a cover-up. It did not occur to him that God knew what he had done—and was displeased. God wants His people to refrain from sinful behavior, but He also knows we are sinners by birth (see Psalm 51:5). However, when we fall into sin, the Lord calls us to confess and repent of those sins immediately and not try to conceal them. Confession leads to forgiveness and reconciliation, while attempted cover-ups lead to further sin and suffering.

Guard your heart against the world's seductions. One of the more tragic elements in Absalom's story of treason is the ease with which God's people turned against David. However, this is not hard to understand from a human perspective, given that Absalom was a charismatic leader who played politics quite skillfully. He played on the people's discontentment and fears, promising them a solution that he could not deliver. The world has not changed since David's day. It still appeals to our vanity, just as Absalom did when he paraded himself through Jerusalem, and it plays on our fears and dissatisfactions, just as Absalom did with those he met at the city gates. Yet true satisfaction and fulfillment are found only in God. What the world promises cannot compare with what He promises.

> Do not love the WORLD or the things in the world. If anyone LOVES the world, the love of the FATHER is not in him.
>
> 1 JOHN 2:15

Wisdom comes through God's Word. When Solomon asked the Lord for wisdom, God gave it to him in abundance. Today, God's wisdom is available to everyone through the gospel. In 1 Corinthians 1:24, Paul calls Jesus "the wisdom of God," and in Colossians 3:16, he says this wisdom is gained through the study of "the word of Christ." God is eager to bestow wisdom on us—and that wisdom is found in Scripture: "If any of you lacks wisdom, let him ask of God, who gives to all liberally" (James 1:5).

STUDY QUESTIONS

1. What were the events that led David to be tempted by sin (see 2 Samuel 11:1–4)? What are some things that David might have done to avoid the temptation?

2. How did the parable that Nathan told expose the true nature of David's sins (see 2 Samuel 12:1–14)? What elements in the parable related directly to those sins?

3. What should Amnon have done about his desires for Tamar (see 2 Samuel 13:1–22)? What would have been a godly way of dealing with the situation?

4. What events led to Absalom rebelling against his father and attempting to take the throne of Israel? What part did David's sin play in setting the stage (see 2 Samuel 15:1–12)?

5. What events ultimately led to the failure of Absalom's rebellion (see 2 Samuel 16:15–17:16; 18:6–18)? How was the hand of God at work in orchestrating all the events?

6. What was the source of the dispute between the tribes of Israel and Judah? How did this so suddenly lead to another rebellion (see 2 Samuel 19:40–20:2)?

7. What words did God give to David in 2 Samuel 23:1–7? How did David acknowledge the failure of his own house to live up to God's standards of righteous obedience?

8. Why did Solomon ask for wisdom when he came to the throne instead of power, wealth, or freedom from his enemies (see 1 Kings 3:1–15)? Why did God grant his request so generously?

WEEK 10

GOD REVEALS HIS POWER

1 KINGS 5–22

READING PLAN: **64** | 1 Kings 5–6 **65** | 1 Kings 7–9 **66** | 1 Kings 10–11
67 | 1 Kings 12–14 **68** | 1 Kings 15–16 **69** | 1 Kings 17–19 **70** | 1 Kings 20–22

Solomon, the second child of David and Bathsheba, not only succeeded his father as king but also became the wisest man who ever lived. People from all over the world traveled to Jerusalem to learn from him. They saw that "the wisdom of God was in him" (1 Kings 3:28).

Solomon sincerely desired to be a good king. He loved the Lord and followed his father's example of walking in His ways. Armed with God's wisdom and His blessings for wealth and honor, Solomon set up his government—choosing men who were loyal to him and had served his father faithfully. Solomon also chose men who were skilled in areas necessary to the functioning of a strong government, including priests, recordkeepers, and administrators.

Solomon's reign ushered in a time of peace and prosperity for Israel, and its borders encompassed most of the lands that God had promised to Abraham (see Genesis 15:18–21). The stage was set for the son to begin the work his father was not allowed to undertake: building a temple in Jerusalem for the Lord. To do so, Solomon called on an old ally of his father's, Hiram, the king of Tyre, to obtain the necessary lumber for the construction.

Solomon understood the importance of this task, for it represented the place where all the people of Israel would come to present their sacrifices to God. Although the heavens themselves could not contain God, the temple would remind the people that He was always present in their midst. Furthermore, the shedding of blood for the sacrifices would inform the Israelites of the cost of their sins.

It took Solomon seven years to build the temple. He spent thirteen years building his own palace. During his rule, he also directed the construction of many other grand buildings in Israel.

Unfortunately, Solomon—much like his father before him—chose to marry a great number of women throughout his reign: "He had seven hundred wives, princesses, and three hundred concubines" (1 Kings 11:3). Solomon wed many of these women in order to establish political alliances that would ensure Israel's peace with neighboring nations. Such unions were commonplace in the world, so Solomon might have told himself that these marriages with foreigners were just part of being king.

However, the Bible reveals that Solomon came to love these wives more than he loved God—they "turned away his heart" (verse 3). He allowed the "high places" where Canaanite gods were worshiped to continue, mixing the pagan practices of his wives with the worship of God. The Lord had forbidden His people to intermarry with the world around them for this very reason. He knew these marriages would lead Israel into idolatry. In this way, Solomon's love for the Lord grew lukewarm. In contrast, David's love for God had grown stronger and deeper the longer he walked in obedience. The difference was that David repented of his sinful behaviors, while Solomon continued to excuse them.

Solomon's paganism eventually led to the loss of his kingdom for his heirs. After his death, the united kingdom of Israel split into two separate parts. The southern tribes of Judah and Benjamin remained loyal to Solomon's son Rehoboam and become known as the kingdom of Judah. The ten northern tribes took a man named Jeroboam as their king and became known as the kingdom of Israel.

The book of 1 Kings records summaries of the reigns of the mostly ungodly kings in both kingdoms of Israel and Judah. King Asa of Judah was one exception. His son Jehoshaphat was even godlier, except that he did have a weakness for making bad alliances. One such alliance was with the wicked King Ahab of the northern kingdom of Israel who, together with his evil queen, Jezebel, had led Israel into idolatry and murdered God's prophets. Jehoshaphat allied himself with Ahab by marrying his son to Ahab's daughter. He then joined with Ahab in a military alliance against Syria that almost cost him his life.

It was during Ahab's reign that the prophet Elijah appeared. He prophesied that God would send a drought to Israel and the surrounding nations as a judgment for the peoples' sin. This came to pass, but God protected His servant by sending Elijah first to a brook near the Jordan River and then to the home of a widow in a distant land. Ultimately, Elijah returned to Israel and engaged in a "showdown" with the prophets of Baal at Mount Carmel, revealing that the God whom he served held all the power.

This event led the people to declare, "The Lord, He is God!" (1 Kings 18:39). It also brought an end to the three-year drought. Yet, sadly, idolatry continued to persist in the land.

First Kings ends with the death of King Ahab, who was struck by a soldier's arrow during a battle against Syria. Ahab had tried to thwart God's prophecies that had predicted his death by wearing a disguise—but God was not fooled. The dogs licked up his blood, just as the word of the Lord had said.

REFLECTIONS

Don't confuse activity with obedience. Solomon honored the Lord by building a magnificent temple, but he was less attuned to the purpose of that temple. God reminded Solomon that faithfulness to Him was the requirement for His presence—not the building itself (see 1 Kings 9:6–7). As believers in Christ, we can become so wrapped up in doing the things we think will honor God that we fail to live in obedience to His commands. When we focus on just the outward acts of religion, our busyness and distraction can actually pull us away from the Lord. However, when our hearts are turned toward God and we are acting according to His will, we will bring Him glory and serve as an example of His love to the world.

We are called to serve one another. Rehoboam's elder counselors advised, "Be a servant to these people today . . . and answer them, and speak good words to them" (1 Kings 12:7). This was wise counsel, and Rehoboam should have heeded it. Servanthood is not an option for followers of Christ or something that some of us are called to do while others are not. It is a command the Lord gives to *all* His followers. If we want to follow Jesus, we must obey Him, and part of that obedience includes being a willing servant to others (see John 13:14–15).

Be bold to speak God's truth. Imagine how the prophet Elijah must have felt when he stood on Mount Carmel facing 850 hostile pagan priests, a powerful king who was looking for an excuse to execute him, and a crowd of Israelites who were indifferent to his fate. As Elijah argued loudly and urgently against the false teachings of the world around him, nobody came up and stood beside him. However, while Elijah may have felt alone, the Lord, in fact, had preserved a remnant in Israel who had remained faithful to Him. Furthermore, Elijah stood in the presence of the *Almighty*. The anger of those around him was ultimately not directed at him but at the Lord God, and God would never abandon His devoted prophet. When we remember that we serve an omnipotent God who is always holding us in His hand, we will be encouraged to stand up boldly—even if we are standing up alone.

SOLOMON'S TEMPLE

Solomon constructed what is called the "First Temple" on Mount Moriah, which was located north of the City of David, according to the plans that his father had received from the Lord and passed on to him (see 1 Chronicles 28:11–13, 19). The Temple was divided into a sanctuary and an inner sanctuary, which corresponded to the division of the tabernacle into the Holy Place and Most Holy Place.

STUDY QUESTIONS

1. What reminder did God give Solomon as he was building the temple (see 1 Kings 6:1–13)? What does this tell you about God's priorities for Israel?

2. What role did Solomon's marriages play in his downfall? How might his life have ended differently if he had not married so many women from foreign lands (see 1 Kings 11:1–8)?

3. If you had been in Rehoboam's position, how might you have responded to the Israelites' complaints? Why was it tempting for him to follow his friends' advice (see 1 Kings 12:1–15)?

4. Why did Jeroboam send his wife to the prophet Ahijah instead of to one of the priests whom he had appointed (see 1 Kings 14:1–18)? What does this reveal about his syncretistic beliefs?

5. What happened in Asa's later years (see 1 Kings 15:9–22)? What might have caused him to move away from faith in God? How might this principle apply in your own life?

6. Why did God send a drought on Israel? How did this lead to a dramatic confrontation between Elijah and the prophets of Baal (see 1 Kings 16:29–17:1; 18:1–40)?

7. Why did Elijah flee to the wilderness after the confrontation with the priests of Baal? What did he hope to find there—and what did he actually find (see 1 Kings 19:1–8)?

8. How did Jezebel gain such power and influence in Israel (see 1 Kings 21:1–16)? How might things have been different if Ahab had not married her?

WEEK 11

GOD ALLOWS US TO FACE CONSEQUENCES

2 KINGS 1-20

READING PLAN: **71** | 2 Kings 1-2 **72** | 2 Kings 3-4 **73** | 2 Kings 5-8 **74** | 2 Kings 9-11 **75** | 2 Kings 12-15 **76** | 2 Kings 16-17 **77** | 2 Kings 18-20

The nation of Israel began as a unified state composed of twelve tribes of God's chosen people living in the Promised Land. But that changed when Solomon added pagan elements to the proper worship of the Lord and led Israel away from God. The Lord responded to this sin by dividing the nation in two: ten tribes in the north (who retained the name Israel), and two in the south (the tribes of Judah and Benjamin, who called themselves Judah).

The books of 1 and 2 Kings depict more than 400 years of the reigns of these rulers as well as the events that led to the demise of both kingdoms. The books also highlight some of the individuals who stood against polluted Israel—prophets such as Elijah and Elisha and priests such as Jehoiada and Azariah.

Following the death of King Ahab at the close of 1 Kings, the rule of Israel fell to two of his sons—Ahaziah and Joram, respectively—who both did evil in God's sight. Meanwhile, Elijah's departure from this world was at hand. But "departure" in this case did not mean death, for God had revealed to Elijah that he would not die but would instead be translated

KINGS OF JUDAH AND ISRAEL

JUDAH		ISRAEL	
Rehoboam	931-913 BC	Jeroboam I	931-910 BC
Abijah (Abijam)	913-911 BC	Nadab	910-909 BC
Asa	911-870 BC	Baasha	909-886 BC
		Elah	886-885 BC
		Zimri	885 BC
		Tibni	885-880 BC
Jehoshaphat	873-848 BC	Omri	885-874 BC
		Ahab	874-853 BC
		Ahaziah	853-852 BC
Jehoram (Joram)	853-841 BC	Joram (Jehoram)	852-841 BC
Ahaziah	841 BC	Jehu	841-814 BC
Athaliah (queen)	841-835 BC		
Joash (Jehoash)	835-796 BC		
		Jehoahaz	814-798 BC
Amaziah	796-767 BC	Jehoash (Joash)	798-782 BC
Azariah (Uzziah)	790-739 BC	Jeroboam II	793-753 BC
Jotham	750-731 BC	Zechariah	753 BC
		Shallum	752 BC
Ahaz	735-715 BC	Menahem	752-742 BC
		Pekahiah	742-740 BC
Hezekiah	715-686 BC	Pekah	752-732 BC
		Hoshea	732-722 BC
Manasseh	695-642 BC		
Amon	642-640 BC		
Josiah	640-609 BC		
Jehoahaz	609 BC		
Jehoiakim	609-597 BC		
Jehoiachin	597 BC		
Zedekiah	597-586 BC		

directly into heaven in bodily form. Elijah's servant Elisha had already been appointed by God to carry on his mentor's great ministry, yet Elisha may well have felt inadequate for the daunting task that lay ahead. So he made a bold request of his mentor before their parting: a double portion of Elijah's spirit.

Elisha didn't make this request out of a desire for power but because he knew the work ahead would require it, and he knew where Elijah's power came from. The Lord granted this request, and the Bible records twice as many miracles performed through Elisha than through Elijah. One of these miracles included the healing of Naaman, the commander of the army of Syria.

The Syrians had long been one of Israel's enemies, engaging in border raids and frequently carrying Israelites into slavery. The Lord wanted His people to recognize His sovereign ability to control events to accomplish His purposes, so He leaked the king of Syria's military plans to Elisha—and kept leaking them. Elisha, in turn, reported everything to Joram, Ahab's younger son who was ruling over Israel.

This unexplained "subterfuge" frustrated Ben-Hadad II, the Syrian king, so he sent an army to take Elisha prisoner. The Syrians surrounded the town where Elisha was staying. This brought Elisha's servant to despair, but the prophet told him not to fear, for there were angelic hosts surrounding the city. God then opened the servant's eyes to the spiritual reality—and simultaneously blinded the Syrians to the physical realm, enabling Elisha to deliver the entire army into the hands of Joram.

Joram would have been justified in enslaving or slaughtering these soldiers to prevent them from regrouping and returning in greater force at a later date. Instead, the Lord commanded him to set the army free and send them home in peace. God further commanded Joram to give these men a great banquet and treat them as honored guests.

In spite of God's grace and mercy, Ben-Hadad II was displeased at his failure to conquer the people of Israel, so he gathered his entire army for a massive siege against Samaria. Syria's chariots and soldiers surrounded the city, cutting off food and supplies and causing a great famine. This turn of events caused Joram to blame the prophet Elisha and seek to take his head. However, the next day the Lord miraculously sent the army of Syria fleeing in fear, leaving their garments and weapons behind.

Ben-Hadad II was murdered shortly after by a man named Hazael, who took his place as Syria's new king. Hazael then went to war against Israel and Judah. By this time, the king of Judah was Ahaziah, a grandson of Ahab and Jezebel through his father's (Jehoram's) marriage, while Joram was still the king of Israel. The Bible doesn't tell us the outcome of the battle, but we do know that Joram was wounded in the fight and had to retreat to the city of Jezreel to recover.

At this point, the Lord intervened. God had previously told Elisha that a man named Jehu would rise up to become king over Israel, and that he would put to death those involved in the worship of Baal. Elisha covertly oversaw the anointing of this new king. The Lord then used Jehu to end the house of Ahab and strike down both Joram of Israel and Ahaziah of Judah. While Jehu did not walk in God's ways, the Lord used him to fulfill His divine purposes.

Upon Ahaziah's death, his mother, Athaliah, seized her opportunity to take the throne. She quickly murdered all her grandchildren so no one would be left to displace her. Fortunately, there were still godly people left in Judah at this time, including the high priest Jehoiada. He and his wife rescued

SYRIAN KINGS	
Hezion (Rezon)	c. 990-930 BC
Tabrimmon	c. 930-885 BC
Ben-Hadad I	c. 885-860 BC
Ben-Hadad II	c. 860-841 BC
Hazael	c. 841-801 BC
Ben-Hadad III	c. 807-780? BC
Rezin	c. 780?-732 BC

ASSYRIAN KINGS	
Assur-nasirpal II	883-859 BC
Shalmaneser III	858-824 BC
Shamshi-Adad V	823-811 BC
Adad-nirari III	810-783 BC
Shalmaneser IV	782-773 BC
Assur-dan III	772-755 BC
Assur-nirari V	754-745 BC
Tiglath-Pileser III	745-727 BC
Shalmaneser V	727-722 BC
Sargon II	722-705 BC
Sennacherib	705-681 BC
Esarhaddon	681-669 BC
Ashurbanipal	668-627 BC

Jehoash, one of Ahaziah's sons, and hid him in the temple. For the next six years, Jehoiada trained the boy to be a godly king who would break the wickedness perpetrated by his father and grandfather.

Once the seven-year-old Jehoash ascended the throne, Jehoiada continued as one of his chief advisors, and Jehoash led the people of Judah in righteousness. Tragically, after Jehoiada died, Jehoash did not remember his mentor's godly counsel and committed a great sin. His reign ended in disgrace.

God endured the unfaithfulness of His people for centuries. But by 722 BC, the time for His judgment was at hand, and the kingdom of Israel fell to the Assyrian Empire. The kingdom of Judah—its kings descended from David's line—remained in the south, ruled by the godly king Hezekiah. The Bible tells us that Judah had never had a king like Hezekiah. He went farther in righteousness than any of Judah's other kings by tearing down the high places that had plagued the nation.

God would often bless obedience with times of peace and prosperity. Yet God had a different plan for Hezekiah. Fourteen years into his reign, the Assyrians invaded Judah, intending to do with them as they had done with Israel. The nation's fate hung in the balance, but Hezekiah knew how to respond. He took the burden to the Lord and trusted Him to fight the battle. God responded by striking down the Assyrian troops, compelling the Assyrians to depart. Judah had been spared . . . for now.

REFLECTIONS

God makes us His heirs through Christ. Elisha's request to inherit a double portion of Elijah's spirit was the equivalent of asking to be made Elisha's "spiritual heir." In biblical times, the firstborn son was the successor of the head of a family, and he received all the status and power that accompanied that position. Believers in Christ, having received the adoption of the Spirit, are given this same status as heirs. As Paul wrote, "For as many as are led by the Spirit of God, these are sons of God. For you did not receive the spirit of bondage again to fear, but you received the Spirit of adoption" (Romans 8:14–15).

God loves to meet our needs. In 2 Kings 4, we read of five situations of dire need: (1) the widow on the verge of starvation, (2) the barren woman, (3) the grieving mother, (4) the sons of the prophets with the poisoned stew, and (5) the one hundred men on the brink of starvation. God met each need with His gracious provision, which reveals He loves to meet His people's needs. However, when we choose to rely on our wealth or find our joy in our possessions, we miss out on the fact that God is capable of meeting our needs in this way. The same principle applies to our spiritual condition. Only when we realize the depth of our sin can we recognize the graciousness of God in salvation (see Luke 5:31–32).

God is sensitive to our needs. When Elisha's servant saw the armies of Syria around Dothan, he cried out, "What shall we do?" (2 Kings 6:15). In response, God allowed him to see into the spiritual realm—and he was comforted by the angelic hosts he saw. God has a great plan for the nations, but He also turns His attention to individuals. He cared about the servant's fear, which is why He instructed Elisha to say to him, "Do not fear, for those who are with us are more than those who are with them" (verse 16).

We must train the next generation to serve the Lord. We have seen many mentors in this week's study. Elijah trained Elisha. Elisha trained Gehazi. Jehoiada trained Jehoash. Yet one critical step is that the mentor trains the pupil to rely on God rather than human counselors. Elisha learned this important lesson, and it enabled him to take over his mentor's responsibilities. Jehoash did not learn this critical lesson, and it destroyed what had begun as a godly career as king. Apparently, Jehoash never went beyond relying on Jehoiada for direction and counsel. He never learned how to serve the Lord and rely on His Word. This step is vital, as illustrated in Jehoash's life, because it is at the core of Christian mentorship. Teaching others to be faithful servants requires teaching them how to draw close to God themselves.

God sees all things. The people of Israel grew bold in their idolatries, carrying out their false worship on open hilltops and in public groves. Yet they also carried their spiritual rebellion into the secret areas of their private lives. They were undoubtedly able to hide such things from their neighbors, but they were foolish in thinking they could keep them secret from God. When we remember that He sees our hearts and secret actions, we will be more likely to walk circumspectly and quicker to confess our sins.

God hears our prayers. Hezekiah was overwhelmed with the threat facing his people, but he did not give in to that fear. Instead, he went into the house of God and spread before Him the defiant letter from Sennacherib, pouring out his heart and asking the Lord to intervene. This was just what the Lord wanted, and He was pleased that His servant came to Him with his troubles. Hezekiah had taken an unbearable burden—a weight that he was not strong enough to carry—and had given it to the Lord to carry. As Peter would later write, "[Cast] all your care upon Him, for He cares for you" (1 Peter 5:7).

STUDY QUESTIONS

1. What did Elisha mean when he asked to receive a "double portion" of Elijah's spirit (see 2 Kings 2:1–11)? Why did he desire to have such a thing?

2. Elisha instructed the poor widow in debt to close the door to her house (see 2 Kings 4:1–7). Why didn't Elisha want this miracle to be seen by everyone in her town?

3. Why did Elisha instruct Naaman, the commander of the army of Syria, to wash seven times in the Jordan River (see 2 Kings 5:1–14)? What did Naaman gain by obeying?

4. How did Elisha respond to the presence of the Syrian armies around the city of Dothan (see 2 Kings 6:8–18)? What does this tell us about the strength of God?

5. Why did Elisha instruct his younger student-prophet to anoint Jehu as king over Israel? What were God's instructions to Jehu that he was to fulfill (see 2 Kings 9:1–10)?

6. What motivated the people of Judah to give so generously to the rebuilding project (see 2 Kings 12:1–16)? How does their example apply to God's people today?

7. What happened when the Assyrians who resettled into Israel conquered people from other places in their empire (see 2 Kings 17:24–41)? Why did God send lions among them?

8. Why did God allow Israel to be taken into captivity by Assyria? Why did He not allow the same fate at this time for the people of Judah (see 2 Kings 18:1–12)?

WEEK 12

GOD WILL BRING US HOME

2 KINGS 21–NEHEMIAH 13

READING PLAN: **78** | 2 Kings 21–25 **79** | Ezra 1–3 **80** | Ezra 4–6 **81** | Ezra 7–10 **82** | Nehemiah 1–3 **83** | Nehemiah 4–8 **84** | Nehemiah 9–13

The Lord had delivered the people of Judah from the Assyrian army. He had answered Hezekiah's prayer, and He would also later answer Hezekiah's request to heal him from an illness and extend his life by fifteen years. Sadly, when Hezekiah's son Manasseh came to the throne, he rebuilt the high places his father had torn down. It is possible he even destroyed all copies of God's law that were not hidden. His son Amon followed in his footsteps.

The Lord had given the Israelites a sacred trust when He revealed Himself to them through His law. They were the only people on earth who possessed God's Word spoken directly through His servant Moses. He had commanded them to preserve the Law, guard it, and pass it on faithfully. Instead, they forsook God's Word, first adding elements from pagan religions into their worship and then gradually giving those elements precedence.

By the time Amon's son Josiah came to the throne, the people had been disregarding God's Word for so long it had been all but forgotten. But Josiah, like his great-grandfather Hezekiah before him, would be a godly king who did what was right in God's sight.

During Josiah's reign, he commissioned a new building project to repair the temple, which led to the priests uncovering a lost book of God's law. When this book was read to Josiah, he tore his clothes in mourning, for he knew the Lord's wrath had been aroused against the people for not obeying His law. Yet the Lord, seeing Josiah's humility, promised His judgment would not fall during Josiah's lifetime.

Instead, this judgment came after Josiah was killed in battle. During the reign of Josiah's sons—Jehoahaz and then Jehoiakim, respectively—the people reverted to paganism. It was during the rule of Jehoiakim that God sent the Babylonians against Judah. When his son Jehoiachin came to the throne, the Babylonians took Jerusalem and carried all the officers, fighting men, skilled workers and artisans, and other prominent people into exile. Zedekiah, the uncle of Jehoiachin, became king of Judah. When he rebelled, the Babylonians returned to Jerusalem and set fire to the temple, palace, and all its houses, carrying even more people into exile. Only the poor were left behind to work the vineyards and fields.

What the Israelites did not know was that God was working behind the scenes to keep them intact as a people group. The time of their exile would be long, but the Lord would raise up leaders to protect

BABYLONIAN INVASIONS

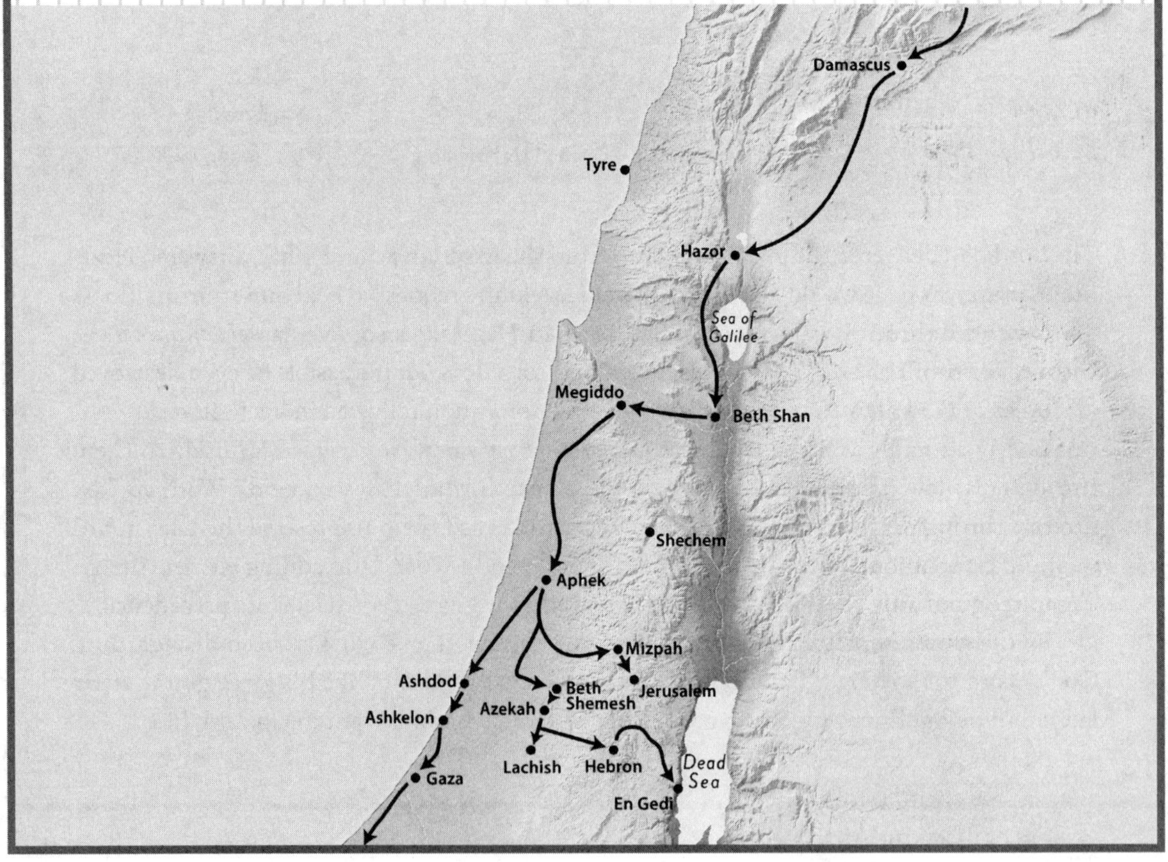

and guide them in their captivity. After seventy years, He moved the heart of a Persian king named Cyrus to allow them to return home. God further raised up leaders like Ezra and Nehemiah to not only champion the rebuilding efforts but also to turn the people's hearts back to the worship of the Lord.

Ezra, a priest and scribe, was unique in that he had access to the royal archives of the Persian Empire. Few were given this access, but Ezra was an exception. The book that bears his name begins with the decree from Cyrus that allowed the Jewish people to return to Jerusalem. It then chronicles the reestablishment of Judah's calendar of feasts and sacrifices, including the rebuilding of the temple.

There had been three waves of deportation from Israel into Babylon, and now there would be three returns to Jerusalem during a nine-decade span. Zerubbabel led the first return in 538 BC, Ezra led the second return in 458 BC, and Nehemiah led the third return in 445 BC. The book of Ezra reports the first two of these three returns and documents how Ezra re-established the Aaronic priesthood, reinstituted the Law, and dealt with the people's sin of intermarriage with foreigners. More importantly, the book describes how the sovereign hand of God moved pagan kings and overcame opposition to reestablish Israel in the land. The Lord had raised up Nebuchadnezzar to carry the nation into Babylon—and then raised up Cyrus to absorb Babylon into Persia and set His people free.

> For ALL that is in heaven and in earth is YOURS . . . You are exalted as head over ALL.
>
> 1 CHRONICLES 29:11

The book of Nehemiah reports the third return of the exiles. The events depicted in the opening chapter begin in the twentieth year of the Persian king Artaxerxes's reign. At the time, Nehemiah held a post in the king's court as his personal cupbearer, or "food taster." The position came with a great degree of trust and intimacy with the king, which Nehemiah used to secure the release of the exiles. The Lord even moved the Persian king to grant assistance and supplies to Nehemiah for the endeavor.

Once in Jerusalem, Nehemiah set about mobilizing the people to rebuild the wall around the city. In this, God worked through Nehemiah's faithfulness, through the people's efforts to rebuild, through the diligent reading of His Word . . . and even through the wicked hearts of His people's enemies. As the Jewish exiles were rebuilding the wall, they were openly mocked, falsely accused of evil motives and rebellious plans, subtly infiltrated by men who sought to discourage them and hinder their work, and even threatened with murder. However, in every instance under Nehemiah's leadership, the people turned to the Lord in prayer for their safety and security, and God brought all the plots to nothing.

In spite of opposition from without, and corruption and dissension from within, the people of Judah completed the wall in only fifty-two days. Now they could finally settle back into their homes. In celebration, they gathered together to observe the Feast of Tabernacles, which had not happened "since the days of Joshua" (Nehemiah 8:17). At the end of that feast, the people gathered once more to worship God as a reunited nation, humbling themselves and acknowledging their dependence on Him.

The Israelites had certainly endured many trials. Yet they had endured because of God's protection and provision for them. In the end, through everything, the Lord revealed that He was sovereign over all the affairs of mankind—and faithful and true to His Word.

REFLECTIONS

Choose to seek the Lord. Some of the kings of Judah sought God . . . and many did not. But in both cases, the seeker always found what he was seeking. King Josiah sought the Lord, and he found him. His son Jehoahaz put his trust in idols, and he found them. The end result of each choice is self-evident: seeking God leads to life, while seeking idols leads to death. The good news is that seeking God is not burdensome. Indeed, He is busier seeking us than we are seeking Him, and He so wants us to find Him that He was willing to sacrifice His Son on the cross to make it possible. All that is required of us is to humble ourselves, confess our sins, and submit to His lordship in our lives (see James 4:8, 10).

God will put an end to mourning. When the exiles laid the foundation for the temple, there was a mixed response from the people. Many shouted with joy at seeing the Lord rebuilding what had been destroyed, while others wept over their memories of what had once been. Ironically, both responses were valid—but in the long run, the joyful shouting drowned out the tears. The people of Israel had good reason to mourn, because it was their own sin that had led to the destruction of the temple and all that it contained—including the ark of the covenant. Yet God had not abandoned His people nor forgotten His promises of faithfulness and blessing. He was still at work, and what mattered most was that Israel still existed, due to the promise of God. Tears had a place, but the shouts of joy would last far longer.

Be STRONG and of good COURAGE; do not be afraid, nor be DISMAYED, for the LORD your God IS WITH YOU.

JOSHUA 1:9

God commands us to resist discouragement. The enemies of God's people tried to interrupt their work by causing them to become discouraged. The essence of discouragement is to become weak, sink down, lose the ability to carry on, and let God's projects drop from despair—and fear is at the root of this. When we are suddenly faced with a circumstance that is beyond our control, we can quickly begin to fear it is beyond God's control as well. And if it is beyond God's control, we might as well just give up now—which is, of course, precisely what Satan is hoping we will do! However, God commands us to not give in to fear but strengthen our hands when they become weak (see Isaiah 41:10).

Study, obey, and teach. In Ezra 7:10 we read, "Ezra had prepared his heart to seek the Law of the LORD, and to do it, and to teach statutes and ordinances in Israel." Ezra made it a priority to study God's Word, meditate on it daily, and look for ways to apply it in his life. He probably had also taken great pains to memorize it, as history claims that he could write the Law of Moses from memory. However, even beyond these pursuits, Ezra had applied God's Word to his life, deliberately obeying His commands on a daily basis. These habits are what equipped Ezra to become a great teacher to the exiles who had returned to Jerusalem. The process we see illustrated by Ezra is threefold: study God's Word, obey God's Word, and teach God's Word. This is the process that all Christians are likewise called to emulate.

Be alert and prepared for battle. Nehemiah did not take the enemy's threat lightly when he learned they were planning to attack. He knew the protection of God's people lay solely in God's hands, but he also understood he had a responsibility for the safety of those under his authority. So, he took steps to prepare for the threat of battle. He also expected all those working on the Lord's project to remain alert and well-armed. Christians must likewise be prepared for battle. Well-armed and vigilant Christians spend time reading and meditating daily on the Word of God. And like all well-trained soldiers, believers in Christ also stay in close contact with the Commanding Officer through prayer and obedience.

ATTEMPTS TO STOP THE WORK IN NEHEMIAH
❶ Sanballat, Tobiah, and Geshem mock Nehemiah (2:19)
❷ Sanballat and Tobiah mock Nehemiah (4:1–3)
❸ The enemy threatens a military attack (4:7–23)
❹ Sanballat and Geshem try to lure Nehemiah to Ono (6:1–4)
❺ Sanballat threatens Nehemiah with false charges (6:5–9)
❻ Shemaiah, Noadiah, and others prophesy falsely to discredit Nehemiah (6:10–14)
❼ Tobiah writes letters to Nehemiah in order to frighten him (6:17–19)

A godly leader leads by example. Nehemiah was a great leader. He organized more than one trip from Persia to Judah, gathering the resources needed to undertake the work of rebuilding the city walls. He also governed with wisdom, leading God's people through difficult circumstances. But one of the strongest elements of his leadership was his own life, as he demonstrated through his own example what it meant to be a godly man. This is the prime quality of a godly leader and teacher. A good leader does not simply give lectures on how to master a skill but also demonstrates that mastery by performing the skill in front of the students. The godly leader says, "Watch my example . . . and then learn to do the same."

God is gracious, even with the presumptuous. The constant theme of the Levites' praise in Nehemiah 9:5–38 was the graciousness of God. In fact, the entire prayer is a litany of God's acts of compassion toward His people. God was gracious to His people in Nehemiah's day, and He is still gracious to His people today. The difference is that now God has sent His Son as the ultimate act of His graciousness. Jesus came as a sacrifice for sin, and in the consummate act of kindness, He gave His life for *all* people. As a result, the news of the gospel is really the news that God's graciousness has conquered the hearts of presumptuous sinners. Jesus' grace is stronger than the hardest of sinners' hearts.

STUDY QUESTIONS

1. What made the Book of the Law that the priests found so valuable? What might have led to its being lost? How did its being misplaced likely affect the people (see 2 Kings 22:3–13)?

2. Based on 2 Kings 23:26–27, what was God's involvement in the fall of Judah? What events occurred that reveal God had indeed withdrawn His presence from His people?

3. Why did the returning Jewish exiles build the altar before the temple that would house it (see Ezra 3:1–7)? What does this indicate they knew about God's priorities?

4. Why did Ezra respond so vehemently to the Jews' marrying foreigners (see Ezra 9:1–4)? Why was that such a big problem for God's people?

5. What risks did Nehemiah take to help the exiles in Judah (see Nehemiah 2:1–10)? What were some of his motivations in taking these risks? What would you have done in his situation?

6. Why did Nehemiah command for the workers to always be armed (see Nehemiah 4:15–23)? What effect did this have on the work? What effect did it have on the enemies?

7. What methods did Sanballat, Tobiah, Geshem, and other enemies employ to stop the work? How did Nehemiah respond to each attack made against God's people (see Nehemiah 6:1–15)?

8. Why did the Levites work chronologically through the history of Israel in their worship (see Nehemiah 9:7–31)? How might this have helped the people recognize God's goodness and their sin?

WEEK 13

GOD SEES OUR SUFFERING

ESTHER 1 - JOB 42

READING PLAN:	**85** | Esther 1-4	**86** | Esther 5-8	**87** | Job 1-3
88 | Job 4-7	**89** | Job 18-21	**90** | Job 27-31	**91** | Job 38-42

Although God is nowhere mentioned in Esther, He is everywhere apparent as He providentially moves kings, queens, and nobles to foil Satan's schemes and preserve His people from annihilation. The genesis for the drama goes back 1,000 years when the Jews left Egypt and were attacked by the Amalekites (see Exodus 17:8–16). God pronounced His curse on the Amalekites: they would be totally eliminated as a people. Hundreds of years later, Saul received orders to kill all the Amalekites, including their king, Agag (see 1 Samuel 15:1–3). But he disobeyed and incurred God's displeasure, leaving Samuel to hack Agag into pieces.

Several centuries later, King Ahasuerus of Persia (also known as Xerxes, his Greek name) gathered nobles from all over his empire at his winter palace in Susa. This gathering might well have been the planning session for a later Greek invasion. Near the end of the 180 days of feasting and celebration, the king hosted a weeklong banquet. In his drunkenness, he sent for his queen, Vashti, but his reason for wanting her and his forceful tone made her uncomfortable and she refused to appear. When she openly defied him, Ahasuerus became so angry that Vashti was deposed. To choose a new queen, the royal advisors counseled the king to hold a beauty pageant and bring in young women to participate from all provinces in the empire.

Once Esther arrived on the scene, God orchestrated the events so she would be chosen. Esther found favor with both the king's eunuch and with Ahasuerus himself, positioning her for when the king's second-in-command, Haman (a descendant of King Agag), would seek to have all the Jews in Persia annihilated. This came about when another character in the story, Mordecai, refused to bow down before him. Mordecai was Esther's cousin (though he served more as Esther's adopted father) and a descendant of Saul's tribe. Haman's hatred for the Jews, though deep-seated, was sparked because of Mordecai's actions. At this offense, Haman unwittingly set a series of events in motion that would bring about his own destruction—rather than the destruction of all the Jews in the empire that he intended.

Esther was the only person who could influence the king to prevent Haman's plan for genocide. God had raised her up for such a time as this, and she risked her life to go before Ahasuerus, cunningly play into Haman's pride, win the king's confidence, and make her request on behalf of the Jews.

Mordecai obeyed the Lord's Word by not bowing before Haman. He did so knowing he was making a powerful enemy—yet he obeyed just the same. This attitude lay at the root of his admonition to Esther to approach the king even at the risk of her life, and God was able to work through her obedience to save the Jewish people in exile. As a result of their actions, "On the day that the enemies of the Jews had hoped to overpower them . . . the Jews themselves overpowered those who hated them" (Esther 9:1).

Although the events in the book of Job occur at a different time and in a different place, the same evil forces are at work. Job, in fact, pulls the curtain back on some of Satan's efforts in our world, revealing his role behind some of the suffering that God's people endure. The story begins in the throne room of heaven. Satan comes before the Lord and makes an accusation that Job—a steadfast servant of God—would not remain so spiritually faithful if his material blessings were removed. So God allows Satan to strip Job of everything—his children, his servants, and his wealth—in the course of a single day.

Later, God allows Satan to strike at Job's health. Three of Job's friends, sensing that his grief is great, come to mourn with him and sit with him in silence for a week. Sadly, after this, these three friends offer Job little comfort. Instead, they advise him to remove himself from God's "doghouse" by confessing whatever great sin has caused such loss. When Job protests that he has *not* violated his integrity, his "comforters" push even harder for him to repent. In three escalating cycles of debate between them, Job maintains his innocence and increasingly appeals to God—because while he understands himself to be a sinner, he knows that he has not intentionally departed from God's will or His statutes.

Job, having endured these debates, engages in two monologues to clarify his point and support his claims. Then a new participant, Elihu, enters the scene. Elihu is evidently a younger man who has been listening nearby, and he is clearly angry at both Job *and* his three companions: angry at Job's continued appeal to his own integrity, and angry at the other men for failing to prove Job wrong. Chapter after chapter, these five men speak at one another, making accusations, offering rebuttals, and revealing the futility of human wisdom. But then, the situation abruptly changes when God shows up on the scene. In many ways, Job's entire story has been building to this moment when he gets to plead his case to God.

God offers four responses in the final chapters of Job. First, he asks a series of rhetorical questions such as, "Where were you when I laid the foundations of the earth?" (38:4). He does this to highlight His power and wisdom in relation to Job's weakness and humanity. Second, God uses two mighty creatures—the "behemoth" and "leviathan"—to illustrate His power. Third, He confronts Job's four companions, declaring them to be wrong in their assertions about Job's character. Finally, He floods Job with blessings, restoring his health, wealth, and family to levels beyond what he had previously known.

The critical question at the heart of Job's story—why suffering exists in the world—is never answered, not even by God. Throughout Job, we are shown sources for suffering and see that sometimes the wicked prosper while the righteous suffer *in this life*, but there is no universal cause for suffering. There is, however, a universal response to suffering, and that is to leave the question of "why?" in the hands of the One who promises to balance the scales of justice. We simply trust that our God is always in control.

REFLECTIONS

God puts us where He wants us. Esther was a young Jewish woman who was whisked from obscurity to become queen of the world's most powerful empire. It seems surprising that she could rise to such a position—but it was no surprise to God. He had placed Esther exactly where He wanted her to be so He could work out a bigger plan that He had for His people's salvation. In the same way, God placed Mordecai exactly where He wanted him to be so that he could influence Esther. Esther and Mordecai could not have seen what God intended to do through them, and neither can we. Our job, like theirs, is to work faithfully wherever the Lord has placed us and allow Him to take care of the future.

God is more powerful than evil. Even when we don't understand the *why* of suffering, we can know that God is more powerful than the forces of evil. Notice the limits that God placed on Satan's attacks against Job: "All that he has is in your power; only do not lay a hand on his person" (1:12). God commanded Satan—and Satan had no choice but to obey. This may seem surprising at first, because we know that Satan is God's fiercest and most determined enemy. His entire existence is defined by rebellion against God and everything that God represents. Yet in spite of all Satan's evil and all his malice, he cannot resist God's command. This is because God is sovereign and greater than His enemies.

God Himself is the answer to the question of suffering. *Why does suffering exist in the world?* This is the question at the heart of Job's story. Yet it is never answered. Throughout Job, we are shown sources for suffering. Sometimes, we experience tragedy because of Satan's attacks. Sometimes, we suffer because we are being punished for sin. Other times, we suffer because God wants to catch our attention or because we are affected by the choices of others. In short, there is no universal cause for suffering. But there is a universal *response* to suffering, and that response is to trust in God. No matter what we experience in this life, we can leave the question of *why* in His hands and trust that He is in control.

STUDY QUESTIONS

1. Why did King Ahasuerus command his wife to appear at the feast? What reasons might she have had for refusing his request (see Esther 1:1–12)?

2. In what ways did Haman deceive the king regarding the Jews (see Esther 3:8–15)? How might the king have ruled more wisely in this situation?

3. Why did Esther invite King Ahasuerus to a banquet instead of asking him outright to save her people? Why did she also invite Haman to attend the banquet (see Esther 5:1–8)?

4. How did God ultimately protect His people from destruction? How did He use all of the evil that had been intended against His followers for good (see Esther 7:1–10; 9:1–5)?

5. What were some of the blessings that Job enjoyed at the beginning of his story? In what ways did he respond well after he lost everything he valued (see Job 1:1–22)?

6. What reasons did Job have to feel frustrated by his companions (see Job 16:1–5)? What reasons did he have to feel frustrated with God?

7. What are your impressions of Elihu based on his speeches in Job 32–34? How are his arguments similar to those of Eliphaz, Bildad, and Zophar? How are they different?

8. What are some of the key points God raised in His response to Job in Job 38–39? What stands out the most to you about Job's response to God in Job 42? Why?

WEEK 14

GOD GUIDES OUR LIVES

PSALMS 1–41

READING PLAN: **92** | Psalms 1–2; 5–6 **93** | Psalms 8–11 **94** | Psalms 12–15 **95** | Psalms 16–17; 19–20 **96** | Psalms 22–25 **97** | Psalms 26–27; 31–33 **98** | Psalms 34; 37–40

For thousands of years, the book of Psalms has served as the gold standard for worship. Contained within its pages are poignant and powerful expressions of praise, honest and authentic cries from the human heart, artistic expressions of God's character, and much more. But this deeply emotional book of praise manifests a very practical theology.

The basic theme of Psalms is living real life in the real world, where two dimensions operate simultaneously: a horizontal (or temporal) reality and a vertical (or transcendent) reality. Without denying the pain of the earthly dimension, the people of God are to live joyfully and dependently on the One who stands behind the heavenly/eternal dimension. All cycles of human troubles and triumphs provide occasions for expressing human complaints, confidence, prayers, or praise to the sovereign Lord.

The songs and poems that comprise the book of Psalms were divinely authored by God, but many human composers were involved over a period spanning about 900 years of Jewish history. It is believed that King David wrote at least seventy-three of the 150 psalms. Fifty psalms are anonymous in their authorship (though Ezra is thought to be the author of some of them). Among the recurring genres in the Psalms are wisdom, with instructions for right living; lamentation, which deals with the pangs of life, usually arising from enemies without; penitence, mostly dealing with the "enemy" within—that is, sin; and thanksgiving.

The 150 psalms of the Bible were organized quite early into five "books," each of which ends with a doxology (a short hymn of praise to God). There is no discernible reason for these divisions. Many authors have psalms in several books, so they are not arranged by writer. Nor are they arranged by topic. Jewish tradition alleged these divisions echoed the five books of Moses. Book I, which we will cover this week, includes Psalms 1–41. Most of these psalms (potentially all of them) were composed by David.

> BLESSED is the man who walks not in the counsel of the UNGODLY . . . but his delight is in the LAW of the LORD, and in His law he MEDITATES day and night.
>
> PSALM 1:1–2

The book of Psalms opens with four wisdom psalms in succession. One of the core themes repeated in the Bible from the very beginning, when Adam and Eve were placed in the garden of Eden, is that God's people have a choice. They can choose to live in obedient submission to God and receive blessing, or they can choose to live in rebellion against God and receive curses. Psalms 1 and 2 again present the reader with that choice. In Psalm 1, the psalmist offers a stark comparison between those who choose righteousness and those who choose wickedness. Those who choose righteousness will be "blessed"—a word that is rich in depth and promise—and will be like trees that bear much fruit. The wicked, however, will be like the chaff that the wind blows away.

While Psalm 1 is a personal reflection about righteousness and rebellion, Psalm 2 carries those themes to a broader audience: the nations and civilizations. The picture being painted is of rulers and armies stirring themselves up in rebellion against God. The psalm ends with a call for those who consider themselves powerful to submit to the only Being in creation who truly carries authority. Psalm 3 is a wonderful example of David's ability to turn real-life events—including moments of acute crisis—into opportunities for praise. Psalm 4 is another compact expression of wisdom as David moves from anxiety to assurance on the road of prayer and trust in God. Psalm 37, also a wisdom psalm, is similar in both thought and ethos to the Proverbs.

Several of the psalms in Book I (such as Psalms 16; 19–21; 23; 27) were written to offer comfort to those who read or sang them. King David wrote many of these comfort psalms. In Psalm 19, he depicts the Lord as author of both His world and His Word, showing how God has revealed Himself to mankind through these two avenues. David's beautiful expressions of admiration and adoration for the Scriptures remind readers of the comfort that can be found in God's Word.

Some of the comfort psalms are connected to specific events or circumstances, such as Psalms 20 and 21, which directly address God's people before and after a battle. Other psalms in this group more generally offer comfort based on God's character. Psalm 23, for example, is perhaps the most famous passage of the Old Testament because it is a compact, visual, and beautiful expression of God's goodness even in the face of difficult circumstances. It also, in an interesting but often-overlooked detail, suggests the comfort that can be found in God's direction through even His rod and His staff.

How do those instruments provide comfort? In the ancient world, the rod and staff (sometimes called the club and crook) were two of the tools that shepherds used to carry out their duties. The former was for protection. If the sheep were under attack, the shepherd could strike the antagonists with the club and drive them off. The staff was typically a tall pole with a curve at the end. If a sheep wandered off in the wrong direction, the shepherd could "hook" the end of the staff around its neck and pull it back into line. How reassuring to know that Christ Himself, the Good Shepherd, is not only watching over His sheep but also provides direction and even redirection when we need it.

There are also messianic songs in Psalms, which contain prophecies about the life and ministry of Christ. Psalm 22 is likely the most prominent because of its connections to Jesus' crucifixion.

Besides composing psalms centering on themes of wisdom and comfort, David also wrote psalms that lift up the theme of repentance, such as Psalms 30–32. His public adultery with Bathsheba is perhaps the most infamous episode in his life. David used his authority as the king of Israel to commit adultery with Bathsheba, and then arranged for her husband to be killed in battle after she conceived.

Psalm 32 is believed to be connected with that incident. We see David's initial attempts to hide his sin, which caused a rift in his relationship with God and a growing burden within his heart. David then makes the choice to repent, and that repentance leads to God's forgiveness. Having confessed his sin, David reflects on the joy of forgiveness in this penitential psalm. Book I ends with this song of praise: "Blessed be the Lord God of Israel from everlasting to everlasting! Amen and Amen" (Psalm 41:13).

REFLECTIONS

We have a choice. One of the core themes in the Bible is that we have a choice. We can be obedient to God and receive blessings, or we can live in rebellion and receive curses. Psalm 1 presents us with that choice. In this case, those who choose righteousness will be "blessed" (verse 1)—a word that is rich in depth and promise. The wicked, however, will be "like the chaff which the wind drives away" (verse 4).

God provides direction and redirection. David writes, "Your rod and Your staff, they comfort me" (Psalm 23:4). In his day, if a sheep were attacked, the shepherd would strike the antagonist with the rod. If a sheep went the wrong direction, he would "hook" the staff around its neck and pull it back into line. Likewise, Christ, our Good Shepherd, provides direction and even redirection when we need it.

Repentance requires humility. David concluded Psalm 39 with a plea: "Remove Your gaze from me, that I may regain strength" (verse 13). Repentance requires humility because we must recognize we have violated God's law, confess our sin, and renounce it. Beyond that, repentance requires humility because it is a gift from God, and in order to recognize that and praise Him for it, we must humble ourselves.

STUDY QUESTIONS

1. What are the key images in Psalm 1, and what does each communicate? What specific aspects of God's character are communicated in Psalm 2?

2. What does David realize about himself—and humanity as a whole—when he considers "the moon and the stars," which God has ordained (see Psalm 8)?

3. What does David say about God's Word ("the law of the LORD)" in Psalm 19? What does he say in this psalm about the judgments of the Lord?

4. The opening line of Psalm 22 was quoted by Jesus on the cross: "My God, My God, why have You forsaken Me?" (Matthew 27:46). How would you describe the overall tone of this psalm?

5. Psalm 23 is a familiar passage to many of us, but reread it carefully. What main point is David expressing? How does God act as a "Good Shepherd" in our lives?

6. What reasons does David give in Psalm 27 for not needing to fear his enemies? What does David desire for the Lord to teach him as goes through his life?

7. What does David reveal about God's character in Psalm 30—especially in connection with the confession and repentance of His people?

8. What does David say about God's mercy and faithfulness in Psalm 38? What does David want to "guard" and "restrain" in Psalm 39?

WEEK 15

GOD PROTECTS US FROM ENEMIES

PSALMS 42–72

READING PLAN:	**99** | Psalms 42–45	**100** | Psalms 46–48; 51	**101** | Psalms 52–55
102 | Psalms 56–59	**103** | Psalms 60–62; 65	**104** | Psalms 66–68	**105** | Psalms 69–72

Historically, the psalms range in time from the origin of life to the joys of the Jewish people who had been liberated from Babylon. Thematically, the book covers a wide spectrum of topics from heavenly worship to earthly war. Yet through the ages, the psalms have always retained their primary purpose: to engender the proper praise and worship of God.

As we noted last week, Psalms is organized into five individual "books." Book II, which we will cover this week, includes Psalms 42–72. Right at the beginning of Book II, we meet a new group of contributors: the sons of Korah. Eleven total psalms are attributed to them (Psalms 42 and 44–49 in Book II and Psalms 84–85 and 87 in Book III). It is quite probable that the sons of Korah were not the authors of these psalms but rather their performers.

While we do not know a lot about the sons of Korah, they carry an ignoble name. In Numbers 16:1–40, Korah was one of the leaders of a rebellion against Moses. He challenged the authority of Moses and Aaron and the priesthood they had established. As a result, Korah and his followers were swallowed up by the ground during an earthquake.

The sons of Korah operated during the time of King David. They were likely legitimate descendants of that original Korah, who was a Levite. They participated in the work of the tabernacle and temple—work that included vocal worshiping and praising the Lord through song.

Their very existence should give us pause. In the midst of a vast sacrificial system—with different groups of the Levitical tribe tasked with all manner of jobs—this group was given the assignment of singing God's praises and leading others to do the same. Why? Because worship is a priority! David made worship a priority too. From the time he was an unknown shepherd all the way through his glorious accomplishments as king, David worshiped God and helped others express their worship to Him as well.

Psalms 42–44 and 46–47 declare God's strength and protection. As Psalm 46 makes clear, the Lord God not only uses His strength to protect His people from nature's threats and national threats but also extends His strength to us. God is not like the capricious kings of old who would only intervene on the side of justice when forced to do so or when they saw personal benefit to it. Instead, God is always present with us. Therefore, as the psalmist declares so well, "we will not fear" (verse 2).

While it is true that God seeks justice, and His wrath is a legitimate expression of His justice, it is also true that God often uses His power to establish peace and end the consequences of violence and strife, which is what the author of Psalm 46 emphasizes. Throughout the song, he describes God's powerful interventions in the world. What is the end result of God expending His strength? He breaks the bow, cuts the spear in two, and burns the chariot in the fire (see verse 9). Chariots were the supreme weapons of war in the ancient world, so melting them was akin to removing the most brutal weapons of an enemy's arsenal. God often uses His strength to end struggles and build peace, just as He did with Christ's death on the cross—which leads to peace with God for those who repent and believe in Him.

Psalm 51, like Psalms 38 and 39, is an expression of penitence from David that reveals the intentionality and humility that repentance requires. (In Psalm 38, we find David feeling crushed by the weight of calamity, a situation he believed to be at least in part due to his personal sin, while Psalm 39 is a heavy lament, expressing David's awareness of his smallness in comparison with God.) Psalm 51 is David's public confession after the sinful choices he made regarding Bathsheba and Uriah (see 2 Samuel 11). Notably, David begins by acknowledging God's forgiving character. Spiritual repentance constantly realigns our mind, affections, and will with God's. Ultimately, it leads to God's forgiveness.

SPIRITUAL CLEANSING (PSALM 51)

"Wash me, and I shall be whiter than snow" (Psalm 51:7). Ritual washing was an important step in the purification of the priests for service in the tabernacle (see Exodus 40:12). Washing with water symbolized spiritual cleansing, the preparation necessary for entering God's presence (see Psalms 26:6; 73:13). The ancient custom of washing a guest's feet was a part of hospitality that was still practiced in Jesus' day (see John 13:5). Paul also described redemption in Christ as "the washing of regeneration" (Titus 3:5).

Psalms 57–58, 61–63, and 66 reflect another theme within this collection of songs and poems: the need to trust in God. Some of these psalms were written either during or as a response to notable historical events. For example, it is believed that David wrote Psalm 57, a prayer for safety, while hiding out in the wilderness from King Saul, who wanted to kill him. Psalms 61 and 62 were likely written during the national revolt led by David's son Absalom. In psalms like these, David often describes God as his rock or shelter or a strong tower. In doing so, he rightly understood a key aspect of God's character: God does not change, nor can He be moved. For these reasons, and many more, God is worthy of our trust.

In Psalm 63, David recalls God's acts of faithfulness: "Because You have been my help, therefore in the shadow of Your wings I will rejoice" (verse 7). Psalm 66, by an unnamed author, then bursts forth in praise and worship because of God's mighty works on behalf of His people. God certainly is worthy of trust simply because of His power, character, and authority. Yet His children don't need to trust blindly. Believers can look back at the journey of their lives and note those moments when God stepped in and worked on their behalf. Those moments are the foundation for every Christian's trust in Him.

REFLECTIONS

Worship must be a priority. In the midst of a complex sacrificial system, worship was a priority, as seen in the fact that the sons of Korah were assigned to sing God's praises and lead others to do the same. Worship was also a priority for David. From the time he was a shepherd to his most glorious accomplishment as king, he worshiped God and helped others express their worship to Him. Similarly, in our journey of following Christ, we must always remember that worshiping God is more than singing a few songs every Sunday. Worship is the posture of our lives as we praise and appreciate our sovereign Lord.

We can be honest with God about our difficulties. David refused to sugarcoat his sorrows and joys in his psalms. "My soul is among lions," he wrote in Psalm 57; "I lie among the sons of men who are set on fire, whose teeth are spears and arrows" (verse 4). David was also honest about those who wronged him: "Break their teeth in their mouth, O God! Break out the fangs of the young lions, O LORD!" (Psalm 58:6). Often, we equate spirituality with stoicism, believing that expressing emotions, fears, or doubts is akin to a lack of faith. As a result, we remain silent about our struggles. But in doing so, we forfeit a precious gift and disobey what God has called us to do, namely, seeking His help, just as David did.

We can trust in God, our Rock. In his psalms, David relied heavily on a specific type of imagery to describe God: "From the end of the earth I will cry to You, when my heart is overwhelmed; lead me to the rock that is higher than I" (Psalm 61:2). David often described God as his rock, shelter, or strong tower. In doing so, he rightly understood a key aspect of God's character: He does not change, nor can He be moved. For these reasons, among many others, God is worthy of our trust. As David wrote: "Trust in Him at all times, you people; pour out your heart before Him; God is a refuge for us" (Psalm 62:8).

STUDY QUESTIONS

1. Psalms 42 and 43 are often considered to be two halves of a single song. What do you see as being the connections between them?

2. The author of Psalm 44 declares God's strength. How has God used His strength to bless you? What does it mean to rely on His strength and not your own?

3. What evidence points to Psalm 47 being written for a corporate setting? How is the language used in this psalm different than in some of the previous psalms?

4. Psalm 51 is believed to have been written by David after he was confronted for his sin. How does this psalm help you understand the nature and process of repentance?

5. In Psalm 57, what reasons does David give for trusting in the Lord? What attributes of God necessitate His faithfulness?

6. What does David mean in Psalm 62 when he says that his "soul silently waits for God" (verse 1)? What is David "expecting" from the Lord?

7. Psalm 66 is an explosion of praise. What is the connection the psalmist gives between trusting God and praising God?

8. Psalm 72 is a coronation psalm, dedicated to the prosperity of Solomon at the beginning of his reign. What is Solomon's request to God in this psalm?

WEEK 16

GOD IS JUST AND MERCIFUL

PSALMS 73-106

READING PLAN:	**106** | Psalms 73-76	**107** | Psalms 77-80	**108** | Psalms 82-85
109 | Psalms 86; 88-89	**110** | Psalms 90-92	**111** | Psalms 93-94; 97-99	**112** | Psalms 100-104

Eleven of the psalms in Book III, which consists of Psalms 73–89, are connected to a man named Asaph (see Psalms 50; 73–83). What little we know about this man is that he was a Levite, a contemporary of David, the leader of a specific tabernacle choir, and a skilled poet and singer. It is also possible that Asaph was not the direct author of these psalms but perhaps performed them or led his choir to perform them.

Psalm 73 is a study of why the wicked seem to have such blessed lives in spite of their rebellion against God. Asaph had evidently wrestled with this question for some time, and so he begins with the conclusion that God is good to Israel and to the pure in heart. He then looks back to his time of struggle, when he wondered if he had even chosen the wrong path. The turning point was an encounter with God in the sanctuary, where the psalmist realized that the blessings of the wicked are fleeting but serving God offers value for all eternity.

In Psalm 75, Asaph praises God's ability and willingness to bring judgment against evil. The psalm begins with an expression of praise, but it is apparent that the "wondrous works" under discussion are primarily God's decision to act in judgment against the wicked. Psalm 78 demonstrates God's goodness in withholding judgment. It was written to teach the younger generations of Israelites how gracious the Lord had been in spite of their ancestors' rebellion and ingratitude during Israel's forty years of wandering in the desert. God forgave their iniquity and did not destroy them.

All of Asaph's psalms in Book III focus on aspects of God's goodness. Other songs in Book III, emphasizing the wonders of God, were written by different authors. Psalm 84 is connected to the sons of Korah, as are Psalms 85 and 87. Psalm 88 was written by Heman the Ezrahite, and Psalm 89 was written by Ethan the Ezrahite. Ethan and Heman were likely contemporaries of David and Solomon. They were known for their wisdom and, apparently, both men were gifted musicians.

Psalm 84 opens with a burst of gladness and expectation. What was the source of this elation? The psalmist was on his way to worship God at the temple. Yet it was not the temple that was the source of the psalmist's expectant joy; rather, it was the opportunity to spend time in God's presence. Psalm 88, on the other hand, is a lament—an outpouring of grief and sorrow. During a period of intense pain, Heman cried out to God for comfort and understanding. Importantly, he had the privilege of spending time in God's presence, and he took advantage of that privilege, approaching God day and night.

In Psalm 89, Ethan contemplates what feels like a conundrum. God had chosen Israel as His covenant people and promised to bless David's descendants forever, yet as Ethan looked at his world, he saw Israel divided and David's dynasty in tatters. How could he reconcile these two truths? Although Ethan never found a resolution to his questions, he began his contemplation on what he knew was solid ground—that God is sovereign and worthy of praise—and then left the matter open for future resolution. Of course, with the benefit of history, we know the answer to his questions; namely, through Christ, God has partially fulfilled His promise to Israel and will one day restore them as a nation in the Promised Land.

Many of the psalms in Book IV (90–106) are not attributed to a specific author. A notable exception is Psalm 90, which was written by Moses, making it the oldest known song in the book. This psalm was likely recorded while the Israelites were wandering in the wilderness—a stressful and dangerous time. Moses begins by proclaiming God's unchanging nature and comparing that with the fleeting lives of humanity. He notes that God's eternal nature makes Him completely separate from us and far above us. Yet incredibly, despite the gulf between us, God deals with us mercifully.

IMAGES OF GOD IN THE PSALMS

Avenger (26:1)
Creator (8:1, 6)
Deliverer (37:39–40)
Fortress (31:3; 71:3)
Healer (30:2)
Judge (7:11)
King (5:2; 44:4)
Protector (5:11)
Provider (78:23–29)
Redeemer (107:2)
Refuge (46:1; 62:7)
Rock (18:2; 95:1)
Shepherd (23:1; 80:1)
Shield (3:3; 28:7)

The unknown author of Psalm 98 proclaims the earth's joy over the rule of the Lord. In Psalm 99, the writer looks back on Israel's history and highlights three leaders who spoke to God as representatives of the people: Moses, Aaron, and Samuel. The psalmist states these men called upon the Lord, "and He answered them" (verse 6). He was to them the "God-Who-Forgives" (verse 8), meaning that forgiveness is an expression of God's character.

Psalms 101 and 103 were written by David. Many scholars believe that Psalm 104 is a continuation of Psalm 103 and was also written by David. The origins of Psalm 106 are unknown, though David is also a candidate for its authorship. These psalms have the particular goal of leading others to join with the author in exalting God and declaring His praises.

David begins Psalm 101 by stating he will sing praises of God's mercy and justice. But the remainder of the psalm focuses on David's actions and attitudes. Later, he adds promises regarding his conduct; for example, he will look at nothing wicked and will not allow liars to remain in his presence. This psalm is David's declaration that his daily decisions and attitudes will serve as an offering of worship.

David also takes care to be specific in his praise. Between the two wonderful injunctions to bless the Lord that bookend Psalm 103, David extols God's forgiveness of all our iniquities and healing of all our diseases, and he praises specific aspects of God's character. Psalms 104 and 106 both show that there is power in raising our voices to verbally worship the Lord Almighty. There is also power in gathering corporately to praise His name and proclaim His glory throughout the nations.

REFLECTIONS

We have access to God's presence. In Psalm 84, the author expresses his joy in worshiping God in the temple. He writes, "I would rather be a doorkeeper in the house of my God than dwell in the tents of wickedness" (verse 10). Sometimes, we forget that we also have an incredible opportunity when it comes to God's presence. In Christ, we have unlimited access to our heavenly Father. Let us never take such a gift for granted—and let us continually avail ourselves of this wondrous joy!

Without God's compassion, we are lost. In many ways, Moses' prayer in Psalm 90 is a foreshadowing of the gospel. Specifically, Moses understood our inability to deal with our own sin. As Paul would write in Romans 3:23, "For all have sinned and fall short of the glory of God." Because of this understanding, the final portions of Moses' prayer are focused on God's mercy and compassion. "Have compassion on Your servants," he prayed. "Oh, satisfy us early with Your mercy, that we may rejoice and be glad all our days!" (verses 13–14). We are dead in our trespasses, and like Moses, we must appeal to God's compassion for salvation. Yet the wonderful news of the gospel is that salvation has already been accomplished, and it is applied to those who believe it through repenting of their sin and placing their faith in Christ.

Sing praise to the Lord! The psalmists were intentional about *verbalizing* their worship to God. "I will sing to the LORD as long as I live," wrote one author. "I will sing praise to my God while I have my being. May my meditation be sweet to Him" (104:33–34). Sometimes, we are content with reading psalms or other words in praise of God. Sometimes, we think thoughts of praise or appreciation to God—and certainly He does hear them. However, there is power in raising our voices to worship the Lord! There is also power in gathering corporately to praise His name and proclaim His glory on this earth.

STUDY QUESTIONS

1. How does Asaph describe his condition at the beginning of Psalm 73? What does he conclude by the end of the psalm about those who are far from God?

2. What evidence of God's goodness does Asaph provide in Psalm 76? How does God's goodness relate to His action against evil and injustice?

3. What is the picture that Asaph presents of the Lord in Psalm 82? What does this psalm say about God's authority to judge human leaders?

4. What are some of the different blessings from God listed in Psalm 84? What does this psalm teach about God's care for all of His creation—even the lowly sparrow?

5. What is the source of Heman's sorrow in Psalm 88? What is he seeking from the Lord—and why is he seeking it?

6. What does Moses communicate about God's compassion in Psalm 90? Why is this element of God's character so important?

7. The author of Psalm 99 describes the Lord as "God-Who-Forgives" (verse 8). How would you explain the breadth of God's forgiveness to someone who has never encountered Scripture?

8. What commitment did David make to righteous living in Psalm 101? How do you seek to model these same traits in your own life?

WEEK 17

GOD GUIDES THOSE WHO SEEK HIM

PSALMS 107–150

READING PLAN: **113** | Psalms 107–109 **114** | Psalms 110–113 **115** | Psalms 114–118
116 | Psalm 119 **117** | Psalms 120–127 **118** | Psalms 128–134 **119** | Psalms 143; 146–150

Psalm 107 marks the beginning of the final "book" of Psalms, Book V, which extends all the way to the closing psalm. Psalm 109 is what scholars often refer to as an "imprecatory psalm." This is a poem or prayer that implores God to call down judgment or destruction on someone who has violated His commands. There are several examples of imprecatory psalms throughout the book of Psalms. Importantly, the goal of these psalms is not to curse wrongdoers out of anger or vengeance but to enlist God in the administration of justice.

Whereas earlier groupings within Psalms were connected due to a common author or theme, this later section in Psalms features a group joined together by a common journey. Psalms 120–134 comprise the "Songs of Ascent," which were hymns that many scholars believe the Jewish pilgrims sang as they climbed their way up the path to Jerusalem (about 2,700 feet in elevation) during three prescribed festivals each year: the Feast of Unleavened Bread, the Feast of Weeks (also known as Pentecost), and the Feast of Tabernacles. All Jewish males were required to travel annually to Jerusalem to attend these three solemn feasts.

Biblical scholars believe the Songs of Ascent were designed to build excitement as the pilgrims grew closer to Jerusalem and God's temple. David authored four of these psalms (122; 124; 131; 133), Solomon wrote one (127), and the remaining ten are anonymous. It is not known when these psalms were first collected together. It appears the songs began far away from Jerusalem (see the references to the cities of Meshech and Kedar, located in Asia Minor and Arabia, respectively, in Psalm 120:5) and moved toward Jerusalem until the pilgrims reached the temple and finished their worship (see Psalm 134:1–2).

In the ancient world, any kind of long journey was perilous—not only because of ambushes and robberies but also because of the long distances and financial burdens imposed by travel. It is perhaps because of these considerations that the Songs of Ascent begin with a cry for protection. The immediate cause for this cry seems to be the original psalmist's pagan neighbors, who did not share his righteous values nor his desire for peace. Subsequent travelers would have taken up that cry to express their desire for protection as they journeyed out of foreign lands and made their way toward God's temple.

Psalm 121 echoes this desire for protection but places the focus on the One who provides it. And Psalm 132 contains the nation's prayers for David's royal descendants.

The psalmists were intentional about describing God's ability to protect His people: "He will not allow your foot to be moved; He who keeps you will not slumber" (121:3). "'If it had not been the Lord who was on our side,' let Israel now say—'if it had not been the Lord who was on our side, when men rose up against us, then they would have swallowed us alive, when their wrath was kindled against us'" (124:1–3). "Our help is in the name of the Lord, who made heaven and earth" (verse 8).

Another major theme within the Songs of Ascent is God's sovereignty. As the pilgrims journeyed toward God's city, they regularly reminded themselves that He alone was in control of all things. Solomon focuses on that theme in Psalm 127, exploring it from three different angles. First, he describes God's sovereignty using the imagery of building a home. Second, he uses the imagery of a watchman protecting a city. Third, he highlights God's sovereignty in connection with a critical area of human existence: raising children. Bearing children was an especially important responsibility for the Israelites because of God's promise that Abraham's descendants would become a great nation and bless the entire earth (see Genesis 12:1–3). Yet here, Solomon is careful to remind his people that it is God Himself who has sovereign charge over all things—even over the opening and closing of the womb.

The literary characteristic of the Psalms, of course, is that it is all poetry. Hebrew poetry was characterized by logical parallelisms. On a larger scale, some psalms, such as 111, 112, and 119, employ an acrostic or alphabetical arrangement. In the original text, the first letter of the first word of every verse or section begins with a different Hebrew consonant, which advances in alphabetical order until the twenty-two consonants are exhausted. Psalm 119 is the most complete example of this device, as the first letter of each of its twenty-two eight-verse stanzas moves through the Hebrew alphabet. Such a literary vehicle aided in memorization and indicated its subject matter had been covered from "A to Z."

The final eight psalms attributed to David are Psalms 138–145. David composed psalms throughout his life—first as a shepherd, then when on the run from King Saul, and finally as a king. Many of David's psalms were written as corporate expressions of worship, intended to be sung by people who had joined together to praise the Lord. Psalm 139 is one of David's most famous poems. A cursory reading might give the impression he was fearful of or annoyed by God's constant attention. But instead, David takes comfort in God's closeness. He then celebrates that God did not just create humanity as a mass collective but that He also intimately knows and has intricately handcrafted each individual.

In these introspective psalms, David often pleads for God's presence and help. Psalm 141 is a great example. When David needed help controlling his tongue, he sought God. When David needed wise counsel from trusted advisors, he asked God to deliver it. And when David needed protection from the schemes of evil men, he invited God to provide it. His exquisite conclusion to his songs (Psalm 145) celebrates the King of eternity for who He is, what He has done, and what He has promised.

In an appropriate ending to the book, Psalms 146–150 are entirely devoted to the worship of God. Each psalm begins with the same line—"Praise the LORD!"—and then recounts why it is good and necessary to continually offer up worship to the Lord. Psalm 150 concludes by calling on *all* creatures of the earth to recognize their Creator: "Let everything that has breath praise the LORD" (verse 6).

REFLECTIONS

God helps those who seek Him. The author of Psalm 121 is unknown, as are the circumstances that caused him to write it. However, his intent is clear. In the four stages of his psalm, he describes the Lord as a helper (see verses 1–2), as a keeper (see verses 3–4), as a protector (see verses 5–6), and as a preserver (see verses 7–8). Jewish travelers on their way to Jerusalem would have taken up this cry to express their desire for God's physical protection on their journey. In the same way, followers of Jesus are invited today to take up this cry to seek help, support, and protection from their loving heavenly Father.

God is intimately involved with His creation. God not only has perfect knowledge about our thoughts and actions but is also deeply involved in our creation. This is true in a general sense, in that God is Creator of all things—everything that exists has come about because of Him. Yet this is also true in a personal sense. God did not just create humanity as a mass collective but intricately handcrafted each human being. "You formed my inward parts," David wrote. "You covered me in my mother's womb. . . . I am fearfully and wonderfully made" (Psalm 139:13–14). Every person on this earth has been fearfully and wonderfully made. Every person is a treasured masterpiece specially designed by the very hands of God.

For we are His WORKMANSHIP, created in CHRIST JESUS for good works.

EPHESIANS 2:10

Praise God in everything. Psalm 150 offers a fitting conclusion to the book of Psalms, inviting us to praise God in any and every way we can—with the trumpet, lute, harp, stringed instruments, flutes, cymbals, and even in dance. We can glorify God in everything! We simply, "Praise the LORD!" (verse 6).

STUDY QUESTIONS

1. Who are the "redeemed of the Lord" the psalmist describes in Psalm 107? What are some of the mercies that God has shown toward this group of people?

2. How would you describe the relationship between the anger that David expresses in Psalm 109 and his calls to praise and worship God in his previous psalms?

3. What are some of the blessings that the author of Psalm 112 states are given to those who fear the Lord? How have you witnessed those blessings in your life?

4. The longest of the psalms (and chapters in the Bible) is Psalm 119—a meditation on exalting God's Word. What stood out to you the most as you read through this psalm?

5. What are some common themes throughout the Songs of Ascent (see Psalms 120–134)? What are some places and geographical features included in these psalms?

6. It is believed that Solomon wrote Psalm 127. What is the meaning of his song? How would you describe God's sovereignty to someone who had never heard about it?

7. What does the author of Psalm 132 communicate about the temple in Zion? What words does he use to describe God's dwelling place?

8. What does David express in Psalm 139 about the frailty and fragility of humankind? What does he express in the psalm about the value and dignity of humankind?

WEEK 18

GOD CALLS US TO PURSUE WISDOM

PROVERBS 1-31

READING PLAN: **120** | Proverbs 1-4 **121** | Proverbs 5-9 **122** | Proverbs 10-13 **123** | Proverbs 14-17 **124** | Proverbs 18-21 **125** | Proverbs 22-26 **126** | Proverbs 27-31

Proverbs is one of the two books of biblical wisdom that is believed to have been written by Solomon. The book contains 513 of the more than 3,000 proverbs he pondered (see 1 Kings 4:32), along with wisdom sayings from others whom he might have influenced.

Solomon most likely wrote Proverbs 1–9 and the wisdom of Proverbs 10:1–22:16. He is likely only the compiler of the "sayings of the wise" in Proverbs 22:17–24:34, which are of an uncertain date before Solomon's reign. The sayings in Proverbs 25–29 were originally composed by Solomon but copied and included later by Judah's King Hezekiah. Proverbs 30 reflects the words of Agur and Proverbs 31 the words of Lemuel, who perhaps was Solomon.

The book of Proverbs itself is a collection of sayings that teach us how to gain understanding and live wisely. These sayings were not necessarily intended as prophecies or promises but as divine guidelines by which we should live. In studying and applying them, we come to contemplate the mind of God, His attributes, His works, and His blessings. Proverbs is both a pattern for the tender impartation of truth from generation to generation as well as a vast resource for the content of the truth to be taught. It contains the principles and applications of Scripture that the godly characters of the Bible illustrate in their lives.

The two major themes in the book are wisdom and folly. Wisdom—which includes knowledge, understanding, instruction, discretion, and obedience—is built on the fear of the Lord and the Word of God. The recurring promise of Proverbs is that, generally speaking, the wise (the righteous who obey God) live longer, prosper, and experience joy and the goodness of God, but that the fool (the unrighteous who do not obey God) generally suffers shame and death. Many of the proverbs teach wisdom by contrasting these opposites—the wise man versus the fool, or the diligent person versus the sluggard.

> The LORD gives WISDOM; from His mouth come KNOWLEDGE and UNDERSTANDING.
>
> PROVERBS 2:6

Solomon begins the book with insights into the origin and value of wisdom. Before a person can hope to gain wisdom, he or she must first learn a deep reverence for God, because true wisdom is from Him. He personifies wisdom in Proverbs 1 as a woman standing in the public square, calling out to the people passing by. This suggests that wisdom and knowledge of God are readily available to anyone who seeks them. Wisdom warns there are consequences for ignoring her offer. This suggests that gaining wisdom requires effort on our part. But it is well worth the effort, for wisdom protects us from the evil enticements of the world.

Proverbs 3 and 4 make it clear that even though life is filled with obligations and demands, we must always keep wisdom as our top priority. Parents, especially, have a responsibility to train up their children in the ways of wisdom. In Proverbs 5, Solomon reminds us that our words influence our behavior. He then (in multiple chapters that follow) teaches what it means to use our gift of language wisely, lovingly, and truthfully. Finally, he informs us in Proverbs 15 that a wise person's speech "is a tree of life" (verse 4) that will be filled with knowledge drawn from the storehouse of Scripture.

Many of the proverbs address areas of fleshly behavior, warning us of the dangers and admonishing us to instead pursue godliness and wisdom. Solomon and the others who contributed to this book often use caricatures—small word portraits of people who are controlled by carnal desires—to caution us against living according to the flesh. One caricature that Solomon repeatedly uses is that of the sluggard: a lazy person who does not have the energy to do any work, although, ironically, does have the energy to contrive outlandish excuses to avoid it. Laziness leads to poverty, enslavement, and personal destruction. The Lord desires for His children to put these passions to death. For the sluggard, this means throwing off the bedclothes and getting busy with the work that God has provided.

The difference between wisdom and folly is so striking we might wonder why *anyone* would choose to be a fool. The answer is simple: we are all born foolish. True wisdom comes only from God, but every human being is born into sin, separated from God and devoid of wisdom. The only way for us to escape folly and find wisdom is to receive God's forgiveness through the gospel. This brings us into a relationship with the source of wisdom, and the Holy Spirit then begins His work of transforming our lives.

In this, we must remember that wisdom from the Lord is not a one-time acquisition, or merely a collecting of knowledge, but a daily commitment to walk according to the Word of God. If we are not careful, we can easily neglect the Word and stray from the paths of wisdom. This was precisely what happened to Solomon in his later years. Finishing strong means persevering in wisdom, keeping company with the wise, and not fighting against correction.

The first few chapters of Proverbs focus on a father's admonition to his son about leading a life of true wisdom, so it is only fitting the last chapter is a mother's advice to her son about what a godly woman should look like. This woman of virtue may seem intimidating at first. She rises before dawn and works until well after sunset. Her efforts are focused on serving others. She is capable in the domestic arts of creating clothing and gourmet meals, but she is equally competent in commerce, demonstrates shrewdness in financial affairs, and even runs a small business. Very few people possess all the qualities of the Proverbs 31 woman, but all Christians can strive to imitate her example.

The chief quality of the woman of wisdom is that she serves others with a willing heart. This is an aspect of wisdom that all God's people can acquire with the help of the Holy Spirit. As we honor the Lord, following Solomon's advice for putting wisdom into daily practice, the Holy Spirit will guide our steps, helping us discern the wisdom that is from above.

REFLECTIONS

Gaining wisdom takes effort. Practically any field of endeavor necessitates hard work if a person is to advance—and wisdom is no exception. This is balanced with the fact that God gives wisdom freely to those who ask. He is the source of true wisdom, and no one can become wise apart from Him. Yet wisdom and understanding also require effort on our part: the effort of obedience to God's Word and diligence in studying His Word. We must put God's Word into practice if we want to gain wisdom.

We must speak the truth in love. The world teaches that we should speak our minds freely, without regard to the effects our words have on others. But this is not how God wants us to use our tongues! James exhorts us to "be swift to hear, slow to speak, slow to wrath; for the wrath of man does not produce the righteousness of God" (1:19–20). God commands us to speak the truth—but He also instructs us to do so with a gentle and loving spirit (see Ephesians 4:15). Lies and deceptions should never be on the tongues of God's people—and our speech should be seasoned with knowledge and gentleness.

True wisdom comes only through the gospel. People today cite many axioms that purport to be wisdom: "follow your heart," "love yourself," and "to thine own self be true." But this so-called wisdom is absent the *basis* of wisdom: God's love for the world as seen through the death and resurrection of Jesus Christ. When we are lost in sin, we know neither wisdom nor the author of wisdom. We believe lies about the world and think those lies are the embodiment of wisdom. But such wisdom is not from above (see 1 Corinthians 3:19–20). Rather, *true* wisdom comes first from having a heart transformed by God's Spirit and then having eyes that are opened to the truth in God's Word.

STUDY QUESTIONS

1. Why does Solomon warn us not to forget wisdom (see Proverbs 1:20–33)? What causes this to happen? How can it be avoided?

2. What does it mean to "incline your ear to wisdom" and search for it (see Proverbs 2:1–4)? What will you gain if you choose to do this (see verses 5, 10–16)?

3. What does it mean to "keep your heart with all diligence" (Proverbs 4:23)? How is this done? Why is it important for followers of Christ?

4. In what ways does Solomon say an ant differs from a lazy person? What other creatures demonstrate diligence and industry (see Proverbs 6:1–11)?

5. What kind of speaker "winks with the eye" (Proverbs 10:10)? What does this mean? How can we detect such motives in another person?

6. Why is the "scoffer" unable to find wisdom (see Proverbs 14:6)? Why do those who reject Christ deny themselves from ever finding true wisdom?

7. What types of "proverbs" do fools tell themselves (see Proverbs 26:7)? What is the result of this type of wisdom in the hands of a foolish person?

8. How does the wise woman in Proverbs 31 benefit her household? How do her husband and her children recognize her for her diligence and leadership?

WEEK 19

GOD CALLS US TO A VIRTUOUS LIFE

ECCLESIASTES 1–SONG OF SONGS 8

READING PLAN: **127** | Ecclesiastes 1–3 **128** | Ecclesiastes 4–6 **129** | Ecclesiastes 7–9
130 | Ecclesiastes 10–12 **131** | Song of Songs 1–3 **132** | Song of Songs 4–6 **133** | Song of Songs 7–8

There are several conclusions we can reach when we look back on the life of Solomon. Clearly, God had blessed the beginning of his reign by giving him great wisdom, wealth, and prestige in the world. Solomon had used that wisdom, at first, to rule God's people justly. Solomon later fulfilled the task that his father, David, left for him in constructing the temple. This structure, and the palace he built, were considered wonders of the known world.

God also blessed Solomon's reign by giving him great power and victory over his enemies. In fact, the Israelite army was the best equipped and most powerful fighting force on earth during the time of his rule (see 1 Kings 4:21). He was the first leader to solidify control of the trade routes connecting Africa, Europe, and Asia, which enabled him to sample all the world had to offer. There was no pursuit or pleasure that he denied himself.

However, near the end of his life, Solomon solemnly declared that all these worldly pursuits had been empty and meaningless. Looking back, he could see that all the world had to offer had only led to emptiness. Life itself seemed nothing but vanity. Sadly, Solomon had not chosen to love the Lord with his whole heart but had filled his life with compromises. What he valued in life was corrupted by his quest for meaning apart from God.

The book of Ecclesiastes encompasses these conclusions from Solomon. It is a profound book, but if only given a surface reading, it can seem depressing with its repeated refrain of "all is vanity" (Ecclesiastes 1:2; see also 12:8). However, Solomon's point is that the riches of the world, the sexual pleasure found in 1,000 different women, and the power he received as king were unable to give him any kind of eternal meaning. Thus, Ecclesiastes serves as both a warning against pursuing the emptiness of the world and an encouragement to trust that God is sovereign over all of life's events.

LOCATIONS IN SONG OF SONGS

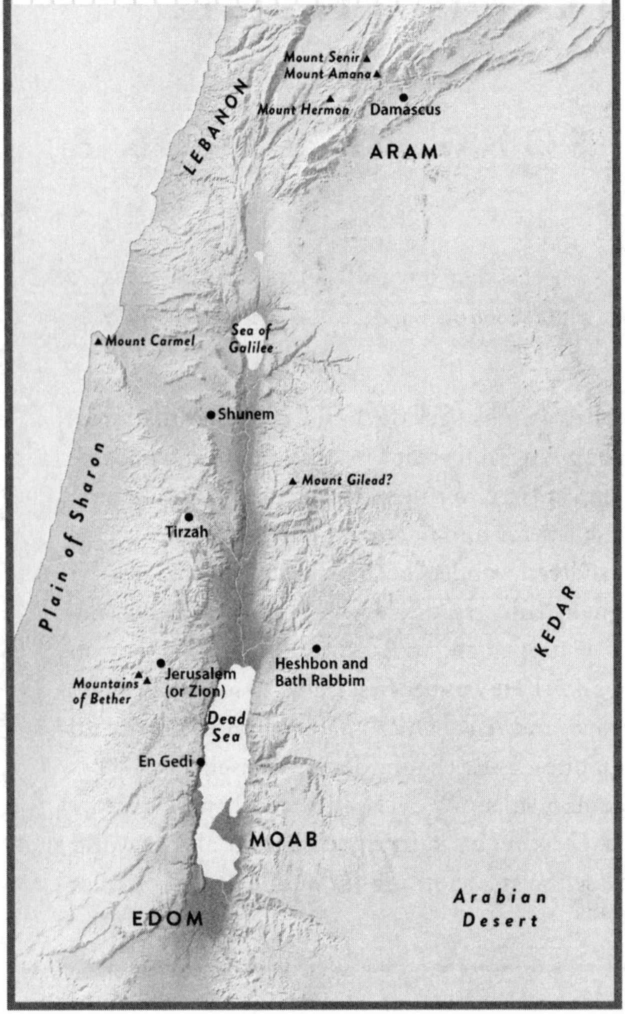

Viewed in this light, the overriding theme of Ecclesiastes is actually a message of hope, not one of despair. There *is* a way for a man or woman to live a fulfilling life—by living for the glory of God! The key to doing this, as Solomon writes at the end of the book, is to "fear God and keep His commandments, for this is man's all" (Ecclesiastes 12:13). When we as followers of Jesus live with this injunction in mind, we will avoid the pessimistic despair of a life filled with vanity.

Song of Songs, also written by Solomon, is different in nature. Penned at some unknown point during his reign, this true-life, dramatic love song is dominated by two people. The first is Solomon, who appears as "the beloved." The second is a Shulamite maiden, whose identity is obscure. Some suggest she was Pharaoh's daughter (see 1 Kings 3:1), though there is no evidence for this conclusion. Others favor Abishag, the Shunammite who cared for David (see 1 Kings 1:1–4, 15). However, her identity as an unknown maiden from Shunem, whose family had possibly been employed by Solomon, seems most reasonable. She would have been Solomon's first wife before he sinned by adding 699 other wives and 300 concubines.

The setting combines both rural and urban scenes. Portions of the story take place in the hill country north of Jerusalem, where the

Shulamite lived and where Solomon enjoyed prominence as a vine grower and shepherd. The city section includes the wedding and time afterward at Solomon's home in Jerusalem. Assuming a chronology without gaps, Song of Songs takes place over a period at least one year in length, but probably no longer than two years.

In contrast to the distorted extremes of ascetic abstinence and lustful perversion outside of marriage, Song of Songs exalts the purity of marital affection and romance. It parallels and enhances other portions of Scripture that portray God's plan for marriage, including the beauty and sanctity of sexual intimacy between husband and wife. The author of Hebrews captures the heart of this song: "Marriage is honorable among all, and the bed undefiled; but fornicators and adulterers God will judge" (13:4).

REFLECTIONS

Life is meaningless apart from God. The world would have us believe that fabulous wealth, power, and the wisdom to use them well are the ultimate goals of our time on earth. Yet King Solomon possessed each of these things in abundance and found them all to be pointless—the "vanity of vanities" as he often proclaimed (Ecclesiastes 12:8). Satisfaction in this life comes not from enjoying the good things on the earth but from walking in a relationship with the Author of all that is good. When we walk in obedience to God's Word, we find contentment with the life that God has provided to us. Apart from such obedience, even the best things of the world are only empty and vain.

Store up treasure in heaven. Human nature is such that we focus on the things we value most, like a king watching over his treasure hoard. Wherever we place our treasure is where we will fix our focus and attention. But our true treasure lies in eternity, where we can never lose the things that God gives us. This is why Jesus said, "Do not lay up for yourselves treasures on earth, where moth and rust destroy and where thieves break in and steal; but lay up for yourselves treasures in heaven, where neither moth nor rust destroys and where thieves do not break in and steal. For where your treasure is, there your heart will be also" (Matthew 6:19–21).

> Provide yourselves MONEY BAGS which do not grow old, a TREASURE in the heavens that does not FAIL.
>
> LUKE 12:33

God honors marriage. Song of Songs has suffered strained interpretations over the centuries by those who claim it has no historical basis and is just an allegory that depicts God's love for Israel and/or Christ's love for the church. However, a more satisfying approach is to take Song of Songs at face value and understand its frequent use of poetic imagery to depict *reality*. When interpreted this way, Song of Songs expands on the ancient marriage instructions given by God in Genesis 2:24: "A man shall leave his father and mother and be joined to his wife." This instruction was given by God to demonstrate His intention for the romance and loveliness of marriage—the most precious of human relations.

STUDY QUESTIONS

1. What are Solomon's conclusions about life in Ecclesiastes 1:1–11? What is his main point about the work we do on this earth outside of God's plans and purposes?

2. Why does Solomon frequently repeat the phrase "under the sun" in Ecclesiastes 2:17–22? To what was he referring? What did this reveal about his priorities?

3. What does King Solomon reveal about the nature of life in Ecclesiastes 3:1–8? How have you witnessed these types of "seasons" in your own life?

4. Solomon states that God "has made everything beautiful in its time" (Ecclesiastes 3:11). When have you seen God make something beautiful out of an unpleasant situation in your life?

5. What solemn conclusion does Solomon make in Ecclesiastes 9:1–8? What he does he advise that people do with their lives in verses 9–10?

6. What is Solomon's purpose in painting such a bleak outlook on old age in Ecclesiastes 12:1–8? What is his message for the young?

7. How does the Shulamite describe her appearance in Song of Songs 1:5–6? How does her Beloved respond to her concerns in verses 8–10?

8. What question did the Daughters of Jerusalem ask the Shulamite in Song of Songs 6:1? What did the Shulamite know was true of her Beloved despite his absence (see verses 2–3)?

WEEK 20

GOD WANTS US TO TRUST IN HIM ALONE

ISAIAH 1-33

READING PLAN: **134** | Isaiah 1-5 **135** | Isaiah 6-10 **136** | Isaiah 11-15
137 | Isaiah 16-20 **138** | Isaiah 21-25 **139** | Isaiah 26-29 **140** | Isaiah 30-33

The writing prophets of the Old Testament fall into two groups: the four major prophets (Isaiah, Jeremiah, Ezekiel, and Daniel) and the twelve minor prophets (Hosea, Joel, Amos, Obadiah, Jonah, Micah, Nahum, Habakkuk, Zephaniah, Haggai, Zechariah, and Malachi). Lamentations falls in the major-prophet grouping because of its connection with Jeremiah.

These prophets emerged on the scene after the united kingdom of Israel under Solomon split into a northern kingdom (which retained the name of Israel) and a southern kingdom (which took the name Judah). As we have seen, the centuries following this split were marked by serious decline, both politically and spiritually, for each kingdom. God's people were continually led by a succession of evil kings who pushed them into idolatry. The failure of each kingdom's political and spiritual leaders led God to send the prophets, who proclaimed a variety of messages from Him, including unpopular words of warning and judgment.

Isaiah, a contemporary of the prophets Hosea and Micah, ministered primarily to the southern kingdom of Judah and its four rulers under whom he served. Raised in Jerusalem, and evidently coming from a family of rank, he was an appropriate choice as a political and religious counselor to the nation. When God called Isaiah after the death of King Uzziah, the prophet supernaturally witnessed a vision of God's heavenly throne room. The sight was both awesome and terrible, and Isaiah recognized the enormous responsibility of his call to service. Even though he knew his ministry would be one of fruitless warning and exhortation, he nevertheless responded with cheerful readiness.

Isaiah, who would speak to both the kings and common people of Judah for nearly sixty years, begins his book with a stunning condemnation of Judah's sinfulness as a society—particularly the empty ritualism of their religious observances—and a proclamation of future judgment as a consequence. After condemning these sins, Isaiah addresses an imminent crisis: the king of Syria and the king of Israel (the northern kingdom) were bringing their armies to the outskirts of Jerusalem to war against Judah.

> Therefore the LORD Himself will give you a SIGN: Behold, the virgin shall CONCEIVE and bear a Son, and shall call His name IMMANUEL.
>
> ISAIAH 7:14

God sent Isaiah to declare that the immediate danger to Judah posed by this alliance would come to nothing. Jerusalem would be spared destruction. The Lord then encouraged Ahaz, Judah's king, by offering to send him a sign. But Ahaz, in false humility, refused—to which God declared that He would choose His own sign. This sign was more than God's plan to save Judah from the immediate threat; it represented His ultimate plan of salvation for all of humanity through the future birth, ministry, redemption, and ultimate reign of a descendant of David, whom the Old Testament prophets knew as the promised Messiah.

Isaiah next focuses on future judgments against two nations that would come to play a major role in the history of God's people. The first nation, Assyria, was already a major player on the world's stage—a warrior nation known for its brutality and its bloodthirsty desire for conquest. The second nation, Babylon, had not yet become a major world power, but it was a known enemy. Both would one day conquer Israel and Judah, respectively. Here, however, Isaiah speaks of Babylon's ultimate destruction at God's hands and how Assyria will serve as a rod of punishment for the Lord's plans, destroying nations such as Philistia, Moab, and Syria.

Isaiah's prophetic gaze then continues across the world as he foretells yet another round of judgments against Babylon, but also against other powerful nations of the day, including Ethiopia (Cush), Egypt, Arabia, and Tyre. These pronouncements would likely have been received as good news by his original hearers. However, Isaiah also includes a proclamation against Jerusalem.

The portion of Isaiah's vision that follows is, in many ways, the culmination of these judgments. Isaiah sees the coming Day of the Lord, when God's wrath will fully fall upon the earth and its inhabitants. Part of God's judgment will include the destruction of our planet: "Behold, the LORD makes the earth empty and makes it waste" (Isaiah 24:1). Ultimately, however, this destruction will lay the groundwork for something wonderful: the final chapters of God's redemption of all His people. The vision that John received in Revelation of this eternal paradise—their future home—will be a new heaven and a new earth, devoid of the corruption of sin, where there will be no more death, sorrow, crying, or pain.

After this look to the day of redemption and restoration, Isaiah returns to the present, focusing on the threat Assyria poses to Israel and Judah. The leaders of God's people had failed. Kings and courtesans were so busy intoxicating themselves with wine that, in many ways, they were oblivious to the threat Assyria posed until its armies were at their door. Isaiah condemns Judah's leaders for considering Egypt their source of rescue rather than God. He correctly prophesies that Assyria will besiege Jerusalem—but not destroy it. And he once again accurately foretells the coming destruction of Israel at Assyria's hands.

Some of Isaiah's prophecies, such as Assyria's defeat, were fulfilled during his lifetime. Many have been literally fulfilled since then, including Jesus' first coming, the Babylonian captivity due to Judah's departure from the Lord one hundred years after Isaiah, and Judah's deliverance from captivity by Cyrus of Persia. Other prophecies, such as Jesus' second coming and the Day of the Lord, are yet future.

REFLECTIONS

Serving God is an awesome responsibility. After the death of King Uzziah, Isaiah witnessed a vision of God's heavenly throne room. The sight caused Isaiah to cry out, "Woe is me, for I am undone! Because I am a man of unclean lips, and I dwell in the midst of a people of unclean lips; for my eyes have seen the King, the LORD of hosts" (6:5). Isaiah's cry mirrors Peter's after he recognized Jesus as the Messiah and exclaimed, "Depart from me, for I am a sinful man, O Lord!" (Luke 5:8). Those of us who serve as disciples of Jesus today will do well to remember that our Savior is also the supreme Lord and Judge of the universe. Our service to Him is not a casual commitment but an awesome responsibility.

We can be confident of a glorious future. The Old Testament prophets were often viewed as "speakers of doom" who railed about bad news and coming judgment. Yet much of Isaiah's prophecy is hopeful—especially when he speaks of the future that God has prepared for His people. In speaking of "that day" when the Messiah will fully reveal His authority in the universe, Isaiah proclaimed, "The wolf also shall dwell with the lamb, the leopard shall lie down with the young goat, the calf and the young lion and the fatling together; and a little child shall lead them. . . . They shall not hurt nor destroy in all My holy mountain, for the earth shall be full of the knowledge of the LORD as the waters cover the sea" (11:6, 9).

We are stewards of God's blessings. In Isaiah 22:15–25, God pronounces a judgment against a man named Shebna. He was the steward over Jerusalem and had been entrusted with a high degree of power and authority. Apparently, Shebna had created a huge tomb in his own honor, similar to the kings of Egypt. God used this tomb as an illustration not only of Shebna's poor stewardship but also of the poor stewardship of the people in Judah in general. Much like Shebna, we as followers of Christ have been entrusted with authority, and we must recognize we are stewards of the blessings God has given to us. Those blessings include our resources—time, treasure, talents—but also the blessings of Scripture and the presence of the Holy Spirit. We have been given those blessings for a purpose. We have work to do.

STUDY QUESTIONS

1. How would you describe the overall tone of Isaiah's prophecy in Isaiah 1–2? What are some of the specific sins of Judah that caught your attention?

2. What do you learn about God from Isaiah's call to be a prophet (see Isaiah 6:8–13)? How long did the Lord instruct Isaiah to prophesy to His people?

3. How should King Ahaz have responded when God offered to give him a sign (see Isaiah 7:12–17)? Why was his response both disobedient and hypocritical?

4. Which elements of Isaiah 9:1–7 has Jesus already fulfilled? Which promises are still to come? What helps you to have confidence that God will fulfill His promises in the Bible?

5. What images strike you in Isaiah's prophecy of Babylon's destruction (see Isaiah 13)? Why would this prophecy of judgment have been encouraging for the people of Isaiah's day?

6. What did God command Isaiah to do as a sign against Egypt and Ethiopia (see Isaiah 20:1–6)? What judgment was God pronouncing against these nations?

7. The restoration of Israel is described in Isaiah 27. Why is that good news for the church? How should the church view and interact with the Jewish people today?

8. Looking at Isaiah 30, what were some of the reasons God's people wanted to turn to Egypt for rescue? What did God think of this plan?

WEEK 21

GOD PROMISES TO REDEEM US

ISAIAH 34-66

READING PLAN: **141** | Isaiah 34-38 **142** | Isaiah 39-43 **143** | Isaiah 44-48 **144** | Isaiah 49-52 **145** | Isaiah 53-57 **146** | Isaiah 58-62 **147** | Isaiah 63-66

As a whole, the Old Testament prophets like Isaiah weren't primarily interested in preserving a detailed historical record in their biblical writings. However, the passages in Isaiah 36-39 are an exception, providing a record of Assyria's attempt to conquer Jerusalem. These chapters also form a transition that closes the first division of Isaiah's prophecy. Isaiah 36 and 37 are the historical consummation of all Isaiah has written so far, describing Jerusalem's deliverance from Assyria. Isaiah 38 and 39 are the historical basis for Isaiah's prophecies that lie ahead, which offer a preview of Judah's captivity at the hands of the Babylonians.

Although Isaiah addresses many different people groups in the first half of his book, he is speaking primarily to the residents of Judah. As such, Isaiah 1-39 addresses the situation in Judah during Isaiah's ministry, which stretched from 739 BC until c. 686 BC. However, a major shift takes place in the second half of Isaiah's book. In Isaiah 40-66, the prophet addresses Judah as though the prophesied Babylonian captivity (foretold in Isaiah 39:5-7) had already occurred—even though that captivity would not begin until 605-586

BC. So, through Isaiah, God was speaking to the people of Judah who would experience captivity a hundred years and more after Isaiah's ministry concluded.

There is also a shift in the tone of Isaiah's prophecies. Rather than primarily speaking words of judgment, he begins to include promises and blessings from God to the people of Judah. These promises would have been encouraging to the people of Isaiah's day. Yet they would also prove to be encouraging to those future residents of Judah and Jerusalem who endured the terror of the Babylonian conquest.

This portion of Isaiah also contains four "songs" that describe the coming of the Messiah—the Servant of the Lord. The first of these songs, recorded in Isaiah 42:1–9, reveals the Messiah as God's servant in whom His soul delights and on whom His Spirit rests. It also points forward to the Messiah's work, including opening the eyes of the blind and freeing prisoners from their darkness. The second song, recorded in Isaiah 49:1–13, tells of the Messiah's mission to the entire world and His spiritual success. The third song, recorded in Isaiah 50:4–11, is the Messiah's soliloquy about being perfected through obedience and sufferings. The final song, recorded in Isaiah 52:13–53:12, contains incontrovertible proof that God is the author of Scripture and Jesus the fulfillment of messianic prophecy.

THE FOUR "SERVANT SONGS" OF ISAIAH
❶ Isaiah 42:1–9: The Servant is chosen by God and has God's Spirit (Matthew 12:18–21)
❷ Isaiah 49:1–13: The Servant's mission is to bring light to the world (Luke 2:29–32)
❸ Isaiah 50:4–11: The Servant will be persecuted yet vindicated (Philippians 2:5–11)
❹ Isaiah 52:13–53:12: The Servant will be a sacrifice for humanity's sin (1 Peter 2:21–24)

Time is a major factor when it comes to understanding the book of Isaiah. The prophecies represent many different layers of time and therefore point to many different audiences to whom God was speaking. The first layer, of course, is the original hearers of Isaiah's prophecy—the residents of Judah and Jerusalem. A second layer includes the surrounding nations—Isaiah's prophecy included words of judgment against those nations, which would primarily be fulfilled in the immediate future. A third layer includes the then-future residents of Judah and Jerusalem who would endure the terror of the Babylonian conquest. A fourth layer includes the first coming of Jesus, the Messiah, into the world. A final layer points to the Messiah's return and further events that remain to be fulfilled in the future.

The final chapters of Isaiah's prophecy alternate back and forth between the first and final layers. Isaiah speaks about the leaders of his day, who ignored justice and allowed God's people to go astray. He then paints vivid pictures of the future glory to be experienced by God's people and reveals the many ways that God will bless those who faithfully follow Him.

In the end, what God communicated through Isaiah is perhaps best summed up in the meaning of the prophet's name: "The Lord is salvation." Most of the people of Isaiah's day were paying lip service to God. They were going through the motions of their religious rituals, but their hearts were far from the Lord. Others had succumbed to the influence of idolatry and forsaken God altogether. They feared the punishment their sin deserved—punishment that, as Isaiah prophesied, would be poured out over generations, culminating in the exile of Babylonian captivity.

Yet the emphasis of Isaiah's prophecy wasn't merely the coming judgment. It was that the Lord is unceasingly faithful to His people and would redeem and restore them in spite of their sinfulness. Perhaps this is best summed up in these words: "But now, thus says the LORD . . . 'Fear not, for I have redeemed you; I have called you by your name; You are Mine. When you pass through the waters, I will be with you; and through the rivers, they shall not overflow you. When you walk through the fire, you shall not be burned, nor shall the flame scorch you. For I am the LORD your God'" (Isaiah 43:1-3).

REFLECTIONS

Temptation strikes at our trust in God. The people of Judah, with a portion of the Assyrian army arrayed against them, gathered in Jerusalem for safety. An Assyrian representative appeared and encouraged them to surrender rather than risk a prolonged siege. The message of this representative (the "Rabshakeh") can be boiled down to a single idea: *God cannot save you.* This man first tried to entice the people with food and comfort (see Isaiah 36:16–17) and then struck at their trust in God, asking, "Who among all the gods of these lands have delivered their countries from my hand, that the LORD should deliver Jerusalem from my hand?" (verse 20). Satan still tries to separate us from God today by suggesting that He cannot be trusted. Don't be fooled! Stand strong and trust in God's sovereignty.

Salvation is for all people. Many residents of Israel and Judah believed they had an exclusive connection with God and that He would always operate with their best national interests in mind. In reality, God's selection of the Jewish people was always intended as the vehicle through which He would reveal Himself to the world (see Genesis 12:1–3). God confirmed this plan in the second Servant Song when He declared, "It is too small a thing that You should be My Servant to raise up the tribes of Jacob, and to restore the preserved ones of Israel; I will also give You as a light to the Gentiles, that You should be My salvation to the ends of the earth" (Isaiah 49:6). God chooses to save sinners from every nation and people group—a gift of salvation made possible through the death and resurrection of Jesus Christ.

God is our Redeemer. In Isaiah 54, God warned that His people would go through trials as a result of their rejection of Him. Even so, God promised they could look forward to a future period of restoration. In describing those future realities, God used the term *Redeemer* to describe Himself: "For your Maker is your husband, the LORD of hosts is His name; and your Redeemer is the Holy One of Israel" (verse 5).

STUDY QUESTIONS

1. How did Assyria's representative (the Rabshakeh) attempt to undermine the people's confidence in both God and their king in his speeches (see Isaiah 36)?

2. How would you summarize King Hezekiah's mistake as related in Isaiah 39? What steps can you take right now to help you from making the same mistake?

3. What words of comfort did God instruct Isaiah to offer to the future residents of Judah who would endure the destruction of Jerusalem and captivity in Babylon (see Isaiah 40)?

4. Isaiah 42 contains a prophecy about the coming Messiah. How do the first nine verses point to Jesus? How does this message encourage you today?

5. How does the second Servant Song in Isaiah 49:1–13 point forward to the life and ministry of Jesus? How do these words bring you comfort today?

6. Why did God's people need to endure a period of suffering and separation from Him? How did God assure them that this separation was temporary (see Isaiah 49:14–26)?

7. What details do you find the most striking from the final Servant Song given in Isaiah 52:13–53:12? What do you learn about Jesus from that song?

8. How do the opening verses of Isaiah 61 also point to the life and ministry of Jesus? What does it mean to be "covered with the robe of righteousness" (verse 10)?

WEEK 22

GOD IS OUR RIGHTEOUSNESS

JEREMIAH 1-52

READING PLAN: **148** | Jeremiah 1-2; 4-6 **149** | Jeremiah 11-13; 16-18 **150** | Jeremiah 19-22
151 | Jeremiah 23-27 **152** | Jeremiah 28-33 **153** | Jeremiah 36-41 **154** | Jeremiah 41-45; 52

The prophet Jeremiah was like a lighthouse set in the midst of God's people. He ministered during the waning decades of Judah, standing against waves of persecution, suffering, rebuke, physical deprivation, and isolation as he declared God's warnings. The life of this "weeping prophet" was full of conflict because of his predictions about coming judgment. He was threatened, put in stocks, forced to flee, publicly humiliated, and thrown into a pit.

Yet it was because the people and their leaders had rebelled against God through idolatry, child sacrifice, and injustice that the Lord's wrath would come against them in the form of an invading army. Jeremiah prophesied not only the military conquest of Judah but also the ruin of Jerusalem—and even the destruction of Solomon's temple.

Jeremiah recounts more of his life in his book than most other prophets. His early chapters offer details on his calling to be a prophet and his first message (2:1–3:5), where he presents God's "case" against the people of Judah—the record of their rebellion and idolatry. His second word from the Lord (3:6–6:30) includes the image of a boiling pot, facing away from the north. The meaning behind the vision was that calamity would break forth from the kingdoms of the north and descend on all the cities of Judah unless they repented. In this message, God compared the rebellion of Judah with the actions of her "sister," the northern kingdom of Israel. Unless Judah repented, they too would be taken captive by foreign adversaries.

Jeremiah's third message (7:1–10:25) was delivered at the temple gate in Jerusalem, where he catalogued the people's idolatry and denounced the false messages of peace being declared by prophets who were not from God. Their claims were that God would never allow a foreign army to invade His city and destroy His temple. Jeremiah reminded them that God had not spared Shiloh in the past—the location of the tabernacle before Jerusalem. Yet God made it clear the horrors Jeremiah was prophesying could be averted if the people repented and returned to Him. Unfortunately, they refused.

Jeremiah's fourth message (11:1–13:27) is interrupted by an autobiographical interlude, in which the prophet recounts the men of his hometown seeking to kill him and God assuring him they would not succeed. This event seems to be the catalyst for a question-and-answer session between the prophet and God. It begins with Jeremiah asking the Lord why the wicked prosper. The prophet even had a suggestion for how God should deal with those who preyed on their fellow Israelites. God confirmed the people of Judah would receive the consequences of their collective sin. "Plunderers" would appear on the horizon to punish His people. This invasion would not be a random attack but rather God's appointed judgment.

> Let not the wise man glory in his WISDOM, let not the mighty man glory in his MIGHT, nor let the rich man glory in his RICHES.
>
> JEREMIAH 9:23

Even at such a late hour, however, God wanted to withhold His judgment. So He told Jeremiah to bury an expensive linen sash next to the Euphrates River (a round trip of more than 1,000 miles) to illustrate the ways the people's pride would be ruined by the coming destruction at the hands of the Babylonians. Living parables like these were not offered for sport or showmanship but as a means of illustrating the truth and capturing the attention of those whom God wanted to reach. Sadly, the people did not listen, and even God mourned the pride of His people.

Jeremiah appears to have given his fifth message (14:1–17:18) during a time of drought. A prolonged drought in Judah should have awakened its leaders to the reality of their sin. The lack of water and fruitfulness was a direct warning from God, but it was a sign that they again ignored. Jeremiah dealt with the people's failure to observe the Sabbath in his sixth message (17:21–24).

His seventh message (18:1–20:18) came shortly after and centered on two object lessons. The first involved the prophet's observations while he watched a potter at work. God declared He was the potter and Israel clay in His hands. The second included a confrontation with priests and elders in the Valley of Hinnom, a fiery refuse dump outside of Jerusalem. It was a vile place where children were sacrificed in the flames to the god Molech. There, Jeremiah smashed the potter's flask to symbolize what would happen to Jerusalem: the Valley of Hinnom would become the Valley of Slaughter. The invaders from the north would bring destruction, ruin, hunger, and captivity on a scale the people had never seen.

Over time, Nebuchadnezzar and his armies were identified as the instrument God would use to humble His people. In 588 BC, the armies of Babylon surrounded Jerusalem. Jeremiah delivered his eighth message (21:1–14) during the days of the final siege. His ninth message (22:1–23:40) included a reference to the throne of David. His tenth message (24:1–10) included an object lesson involving two baskets of figs. An eleventh (25:1–28), twelfth (26:1–24), and thirteenth (27:1–28:17) message followed.

Some of these middle portions of the book include content that spans the earlier years of various kings. In compiling these chapters, Jeremiah placed events from different timelines together to emphasize specific themes—for instance, to show how the obedience of the Rechabites (a semi-nomadic people group) contrasted with the general disobedience of the people and leaders of Judah.

Jeremiah's fourteenth message was written after his countrymen were deported to Babylon. His words, recorded as a letter, were to comfort those taken captive, with the promise that Judah's exile would only last seventy years. The letter also reassured the captives they should seek to flourish in Babylon. But God offered an even greater promise out into the future: He would make a new covenant with His people—a Branch of righteousness would come from David's line to bring salvation.

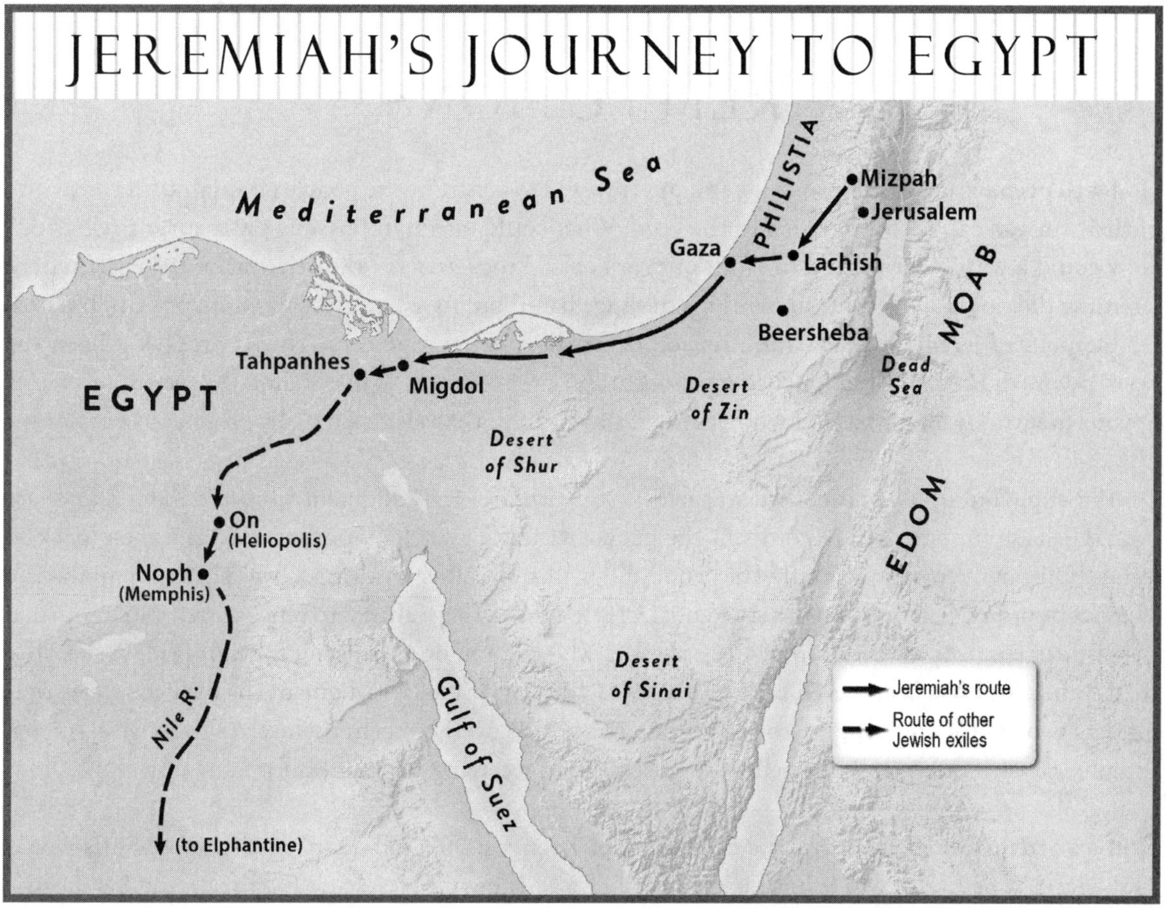

At this point, Jeremiah's narrative shifts in two ways. First, the messages move away from God's judgment and emphasize His compassion and consolation. Second, the prophecies shift from the short-term future to the long-term future—even to events that still have yet to occur. Jeremiah speaks not only of the future restoration of Jerusalem but also of a New Covenant and of the coming Messiah.

Ultimately, most of those who had taken refuge in Jerusalem were killed or taken into captivity, but a remnant were left behind to keep the city functioning. Specifically, a group of poor farmers and vinedressers remained to tend the crops and raise tribute for Babylon. Jeremiah was among this group. God spoke through Jeremiah to this remnant in Judah, extending a season of peace and prosperity over the land through the protection of Babylon's armies so they could rebuild their lives. In time, Jeremiah was forced, against both his will and the Lord's will, to go with a fleeing remnant of Judah to Egypt. It is believed he was taken captive to Babylon several years later when the Babylonians invaded Egypt.

The final chapter of Jeremiah takes a second (and longer) look at the fall of Jerusalem. For decades, Jeremiah had declared that God would use Babylon to accomplish His judgment and that the walls and temple of Jerusalem would be torn down. Jeremiah's purpose was thus to highlight the accuracy of God's message through His prophet. What God said would happen did indeed come to pass.

REFLECTIONS

God will prepare us for His work. Jeremiah's task was to confront the people of Judah with the reality of their sin and call them to return to the Lord. What could one man possibly say to an entire nation? How could a young man stand in front of priests and kings and speak with authority? Fortunately, Jeremiah did not have to come up with his message based on his experience, wisdom, or skill. Instead, God appointed Jeremiah as His mouthpiece, declaring His message through His prophet. "Then the LORD put forth His hand and touched my mouth, and the LORD said to me: 'Behold, I have put My words in your mouth'" (1:9). It was God who provided the message that He desired His prophet to proclaim.

Don't get puffed up by pride. God was willing to withhold His judgment from Judah even at a late hour. He had sent Jeremiah to confront the people with their unrighteousness and call them back to Himself through repentance. Sadly, the people did not listen. Why? One reason was pride. Jeremiah said, "Do not be proud, for the LORD has spoken" (13:15). But still, they refused to repent. Even God mourned the pride of His people: "But if you will not hear it, My soul will weep in secret for your pride . . . because the LORD's flock has been taken captive" (verse 17). Today, pride is still one of the core obstacles that hinders people from responding to the gospel. Those who overly esteem themselves to be wise, strong, or righteous will often refuse to believe the necessity of receiving forgiveness for their sin.

God's words promise hope. At the beginning of Jeremiah 30, God changed the tone of His words spoken to His people: "I will bring back from captivity My people Israel and Judah. . . . And I will cause them to return to the land that I gave to their fathers, and they shall possess it" (verse 3). The prophecies in Jeremiah up to this point are generally negative. The Lord did not renounce those prophecies—the destruction of Jerusalem was still imminent—yet God would not abandon His people. After seventy years of captivity, He would bring them back. Not only that, God promised to bless His people: "Then out of them shall proceed thanksgiving and the voice of those who make merry; I will multiply them, and they shall not diminish" (30:19). These were words of hope in advance of suffering.

Take the course of obedience. Jeremiah juxtaposed two events as a way of highlighting Judah's lack of obedience. The first was an oath taken by the people near the beginning of Nebuchadnezzar's siege. The people at first committed to freeing their slaves, but then they changed their minds and put those who had been freed back into slavery (see Jeremiah 34:8–11). What caused such a drastic shift in behavior? It is likely the people changed their minds after the Babylonians briefly relented in their siege to deal with Egypt (see Jeremiah 37:6–10). Those who had freed their slaves likely believed that their problems had come to an end and so determined to regain their slaves. By contrast, Jeremiah highlights a group known as the Rechabites, who had made a covenant to abstain from alcohol. They remained true to that oath even when Jeremiah urged them to take wine. Their obedience highlighted the disobedience of God's chosen people.

> OBEY the voice of the LORD . . . then the LORD will RELENT concerning the DOOM that He has pronounced AGAINST you.
>
> JEREMIAH 26:13

God has authority over nations. In Jeremiah 46–49, the prophet declares God's judgments over many different nations and people groups. One of the themes of these prophecies was that God would use the Babylonians to punish the evil of the foreign nations—not just the people of Judah. These nations included Egypt, Philistia, Moab, Ammon, Edom, and others. Yet while the Babylonians were the instruments of judgment, it was through God's authority that the judgment was carried out. "The Lord of hosts . . . says: 'Behold, I will bring punishment on Amon of No, and Pharaoh and Egypt, with their gods and their kings'" (Jeremiah 46:25). "'A general lamentation on all the housetops of Moab, and in its streets; for I have broken Moab like a vessel in which is no pleasure,' says the Lord" (Jeremiah 48:38).

We are only a step away from God's forgiveness. Not even Babylon with its military might could avoid God's judgment. Less than fifty years after the destruction of Jerusalem, Babylon was overthrown by the Persians. God predicted this judgment through Jeremiah, and in the middle of that prophecy, He spoke words of encouragement to those among His chosen people who would experience captivity. But more than just encouragement, He also spoke words of forgiveness (see Jeremiah 50:20). This promise of pardon foreshadowed the coming of the Messiah and the message of the gospel—and it remains true of all who follow the Messiah today. As God promised through the apostle John, "If we confess our sins, He is faithful and just to forgive us our sins and to cleanse us from all unrighteousness" (1 John 1:9).

STUDY QUESTIONS

1. What are some specific examples of God preparing Jeremiah and the citizens of Jerusalem for the coming invasion from Babylon (see Jeremiah 1:14–19)?

2. What messages were the false prophets proclaiming to the people (see Jeremiah 8:4–17)? What criticisms did Jeremiah have for those who worshiped idols (see Jeremiah 10:1–10)?

3. Jeremiah at one point asked the Lord, "Why does the way of the wicked prosper?" (Jeremiah 12:1). What is the biblical answer to this question?

4. What lesson was God teaching Jeremiah at the potter's house (see Jeremiah 18:1–11)? How would you apply this lesson to your own life?

5. How would you summarize God's message to the people of Judah in Jeremiah 19? What was the purpose of the broken flask (see verse 10)?

6. What was the situation in Judah as the events of Jeremiah 21 began to unfold? What request did King Zedekiah make of the Lord (see verses 1–2)?

7. What charge did God make against the people of Judah in Jeremiah 25:1–7? What did He reveal about the nature of His judgment and how long it would last in verses 8–14?

8. What does the Lord say in Jeremiah 31:31–34 about the New Covenant that He will bring? What does this reveal about God's character?

WEEK 23

GOD CALLS US TO SERVE HIM

LAMENTATIONS 1–EZEKIEL 19

READING PLAN: **155** | Lamentations 1–2 **156** | Lamentations 3–5 **157** | Ezekiel 1–3 **158** | Ezekiel 4–7 **159** | Ezekiel 8–11 **160** | Ezekiel 12–15 **161** | Ezekiel 16–19

The book of Lamentations is believed to have been written by Jeremiah after the destruction of Jerusalem in 586 BC. The content is thus rooted in a historical moment, but it contains the prophet's reaction to that history rather than a description of events. For example, Jeremiah wrote these words as an expression of grief emanating from that destruction: "For these things I weep; my eye, my eye overflows with water; because the comforter, who should restore my life, is far from me. My children are desolate because the enemy prevailed" (1:16).

Much like the book of Jeremiah, Lamentations focuses on God's judgment against Judah—a judgment that has just taken place. Jeremiah is weeping over the devastation he has *just* witnessed. Yet, importantly, Lamentations also includes themes of hope and the reality of God's faithfulness. "For the Lord will not cast off forever. Though He causes grief, yet He will show compassion" (3:31–32). God had kept His promise to judge Jerusalem; therefore, Jeremiah could hold on to God's promise that He would restore the city in the future.

The prophet Ezekiel was twenty-five when he was taken by Babylon and thirty when called into ministry—and what a calling it was. The opening chapter of Ezekiel is filled with a stunning visual display of God's glory and divine presence. In the vision that Ezekiel received from the Lord, he saw whirlwind filled with "raging fire" (1:4), radiantly colored angelic beings "in appearance like a flash of lightning" (verse 14), and a vision of God seated on a throne of sapphire, surrounded by "the appearance of the likeness of the glory of the LORD" (verse 28).

The display of God's majestic throne assured Ezekiel that he was indeed receiving word from the God of Abraham, Isaac, and Jacob. This assurance no doubt helped him retain his resolve in carrying out a difficult assignment. Ezekiel 2 and 3 offer details about that assignment: God commissioned him to speak His truths to the children of Israel. Ezekiel would experience physical hardships, along with social pressure and rejection, during his ministry as a watchman. For this reason, God strengthened Ezekiel at the beginning of that ministry—and continued to fortify him in the decades that followed.

> Thus shall My ANGER be spent, and I will cause My FURY to rest upon them, and I will be AVENGED; and they shall know that I, the LORD, have spoken it in MY ZEAL.
>
> EZEKIEL 5:13

God often commanded His prophets to dramatize His prophetic words in ways designed to catch the attention of the people and shock them out of their complacency. No prophet used these visual displays more prominently than Ezekiel. In Ezekiel 4, the Lord instructs His prophet to draw (or scratch out) a picture of Jerusalem and then act out a siege against it—including visualizing the extreme methods the residents of the city would use to cook food. God called Ezekiel to cut, weigh, and burn his own air; to prophesy against the mountains of Jerusalem; and to relate a powerful vision of idolatry in the temple.

God used Ezekiel for eighteen months as a visual display of His coming judgment against the people of Jerusalem and Israel. During that time, Ezekiel declared the specifics of that judgment through several prophecies. Ezekiel 8 then marks a turning point. The prophet was lifted by the Holy Spirit between earth and heaven and given a series of visions regarding the idolatry being practiced in Jerusalem, including the detestable rituals of its leaders. Ezekiel's visions included heavenly angels being called to carry out God's judgment against the city. They also include the departure of God's glory from the temple, which occurs in stages. Ezekiel then learns that twenty-five leaders are giving deceptive advice to God's people, and he is given another promise of future restoration once God's judgment is complete.

Ezekiel 12 marks another turning point, as the prophet turns his attention to his fellow captives in Babylon. Much like the residents of Judah, these captives were hard-hearted and refused to believe that Jerusalem would be destroyed. They believed they would soon return to their homes in spite of their continued rejection of God's will. Ezekiel made every effort to show them the error in their thinking and the many reasons for God's judgment. In Ezekiel 15, he even offers an object lesson of Israel as a useless vine, fit only to be burned as fuel. In Ezekiel 16, he then paints a picture of God's deep love for Israel as a nation—and of Israel's deep personal betrayal by pursuing the gods of other nations.

REFLECTIONS

We must honestly assess our wrongdoing. The book of Lamentations reveals that Jeremiah experienced strong emotions following the aftermath of Jerusalem's destruction. He was horrified at the ruin of his beloved city. At first glance, it might seem as if Jeremiah was angry with God. He lamented that God had "spurned His altar" and "done violence to His tabernacle" (2:6–7). Yet a full reading of Lamentations makes it evident that Jeremiah blamed himself and the people of Judah for the consequences of their actions—not God (see 1:8). Speaking on behalf of the city, he declared, "The LORD is righteous, for I rebelled against His commandment . . . my young men have gone into captivity" (1:18).

God calls His people to serve Him. The early chapters of Ezekiel reveal how God called him to serve as His prophet. God's call was not framed as a request but as a *command.* The Lord commanded Ezekiel to carry out a specific role for the rest of his life, and he expected Ezekiel to obey. Other individuals received similar calls in the Old Testament, including kings such as Saul and David, prophets such as Jeremiah and Deborah, and even artisans such as Bezalel and Aholiab (see Exodus 31). Followers of Jesus also live under a broad call to spend their lives obeying the Great Commission: "Go therefore and make disciples of all the nations, baptizing them in the name of the Father and of the Son and of the Holy Spirit, teaching them to observe all things that I have commanded you" (Matthew 28:19–20).

All sin is a form of idolatry. Israel had been blessed with the revelation of God. They had been chosen to reveal God to the rest of the world. Yet, for centuries, they had ignored the reality of their calling and even rejected it. Rather than being a witness of God to the nations, they had turned to the religious practices of those nations. God's words in Ezekiel 5:7–8 are sobering: "Because you have multiplied disobedience more than the nations that are all around you. . . . Indeed I, even I, am against you and will execute judgments in your midst in the sight of the nations." Israel had rejected the true God and turned to false gods, which is idolatry. Similarly, all sin is rooted in idolatry. Even today, our sin is rooted in idolatry. Every time we turn away from God to serve something else—including our own desires or our own purposes—we are elevating that something else above God. We are practicing idolatry.

God knows those who belong to Him. Ezekiel 9 offers a fascinating "behind the scenes" view of the spiritual realm. While physically "seeing" Jerusalem in the middle of a vision, Ezekiel also witnessed six angelic beings charged with carrying out God's judgment against the city. One of the angels was given the task of identifying individuals in the city who still feared the Lord God. This angel was commanded to "mark" the foreheads of those who wept over the evil done there. The rest of the angels were then given a chilling command: "Go after him through the city and kill; do not let your eye spare, nor have any pity" (verse 5). God's judgment against evil is always frightening, but the larger implication of this vision is encouraging for God's people—namely, that He knows those who are His own. Though we live in a corrupt culture, our Savior is faithful toward those who remain faithful to Him.

STUDY QUESTIONS

1. Which sections or elements of Lamentations impacted you the most? What did you learn about God's nature and character from these five chapters?

2. What does Jeremiah say about God's mercy in Lamentations 3:22–27? What reasons does the prophet Jeremiah provide for clinging to God in hope?

3. How would you summarize the assignment that God gave to Ezekiel in chapters 2 and 3? What was Ezekiel called to be and what was he to do?

4. What do you risk when you ignore or reject God's specific and direct call on your life? What rewards can you receive by obeying that call?

5. Picture yourself with the exiles. How would you respond if you routinely encountered a prophet demonstrating a siege against a city, cooking food over dung, shaving off his own hair, and so on?

6. What promises did God make in Ezekiel 5:15–17? What was the purpose of those promises? What do you learn about God's character from Ezekiel 7:1–27?

7. How would you summarize the object lessons Ezekiel carried out in chapter 12? What was the purpose of these object lessons among the captives in Babylon?

8. What emotions does God express toward His people in Ezekiel 16:1–14? What do you learn from those verses about God's care and protection of His people?

WEEK 24

GOD IS HOLY AND SOVEREIGN

EZEKIEL 20-48

READING PLAN:	**162** | Ezekiel 20-23	**163** | Ezekiel 24-27	**164** | Ezekiel 28-31
165 | Ezekiel 32-35	**166** | Ezekiel 36-39	**167** | Ezekiel 40-44	**168** | Ezekiel 45-48

In the law of Moses, God established that sin in one generation would produce consequences in subsequent generations (see Exodus 20:5). In Ezekiel's day, God's people were apparently using this principle to absolve themselves of blame for their current situation. They believed their captivity was the result of the sins of previous generations and there was nothing significant they could do to alter the situation. In Ezekiel 18 and 19, God rejects this way of thinking. The current generation of Israelites had *themselves* chosen rebellion and idolatry.

By this time, Egypt was resisting the advance of Babylon. King Zedekiah of Judah used Babylon's defeats during this time as an opportunity to launch his own rebellion. This rebellion failed, resulting in the siege of Jerusalem and its eventual destruction at the hands of Nebuchadnezzar. It is likely the "elders of Israel," who again inquired of Ezekiel (see 20:1), wanted to know if God was going to use Egypt as a tool to throw off the yolk of Babylon and return them, the captives, to their homeland of Judah. Ezekiel responded that it was God's intention to destroy His holy city through the "sword of Babylon" (see Ezekiel 21).

Ezekiel goes on to issue God's judgments against the nations of Ammon, Moab, Edom, Philistia, Tyre, Sidon, and Egypt. The placement of these chapters (25–32) is likely due to Ezekiel's shocking announcement from the Lord back in chapter 24: "Son of man, write down the name of the day, this very day—the king of Babylon started his siege against Jerusalem this very day" (verse 2). God had told Ezekiel that the city of Jerusalem was under siege—news that normally would not have reached the captives in Babylon for many months. Now that God's judgment against Judah was underway, He was turning His attention to the surrounding nations who were also guilty of great sin.

Ezekiel 33 serves as a transition between the first half of Ezekiel's prophetic record and the second. This transition represents the historical moment of Jerusalem's actual fall and the destruction of the temple—news that Ezekiel and the other captives learned from a single survivor who made it all the way to Babylon. Ezekiel 34 then begins another series of prophecies that continue through chapter 48. In these messages, Ezekiel's theme is the future restoration of Israel, Judah, and Jerusalem. In other words,

THE HOLY DISTRICT OF EZEKIEL

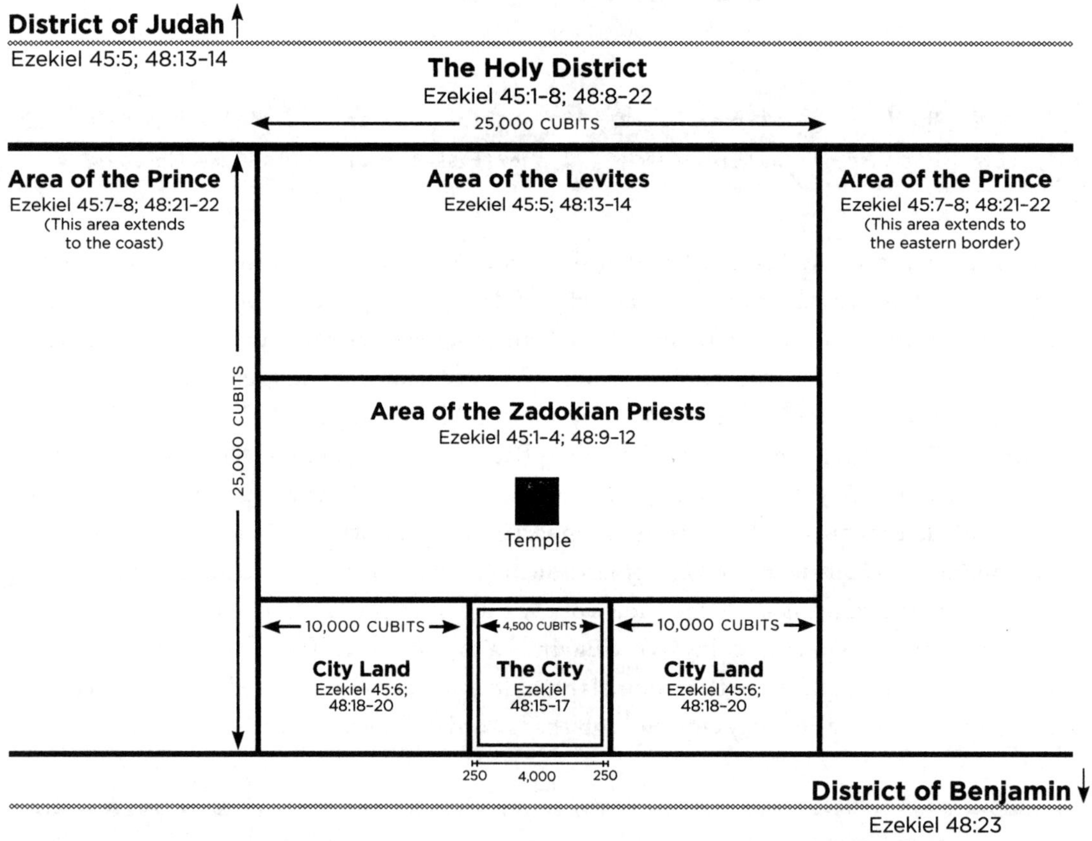

these prophecies from Ezekiel offer *hope* to the people rather than judgment. They emphasize God's grace and mercy and point forward to a future regathering of God's people in the Promised Land. For that reason, many of the prophecies in this section have strong connections to the Millennium.

Ezekiel prophesied several times that the "remnant" of God's people—those who were scattered around the world after the invasions of Assyria and Babylon—would one day be regathered and restored to the Promised Land (see 39:25–26). Ezekiel 40–48 provides details about this millennial reign of Christ, giving more information about the 1,000-year kingdom than all other Old Testament prophecies combined. They form the crowning reality—the climax of Ezekiel's prophecy and Israel's restoration.

The prophet begins by relating how he was taken "into the land of Israel" and set "on a very high mountain" where he could see this new city of God and its temple (40:2). An angel then measured the dimensions of that temple and each of its primary structures. The Lord then revealed the purpose of Ezekiel recording all these measurements: "Son of man, describe the temple to the house of Israel, that they may be ashamed of their iniquities; and let them measure the pattern" (43:10). These glorious future plans revealed to the people of Israel just how much they had forfeited because of their sins.

Ezekiel's prophetic record even describes the new "holy district" that will be created and the role of its "prince" or administrator. There will be a new system of feasts, and the land will be redistributed among God's people. In the end, we find in Ezekiel's prophecies that while the primary audience for his visions were the Jewish people, they still have great relevance and importance for Christians today.

REFLECTIONS

Do not trust in worldly might. In Ezekiel 29, God describes Egypt as "a staff of reed to the house of Israel" (verse 6). Israel had leaned on the Egyptians in military alliances like a person leans on a staff. But when that staff "of reed" broke, Judah was even more vulnerable than before. As King David wrote, "Some trust in chariots, and some in horses; but we will remember the name of the LORD" (Psalm 20:7).

God is the leader of His people. In Ezekiel 34, God pointed to a future moment when He would be the shepherd of His people: "I Myself will search for My sheep" (verse 11), and later, "I will feed them in good pasture, and their fold shall be on the high mountains of Israel" (verse 14). These verses point to the coming of Jesus as the Good Shepherd who would lay down His life for the sheep (see John 10:11). They also point to the millennial kingdom, when God's people will receive blessings in a restored Israel.

God will be present in the millennial kingdom. In describing the land of the millennial kingdom, Ezekiel mentions a district that will be at the center of Israel (see 45:1). This district will include the millennial temple itself, housing for the priests and prince, and more. It will represent a vast increase in God's physical presence in our world. Of course, that presence will be fully realized in the person of Jesus Christ, who will reign from Jerusalem, seated on the throne of King David (see Ezekiel 48:35).

STUDY QUESTIONS

1. Imagine you were one of the captives of Judah when you heard God's declaration in Ezekiel 21:1–17. How would you have responded to those words?

2. What was the point of God's story about the "two women" in Ezekiel 23? What was He communicating to His people through that story?

3. What is the significance of God comparing Egypt to a great tree in Ezekiel 31? What did God say would ultimately happen to this "strong tree" among the nations?

4. How does Ezekiel point forward to Jesus the Messiah (see Ezekiel 34:11–31)? What do you learn from those verses about God's care for His people as their shepherd?

5. How would you describe the forces that will gather against Israel based on Ezekiel 38:1–17? What is the "evil plan" that they will make against God's people?

6. God promises to destroy the armies of Gog and free His people (see Ezekiel 39:1–16). What promise does the Lord then make to the "house of Israel" (see verses 21–29)?

7. The prophet provides detailed descriptions and measurements of the future millennial temple in Ezekiel 40:5–43:12. Which features stand out to you the most? Why those features?

8. Which of the feasts will still be celebrated in the millennial kingdom (see Ezekiel 45:18–25)? Why will the feasts of Pentecost, Trumpets, and Atonement no longer be celebrated?

WEEK 25

GOD SETS US APART FOR HOLINESS

DANIEL 1–HOSEA 14

READING PLAN:	**169** | Daniel 1–2	**170** | Daniel 3–4	**171** | Daniel 5–6
172 | Daniel 7–9; 12	**173** | Hosea 1–3	**174** | Hosea 6–8	**175** | Hosea 11–14

As previously noted, the Assyrians overran the kingdom of Israel in 722 BC and carried the people into captivity. The kingdom of Judah vacillated between obedience and idolatry for a time but eventually was also taken—by Babylon in 586 BC. Daniel was transported to Babylon as a young man in the first group of exiles (c. 605 BC). He would spend his entire adult life as a high-ranking official and confidante of pagan kings. He first served under the Babylonians (Nebuchadnezzar through Belshazzar) and then in the court of the Persian kings.

Upon Daniel's arrival in Babylon, he found himself in a foreign culture, surrounded by powerful slavemasters who worshiped false gods and ate foods that were forbidden to God's people. Yet Daniel firmly believed that God was in control of his circumstances. Therefore, he resolved to obey God, and the Lord rewarded his obedience with stunning success.

Throughout the book of Daniel, God displays His sovereign power. In nine of twelve chapters, Daniel provides revelation from God through the recounting and interpreting of various dreams and visions. The first time occurs when Nebuchadnezzar had a dream of a giant statue of a man composed of various metals. Daniel interpreted the dream as a succession of world powers, beginning with Nebuchadnezzar's own, and stretching out more than 500 years through the age of the Roman Empire. Other miracles include the Lord's protection of Daniel's three friends in a blazing furnace, God writing on the wall during a licentious palace party (and revealing to Daniel the interpretation that Belshazzar's kingdom was about to end), the Lord's safekeeping of Daniel after an engineered plot within King Darius's court landed him in a lion's den, and supernatural prophecies.

> The SAINTS of the Most High shall receive the KINGDOM, and possess [it] FOREVER.
>
> DANIEL 7:18

In Daniel 7, the prophet shifts from telling stories of God's provision for His servants in exile to a recounting of the visions and prophecies he received from the Lord. One dream addresses the Babylonian Empire and the kingdoms to come. However, this time the kingdoms are represented by strange beasts rather than a huge statue. In addition, the events described extend far into the future—culminating in the final triumph of Jesus Christ. The prophecies throughout Daniel reveal that, at some future date, Christ will return and abolish all forms of human government, establishing His earthly throne for 1,000 years, after which He will bring about a new heaven and a new earth and reign eternally.

Daniel was set apart as God's mouthpiece during the seventy years of Babylonian captivity. Hosea, another prophet of God, was set apart as a messenger to Israel during the last six rulers of the northern kingdom before its fall. However, he is best known for his marriage. Hosea was instructed by God to marry and build a family with a woman named Gomer, whom the Lord foretold would be unfaithful. Their marriage served as an illustration of the relationship between God and His people, providing the rich metaphor that clarifies the themes of the book: faithlessness, judgment, and forgiving love.

VISIONS AND DREAMS IN DANIEL

	Image: Daniel 2	Beasts: Daniel 7	Beasts: Daniel 8	Kingdoms Presented
Times of the Gentiles	Head of fine gold	Like a lion with eagle's wings		Babylon
	Chest and arms of silver	Like a bear	Ram with two horns	Medo-Persia
	Belly and thighs of bronze	Like a leopard with four wings and four heads	Male goat with one horn, four horns, and little horn	Greece
	Legs of iron, feet of iron and clay	Beast with ten horns and little horn		Rome
	Stone that becomes a great mountain	Messiah and saints receive the kingdom		Kingdom of God

Hosea's message contains much condemnation, both national and individual. At times, God's words seem harsh. By using the language of a betrayed spouse, God was revealing the reality of Israel's unfaithfulness—and a poignant portrayal of the loyal, covenantal love of God toward His people . . . a love that would tolerate no rival. In the end, the Lord instructed Hosea to pursue his estranged wife and restore their relationship, thus symbolizing how He would restore His relationship with His people.

The primary message of Hosea and Gomer's marriage is the faithfulness of God. In Hosea 4–5, the focus moves away from Hosea's marriage. Instead, God instructs Hosea to bring a charge against the people of Israel. These words function as a judicial proclamation in which they are declared guilty of idolatry. The spiritual leaders are specifically called out, because they have led the people toward "harlotry." In the midst of a call for repentance, the prophet also details the impending consequences of Israel and Judah's idolatry, including the nation's spiritual isolation and eventual exile.

Hosea makes it clear that exile was a certainty for the adulterous kingdom of Israel. He even details what God's people would experience after being removed from their covenantal home. In spite of Israel's current prosperity, their future was sealed as a time of deprivation and distress. Israel's kings would be cut off, the people would eat the fruit of their own wickedness, and the nation would be separated from God's covenantal blessings for the many ways they had violated their covenant with Him. Yet even in this, God lamented the loss of fellowship with His people and clarified His desires for their relationship: not meaningless sacrifices but mercy and their genuine knowledge of Him.

> Come, and let us RETURN to the LORD; for He has torn, but He will HEAL us; He has stricken, but He will BIND US UP. After two days He will REVIVE us; on the third day He will RAISE us up, that we may live in His SIGHT.
>
> HOSEA 6:1–2

Later, in Hosea 11, come more tender words: those of a loving heavenly Father who longs for His people to return to Him. God describes loving Israel as a child, even teaching Ephraim (another name for Israel) to walk. He speaks of healing and feeding His wayward son and of drawing His people forward with bands of love. Perhaps even more poignant is the grief that God expresses regarding the necessity of Israel's destruction and captivity. Notably, God does negate His plan for the Assyrians to conquer Israel—sin still required justice. But Hosea's words reflect the compassion of a parent who knows their children must experience consequences but also desires to shield them from those consequences.

In the last three chapters of the book, Hosea returns to the primary theme of Israel's unfaithfulness to God, contrasting the people with Jacob the patriarch (who sought the Lord with diligence) and revealing the magnitude of grief and pain the Israelites will experience because of their continued rebellion. Still, the Lord affirmed His fierce and faithful love for His people, saying, "O Israel, you are destroyed, but your help is from Me. I will be your King" (Hosea 13:9–10). Finally, the prophet Hosea concludes with a forward look to the restoration of Israel that will take place during the millennial kingdom and exhorts his readers to choose obedience and faithfulness over folly.

REFLECTIONS

Resolve to obey God. We can only imagine the temptations Daniel and his three friends faced living in a pagan culture with strange gods, traditions, and practices. It would have been easy for them to fall into despair and any number of sinful practices. Instead, they resolved to obey God's commands, whatever might come. Life is filled with situations that test our resolve, but God has given us His Holy Spirit to empower us to resist and stand firm against those pressures and temptations. However, the time to make a resolution to walk in God's ways is before the time of temptation comes (see Proverbs 4:23).

Resolve to seek God. Nebuchadnezzar's magicians were filled with dread when the king commanded them to describe his dream, for they recognized no human could accomplish such a thing. "There is no other who can tell it to the king except the gods" (Daniel 2:11). They did not trust the Lord, and so, of course, they did not turn to God for guidance. Daniel knew the magicians were partly right, for the correct interpretation was only available from the Lord God. Daniel had no way of knowing if the Lord would reveal the dream to him, but knew his only hope was to trust in God. So Daniel sought the Lord in prayer and trusted He would guide him through this trial—which is exactly what God did.

No danger can touch us without God's permission. From the world's perspective, Daniel's three friends were foolishly overconfident—if not self-deluded. The furnace was terribly real, as were the flames that leaped from it. Yet Shadrach, Meshach, and Abed-Nego knew that while the flames were real, those fires were under the sovereign command of their Creator. If God so chose, not a hair on their heads would be singed— which proved to be exactly the case. Their attitude is a model for all believers. God will not permit anything to touch us that is not ultimately for our good (see Psalm 121:2–8).

Worship the Creator and not the creation. King Belshazzar threw a drunken party for his friends, and in their licentious frenzy, they ate and drank from sacred vessels that had been dedicated to the temple. But the revelers took their blasphemy one step further: "You and your lords . . . have drunk wine from them. And you have praised the gods of silver and gold, bronze and iron, wood and stone" (Daniel 5:23). Many people today also deny God created the earth and humankind while simultaneously elevating His creation in His place. It is a bitter irony to treat the things of God with disdain, as Belshazzar did, while praising the very things He made. The Bible warns this idolatrous attitude will inevitably lead to the downfall of a nation, just as it did in Babylon during the time of King Belshazzar.

God's people should live above reproach. The events of Daniel 6 present a statement of Daniel's godly character. His enemies wanted to uncover some shortcoming, failure, or character flaw with which to spoil his reputation—but could find nothing! Most of us would cringe if we knew an enemy was trying to discover something we had done wrong. Yet that is exactly what is happening every day of the year! The enemy is the accuser of believers, and he works diligently, day and night, to bring accusations of sin against all who place their faith in Jesus Christ (see Revelation 12:10). The blood of Christ permanently silences the devil's accusations, for through His sacrifice we are found blameless before God. However, this does not give believers the license to indulge in sin . . . quite the opposite, in fact.

DEN OF LIONS (DANIEL 6)

"They brought Daniel and cast him into the den of lions" (Daniel 6:16). The word *den* is related to the Hebrew term meaning "to dig," so it refers to an underground pit that likely had (1) a hole at the top from which to drop food into the pit, and (2) a door at the foot of a ramp or on a hillside through which the lions could enter. The lions we read about in Scripture were smaller than the African lion, but no less feared. Lion hunting was a favorite sport of Near Eastern kings, so Darius was not eccentric in keeping a den.

Be faithful to God. Hosea's marriage was not a metaphor; he actually took Gomer as his wife, and the text indicates he desired her to be faithful to him—and to their children. The connection between God and His people was also not a metaphor. God had entered into a covenant with Abraham's descendants—similar to a marriage covenant—in which He said, "I will take you as My people, and I will be your God" (Exodus 6:7). Followers of Jesus are also expected to maintain a spiritually faithful relationship with God. In fact, the New Testament uses similar imagery of the church as Christ's "bride." As Paul wrote, "Husbands, love your wives, just as Christ also loved the church and gave Himself for her, that He might sanctify and cleanse her with the washing of water by the word" (Ephesians 5:25–26).

Do not ignore God's warnings. According to Hosea, the people had rejected God's messengers, saying, "The prophet is a fool, the spiritual man is insane" (9:7). When the prophets spoke truth in a way the people found offensive, they rejected those messages by labeling them as untrustworthy. As a result, "The days of punishment have come" (verse 7). Jesus warned that His disciples would encounter a similar obstacle: "Brother will deliver up brother to death, and a father his child; and children will rise up against parents and cause them to be put to death. And you will be hated by all for My name's sake" (Matthew 10:21–22). Standing for God often means facing rejection from those in the world.

God's love for His children is tender. The word pictures we find in Hosea 11 are stunning in their tenderness. God describes loving Israel as a child, even teaching Ephraim to walk. He speaks of healing and feeding His wayward son and of drawing His people forward with bands of love. Perhaps even more poignant is the grief God expresses regarding the necessity of Israel's destruction and captivity. The pain is evident as God cries out, "How can I give you up, Ephraim? How can I hand you over, Israel? How can I make you like Admah? How can I set you like Zeboiim? My heart churns within Me; My sympathy is stirred" (11:8). What these verses reveal is that God is by nature a Father. His Fatherness (or His Father's heart) is a vital part of His character and plays a major role in how He relates to His people.

STUDY QUESTIONS

1. Why did Daniel not want to eat the diet of the Babylonians (see Daniel 1:8–14)? What would have been the implications if he had done so?

2. What might have motivated King Nebuchadnezzar to create the giant statue of gold (see Daniel 3:1–3)? Why would he command all the people to worship it?

3. How did Daniel know the meaning of the mysterious message on Belshazzar's wall (see Daniel 5:5–7)? When did he receive the interpretation? What principle does this illustrate?

4. How did Daniel's enemies come up with the idea of creating the new law (see Daniel 6:1–9)? What does this reveal they knew about Daniel's faith in God?

5. What are some of the ways the people of Israel had broken the basic tenets of the Ten Commandments according to Hosea 4:1–2?

6. According to Hosea 6:1–3, what does it mean for an individual to repent of spiritual unfaithfulness? What would it mean for Israel to "return" to the Lord?

7. What do you learn about Judah, the southern kingdom, from Hosea 11–12? How have you experienced God's love? What are the effects of His love?

8. How would you describe Hosea's concluding message or exhortation in chapter 14? What did he want his readers to learn (and do) based on his prophecy?

WEEK 26

GOD EXPECTS OUR OBEDIENCE

JOEL 1–NAHUM 3

READING PLAN:	**176** | Joel 1–3	**177** | Amos 1–3	**178** | Amos 7–Obadiah 1
179 | Jonah 1–4	**180** | Micah 1–3	**181** | Micah 4–7	**182** | Nahum 1–3

We tend to think of an Old Testament prophet as someone standing in opposition to the people, crying out, "Repent!" or "The end is near!" In many ways, Joel operated as this kind of prophet. The immediate context of his prophecy was an invasion of locusts that had decimated the people's crops in the kingdom of Judah. Yet Joel's vision also pointed forward to the future invasion of Judah by the armies of Babylon—"a people . . . great and strong" (2:2)—who would swarm over Jerusalem's walls in numbers similar to those of the locusts.

Beyond this, Joel's prophecy points forward to God's ultimate judgment against sin and evil, which will occur at some point in the future in what is called the "Day of the Lord." In the second half of Joel 2, specifically verse 18, this moment is reached when the prophetic text shifts decisively in terms of its intended timeline. From this point onward, the focus of Joel's prophecy moves from present judgment to future restoration.

Amos ministered during "the days of Jeroboam the son of Joash" (1:1). At the time, the nation was enjoying a time of prosperity, but spiritually, it was a time of great poverty. So

God called Amos, a Judean sheepbreeder, to prophesy away from his homeland in this northern kingdom of Israel. Amos began by speaking judgments against Israel's enemies, which likely were received with a positive response—but each judgment progressively moved closer to Israel's borders. God's judgment against Judah revealed that He would not play favorites. Finally, Amos turned fully to describing God's judgments against Israel. The Lord condemned their irresponsibility, idolatry, and moral decay.

Amos concludes with five prophetic visions. In the first vision, Amos sees a swarm of locusts devouring the people's portion of the harvest, after the king has received his share. In the second vision, Amos sees a fire that consumes the fields and causes the nation's water supply to dry up. In the third vision, Amos sees the Lord holding a plumb line. God tells Amos that He has measured the spiritual nature of Israel and found her wanting. The fourth vision is of a basket of summer fruit, while the fifth vision is of the Lord Himself. All of these visions confirmed God's plan to pour out His wrath on Israel. Yet the book ends on a more hopeful note—with God's promise once again to restore His people.

Obadiah's short book contains a judgment against Edom. The relationship between Israel and Edom was complicated from the beginning. Both nations found their patriarchs in the twin sons of Isaac. Esau, the firstborn, was given the nickname "Edom" because of his reddish appearance at birth

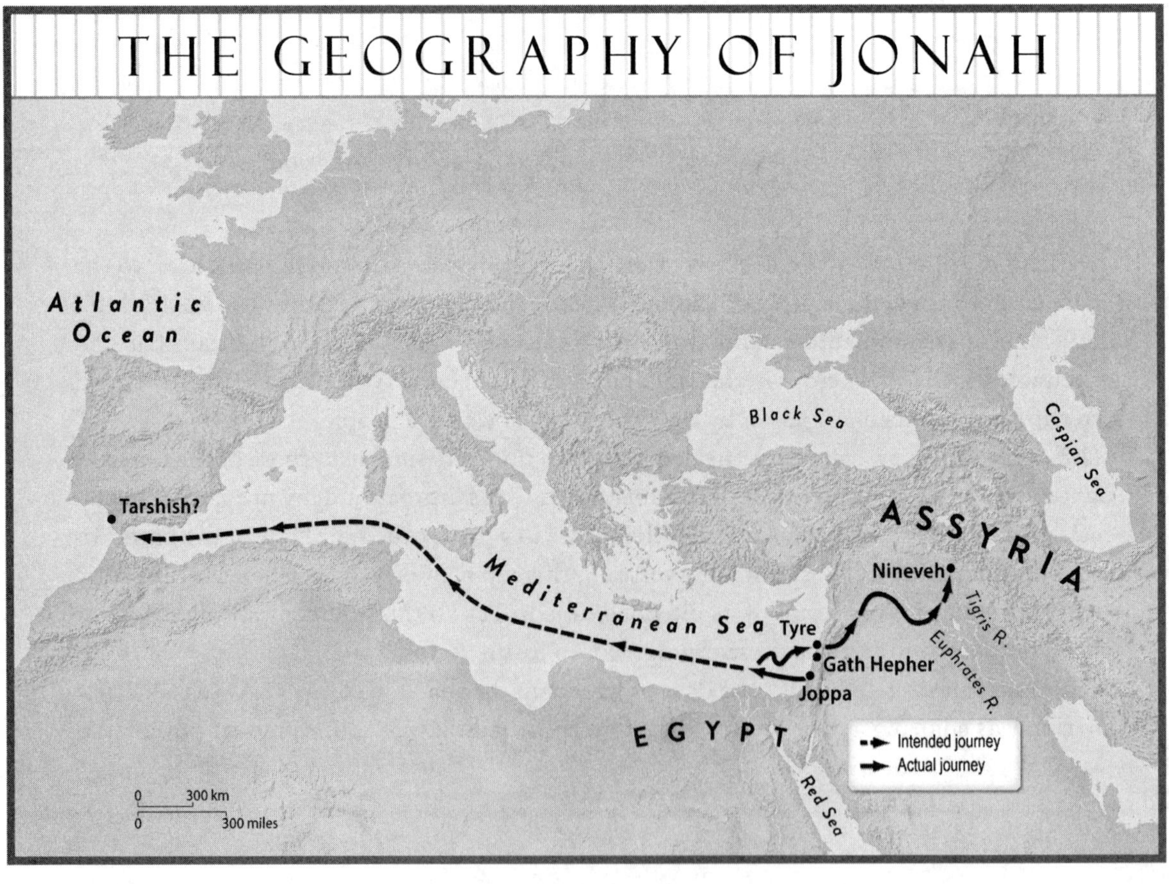

and his affinity for red stew (see Genesis 25:30). The Edomites grew out of his descendants, while the Israelites were the descendants of Jacob. Centuries later, the Israelites encountered the Edomites after their exodus from Egypt. The king of Edom refused to grant the Israelites passage through his territory (see Numbers 20:14–21). From that moment, Edom became an enemy of Israel. Obadiah's prophecy announces God's judgment against them, along with reinforcing the future restoration of Israel.

While many of the prophets ministered to the people of Israel, the Lord sent Jonah (c. 760 BC) to proclaim a message of divine judgment to a foreign nation. God instructed Jonah to go to Nineveh, the capital of Assyria. But instead of obeying God's call, Jonah booked passage on a ship bound for Tarshish—likely in the exact opposite direction from Nineveh. As a result, God sent a great storm on the sea, and the sailors feared their boat would sink. They cast lots and found that Jonah was the cause of the storm, eventually prompting them (at the prophet's insistence) to throw him overboard. God then sent a great fish to swallow Jonah, and he remained in the belly of that fish for three days and three nights.

God caused the fish to vomit Jonah onto dry land, possibly near Joppa where he had started. This time, Jonah went to Nineveh and proclaimed God's word. The people repented, which "displeased Jonah exceedingly" (4:1), for he desired God's judgment to fall on them. In the end, God gave Jonah an object lesson involving a plant that provided shade to show His care for all people, telling His prophet, "Should I not pity Nineveh . . . who cannot discern between their right hand and their left?" (4:11).

Micah was likely alive when the Assyrians conquered the kingdom of Israel in 722 BC. Micah may have also experienced Assyria's unsuccessful siege against Jerusalem in 701 BC. For these reasons and more, Micah understood the stakes involved with Judah's idolatrous pursuits. Even as the residents of Jerusalem stubbornly refused to believe that God would allow true judgment against Zion, Micah knew the truth. His mission was to communicate that truth to those who did not want to hear it.

Micah's book is divided into three "oracles." Each one begins with a command for the people to listen: "Hear, all you peoples!" (1:2); "Hear now, O heads of Jacob" (3:1); "Hear now what the LORD says" (6:1). The first oracle describes the judgment God had declared against Judah because of her disobedience. The second oracle begins with a repudiation of Judah's leaders, with imagery designed to shock them out of complacency, and then points forward to the millennial kingdom and the appearance of the Messiah in Bethlehem. The third oracle follows a tradition that runs throughout the Old Testament of prophets calling on the heavens and the earth to serve as witnesses between humanity and God: "Hear, O you mountains, the LORD's complaint" (6:2). Micah ends this oracle by stating that God will remain faithful to the covenants He made with Israel. A day will come when He completely fulfills His end of the bargain and blesses a future remnant of Abraham's offspring who turn back to Him.

In many ways, Nahum's prophecy is a follow-up to the one delivered by Jonah. Jonah's proclamation of God's judgment against Nineveh led to a revival there. However, forty years later, the Assyrians attacked and conquered the northern kingdom of Israel, and then, in 701 BC, tried to besiege Jerusalem. Nahum's prophecy specifically and graphically set forth doom against both Nineveh and the Assyrian Empire—and not just any doom, but God's judgment. Nahum's prophecies were fulfilled to the letter when a coalition led by Babylon defeated Assyria and destroyed Nineveh in 612 BC.

REFLECTIONS

Return to the Lord with all your heart. The prophets often delivered messages of God's impending judgment. These messages were consistent with God's character, "for the LORD is a God of justice" (Isaiah 30:18), and He punishes evil. Yet God is also merciful, and His desire is for rebels to lay down their arms and repent. Even in the midst of Joel's prophecies about the Day of the Lord, he included this aspect of God's character: "He is gracious and merciful, slow to anger, and of great kindness" (2:13). We all sin at times and "fall short of the glory of God" (Romans 3:23). The remedy for our sinful acts is to repent and return to a right relationship with God—to love Him and serve Him with our whole heart.

God cannot be bribed. Amos was one of many prophets through whom God delivered His message of coming judgment. Ezekiel, Jeremiah, Hosea, and others prophesied about Israel's and Judah's destruction at the hands of foreign powers. So why did the people ignore these warnings? One reason seems to be because they believed their spiritual practices—their offerings, sacrifices, and rituals—would appease God's anger. This is why Amos 5:21 is so shocking: "I hate, I despise your feast days, and I do not savor your sacred assemblies." This was God speaking, and it was just the beginning: "Though you offer Me burnt offerings and your grain offerings, I will not accept them, nor will I regard your fattened peace offerings" (verse 22). The Israelites mistakenly believed they could use external actions to assuage their internal sinfulness. They tried to cover over their sins of their homes through pious activity in the temple. But all these efforts failed. God made their fate clear: "I will send you into captivity beyond Damascus" (5:27).

> For the LORD your God . . . shows no PARTIALITY nor takes a BRIBE.
>
> DEUTERONOMY 10:17

God hears the prayers of His people. In Amos 7:1–3, the prophet had a vision of a swarm of locusts devastating the crops of Israel. In Amos 7:4, he saw God calling for "conflict by fire" that consumed much of Israel's territory. Both times Amos received these visions, he interceded on behalf of the people. He asked God to cease His judgments, and in both cases, he concluded his prayer with this supplication. And, in both cases, God responded by relenting from His wrath. What do we learn from these visions? First and foremost, that God hears the prayers of His people. As the apostle John wrote, "Now this is the confidence that we have in Him, that if we ask anything according to His will, He hears us" (1 John 5:14). God not only hears our prayers but also responds to them in accordance with His sovereign will.

Doing nothing is a big deal to God. There are "sins of commission" and "sins of omission." Sins of commission occur when we actively break God's commands. Sins of omission occur when we fail to do something we know we should do (see James 4:17). We see this principle in operation in Obadiah. The Edomites, by refusing to aid their ancestral kindred, had made themselves a stench not only to God's people but also to God Himself. Although they did not directly attack or harm the Israelites during those critical encounters, they failed to help their "brothers." We have to remember this same principle. Most of us want to avoid doing what we know is wrong, but it has become acceptable in our culture to not do something right. Such an attitude does not align with God's desire for our lives.

God is patient with us. Jonah's second chance to obey the Lord was a reflection of God's patience. The prophet had already failed in following God's first command by attempting to run away from His will—something Jonah should have known to be impossible. Even so, God showed mercy to His prophet. He also showed mercy to the people of Nineveh, who were renowned for their wickedness. Jonah's declaration—"yet forty days, and Nineveh shall be overthrown!" (3:4)—was not a bluff. The Assyrians were deserving of God's wrath, yet, due to His grace, God granted them salvation, which they did not deserve.

Our commission is to share the gospel. The Assyrians were locked in a pattern of paganism and violence, not knowing "their right hand and their left" (Jonah 4:11). They had no hope of reaching God without His intervention. So the Lord commissioned Jonah and instructed him to share the truth with this people mired in their own wickedness. The same is true for every follower of Christ. Jesus commanded His followers, "Go into all the world and preach the gospel to every creature" (Mark 16:15). Like Jonah, we are surrounded by people suffering the consequences of their own unrighteousness and rebellion against God. Such people are lost without God's grace and have no hope for salvation. Also like Jonah, our command is to go and proclaim God's Word to these people who need to hear it.

We have victory in Christ. The situation for the "regular" people of Micah's day was bleak. God was preparing to judge Judah not only for the idolatry of its leaders but also for their injustice and corruption. The powerful had treated those beneath them cruelly—as if their fellow citizens were animals fit to be butchered (see Micah 3:2–3)—and the priests and false prophets had spread a message of prosperity designed to further their own interests. Thankfully, Micah ends his second oracle with a more hopeful message. When God's people abandon their sinful ways, they receive the promise that He will comfort them, protect them, and give them peace. We need not put our faith in the protections of this world. We can trust solely in Jesus, the Messiah, who offers the only protection and safe harbor that we need.

The Word of God is truth. One of the most powerful elements of Nahum's prophecy is the accuracy with which it foretold the destruction of the city of Nineveh. Remember that Nahum delivered this prophecy decades before the city was actually destroyed. Even so, he was able to comment on the different stages of the sack of Nineveh as if he had personally witnessed the events. For instance, Nahum said that Nineveh would end "with an overflowing flood" (1:8), and this happened when the Tigris River overflowed, destroying enough of the city walls to allow the Babylonians to invade. Nahum also prophesied the city would "be hidden" (3:11), and this proved true because the city was not rediscovered after its destruction until AD 1842. Nahum's accuracy was bad news for Nineveh but good news for followers of Christ, for it reveals all God's words are true. We can trust the accuracy and truth of the Bible.

STUDY QUESTIONS

1. What promises did God make to His people in Joel 2:18–27? Why would those promises have been especially important to Joel's original audience?

2. What do you learn from Amos 4:6–13 about God's methods for catching our attention when we have wandered away from Him?

3. God called His people to repent in Amos 5:4–15. What does it mean to "seek the Lord" when you are convicted regarding your sin?

4. How should we understand the grievances described in Obadiah 1:10–14? What are some of the things that Edom had done to earn God's wrath?

5. What do you learn about Jonah's character and motivations based on chapters 1–2? What do you learn about God's character and motivations from these chapters?

6. What is the evidence of revival and spiritual fruit in Nineveh based on Jonah 3:5–10? What are the similarities between Jonah's mission and our mission as disciples of Christ?

7. The language in Micah 3:1–7 is intentionally graphic and shocking. What was Micah communicating through those verses to the leaders of Judah?

8. What does Nahum mean when he writes that "God is jealous" (1:2)? How had God shown that he was "slow to anger" (verse 3) toward Nineveh's transgressions in the past?

WEEK 27

GOD WANTS US TO FULFILL OUR TASKS

HABAKKUK 1–MALACHI 4

READING PLAN:
183 | Habakkuk 1–3
184 | Zephaniah 1–3
185 | Haggai 1–2
186 | Zechariah 1–5
187 | Zechariah 6–9
188 | Zechariah 10–14
189 | Malachi 1–4

The Assyrian Empire was conquered by a coalition of nations in 612 BC led by Nabopolassar, first king of the Neo-Babylonian Empire. Habakkuk ministered during this time. For this reason, he was greatly shocked when he learned that God intended to use the Babylonians as instruments of judgment against Judah. Habakkuk understood the problem of idolatry in Judah, but he was greatly perplexed by God's solution to that problem.

Habakkuk first wanted to know why God had waited so long to bring judgment against the people of Judah. He likely had in mind the curses that Moses had prophesied would come upon the Israelites if they failed to obey the Lord and follow His commands (see Deuteronomy 28:15–68). When God replied that His judgment was already in motion through the rise of the Babylonians, Habakkuk then questioned why God would use such an ungodly nation as a tool against His chosen people.

God's response was that the Babylonians would also not escape His judgment. The Lord even went so far as to proclaim five "woes" that would befall the classes of Babylonian society. Following this response, Habakkuk adopted a posture of prayer and praise, ending his prophetic book by expressing his steadfast faith and trust in the Lord God.

Moving back in time, Zephaniah was a prophet in the kingdom of Judah who ministered during the reign of the godly king Josiah (c. 640–609 BC). However, as we have discussed in this study, Josiah's father (Amon) and grandfather (Manasseh) had been ungodly kings who led the people of Judah into spiritual darkness for more than five decades (c. 695–640 BC). Zephaniah spoke of the consequences the people were about to experience because of their prolonged rebellion and idolatry.

Most cultures in Zephaniah's day had their own system of gods, with the idea that these deities held geographical connections. For instance, certain gods were connected with certain mountains and worshiped in the high places. Other regions worshiped gods connected with rivers or plains. Clashes between nations and armies were viewed as clashes between regional gods. However, Zephaniah proclaimed the God of Israel was not like these would-be gods whom the people worshiped. He was not limited to Mount Zion or the hills of Palestine. He claimed authority over all nations and peoples.

The final three prophets that appear in the Old Testament—Haggai, Zechariah, and Malachi—each ministered after the exile. Haggai most likely returned from Babylon to Jerusalem during the first wave of exiles under the leadership of Zerubbabel in 538 BC. It is possible that Haggai had even been carried into captivity with Daniel in 586 BC. The name Haggai means "festival," which seems ironic given the disciplinary content of his message. However, God had sent His people to Jerusalem to reinstate His worship practices and to rebuild His chosen city, which should have been a festive occasion.

The returned exiles had become discouraged by the opposition of their neighbors and wrongly concluded it was not time for them to rebuild the temple. Instead, they sought to expand their wealth. Like their ancestors before them, they ceased caring about God's kingdom and started building their own. With a biting query, the Lord reminded them it was not right for them to live in paneled houses while the temple lay in ruins. He urged them to consider the consequences of their indifference.

Zechariah was a priest who also traveled back to Judah with the first wave of exiles under Zerubbabel. Tradition holds he was a member of the Great Synagogue, a council of 120 men originated by Nehemiah and presided over by Ezra. (This council later developed into the ruling elders of the nation, called the Sanhedrin.) Zechariah began his ministry two months after Haggai gave his first prophecies. The Lord used Haggai to begin a revival, and He used Zechariah to keep it going strong.

The first section of Zechariah (1–6) is comprised of eight "night visions," followed by four messages that Zechariah received from God to deliver to the people (7–8). The final section of Zechariah's book (9–14) describes the Messiah's rejection at His first advent and His acceptance at His second advent. In truth, Zechariah is the most messianic, apocalyptic, and eschatological book in the Old Testament. Primarily, it is a prophecy about Jesus Christ, focusing on His coming glory as a means to comfort Israel, yet it also deals with issues such as repentance, salvation, and holy living.

After Zechariah, God raised up Malachi to rebuke and condemn the exiles for the abuses they had committed during the period of Nehemiah's absence (c. 433–424 BC). By this time, the second temple had been built and sacrifices were being made there, yet the priests had increasingly become complacent and corrupt. Malachi condemned these abuses, indicting the people and calling them to repentance. When Nehemiah subsequently returned from Persia, he also rebuked these abuses in the temple and priesthood. Nehemiah also rebuked the people for their violation of the Sabbath rest and the men's unlawful divorce of their Jewish wives so they could marry Gentile women (see Nehemiah 13).

The sad truth is that less than one hundred years after returning from captivity, the Jewish people had sunk to a depth of sin that exceeded the former iniquities that brought on the Assyrian and Babylonian deportations. Beyond this, the long-anticipated Messiah had not arrived and did not seem to be in sight. So Malachi wrote the capstone prophecy of the Old Testament in which he delivered God's message of judgment on Israel for their sin and God's promise that one day in the future, when the Jews would repent, the Messiah would be revealed and God's covenant promises would be fulfilled.

Following the ministry of Malachi, there were to be 400 years of divine silence before another prophet arrived on the scene with a message from God. This prophet was John the Baptist, proclaiming, "Repent, for the kingdom of heaven is at hand!" (Matthew 3:2). The Messiah had come.

REFLECTIONS

The time to repent is now. Peter wrote, "The Lord is not slack concerning His promise . . . but is longsuffering toward us, not willing that any should perish but that all should come to repentance" (2 Peter 3:9). God was patient with Judah, sending prophets to warn them what would happen if they did not turn from their sins. But they had persisted in their idolatry. Zephaniah's message was thus, "The time to repent is now!" The same is true for us. God convicts us and gives us the opportunity to repent, but we need to recognize that He is being merciful and not delay in confessing our transgressions.

Adopt God's priorities. God sent Haggai to bring a clear message to His people: obey the Lord even when the circumstances are difficult. The prophet proclaimed, "Consider your ways!" (Haggai 1:5). This command might be translated, "Set your mind on your way of life." In effect, God was proclaiming to His people, "Make your priorities My priorities!" This is an important discipline that we also need to exercise. The priorities and perspectives of the world are not God's views, yet they have a way of seeping into our thinking without our even being aware of it. As Christians, we need to reassess our priorities and views daily, even moment by moment, to ensure that we are thinking the way God thinks.

Jesus is coming again. God's prophecies of blessing in Zechariah had immediate application to the Jewish people of the day but also looked forward to future events. For example, His promise to return to Zion indicated that He would rebuild His temple in Jerusalem during their day, yet it also looked to the day when He would enter Jerusalem in physical form through Christ. The promise has yet another level of fulfillment still to come, when Jesus returns to establish His 1,000-year earthly kingdom in Zion. Jesus is coming again—and He will establish a kingdom that rules all the nations of the earth.

STUDY QUESTIONS

1. Consider Habakkuk's first question to the Lord in 1:1–4. What problem was he addressing with God? What is interesting about God's answer in verses 5–11?

2. God's denunciation of the Babylonians came in five separate woes (see Habakkuk 2:5–20). Which of those "woes" is the most devastating? Why that particular woe?

3. What does Zephaniah 1:4–6 teach about the spiritual condition of Judah? What is the "sacrifice" that the Lord says He has prepared in verse 8?

4. God does not dwell in any physical structure, so why was He angry the people had not rebuilt His house (see Haggai 1:1–11)? What were the larger issues involved?

5. What images stand out to you in the eight visions that Zechariah received (see Zechariah 1–6)? What was God's message to His people through these visions?

6. What did the Lord remind the people of Judah had happened to their ancestors in Zechariah 6:8–14? Why do you think He gave them this message at this time?

7. What prophecy about the coming Messiah is given in Zechariah 9:9–10? How was this fulfilled by Jesus (see Matthew 21:1–11; Mark 11:1–11; Luke 19:28–44; John 12:12–19)?

8. How do the prophecies of Malachi 3:1 relate to John the Baptist? What does Malachi go on to prophesy will happen when the Messiah appears (see verses 2–7)?

THE NEW TESTAMENT

More than 400 years separate the final events (Nehemiah 13:4–30) and the final prophecy (Malachi 1:1–4:6) recorded in the Old Testament from the beginning actions narrated in the New Testament (Luke 1:5–25). Given there was no prophetic word from God during this time, some have called this period "the 400 silent years." However, though the voice of God was silent, the hand of God was actively directing events during these centuries.

For about 200 years, the Persian Empire ruled the Jews (539–332 BC), allowing them to return, rebuild, and worship at the temple in Jerusalem. For about 100 years after the close of the Old Testament canon, Judea continued to be a Persian territory under the governor of Syria, with the high priest exercising a measure of civil authority. The Jews were allowed to observe their religious tenets without any official governmental interference.

Between 334 and 331 BC, Alexander the Great of Macedon defeated the Persian king Darius III in three decisive battles that gave him control of the Persian Empire. The land of Israel thus passed into Greek control in 332 BC. Alexander sought to bring Greek culture, known as Hellenism, to the lands he had conquered. This policy, carried on by Alexander's successors, was as dangerous to the religion of Israel as the cult of Baal had been, for the Greek way of life was attractive, sophisticated, and appealing—but utterly ungodly.

Alexander's empire was divided among his generals after his death in 323 BC. Ptolemy I Sater took control of Israel, and the Ptolemies ruled from 301 BC to 198 BC. Under their reign, the Jews had comparative religious freedom in a setting of economic oppression.

However, in 198 BC, Antiochus III defeated Ptolemy V Epiphanes and took control of Palestine, bringing Judea under Seleucid rule. Antiochus IV Epiphanes, a later Selucid ruler (175–164 BC), desecrated and plundered the temple of Jerusalem in 170 BC. In 167 BC, he ordered a "Hellenization" in Palestine and forbade the Jews from keeping their laws, observing the Sabbath, keeping festivals, offering sacrifices, and circumcising their children. The Jews were also commanded to offer unclean sacrifices and to eat swine's flesh.

An aged priest named Mattathias and his five sons led a Jewish resistance against Antiochus and his Seleucid successors. After war for twenty-four years (166–142 BC), the Jews were able to gain their independence due to growing Roman pressure on the Seleucids. The descendants of Mattathias founded the Hasmonean dynasty, a name derived from Hashmon, an ancestor of the Maccabees. The Hasmoneans soon began to follow Hellenistic ways, the very practices they had at first resisted. The Greek influence continued in Palestine from 142 BC to 63 BC through this native dynasty.

The Hasmonean dynasty ended in 63 BC, when Pompey, a Roman general, intervened in a clash between two claimants to the high priesthood. Continuing unrest led the Romans to make a man named Herod the Great the king of Judea. He was an Idumean by birth, a Jewish proselyte, and thoroughly Greco-Roman in outlook. He ruled Palestine from 37 BC to 4 BC, and was the "king of the Jews" when Jesus was born (see Matthew 2:1–2). In this second half of the year (Weeks 28–52), you will pick up the story from this point in the New Testament, reading one to two chapters each day.

The New Testament can be broken into five sections. The first section (Matthew–John) is known as the Gospels, which means "good news." The four Gospels are the good news about the most significant events in all of history—the life, sacrificial death, and resurrection of Jesus of Nazareth. Matthew wrote primarily to a Jewish audience, presenting Jesus of Nazareth as Israel's long-awaited Messiah and rightful king. Mark targeted a Roman audience. Luke addressed a broader Gentile audience. John, who wrote the last Gospel, emphasized the deity of Christ and wrote to strengthen the faith of all believers.

The second section of the New Testament contains the historical book of Acts. Luke, the author, provides information on the first three decades of the church's existence. He begins with Jesus' ascension into heaven and ends with Paul's arrest and journey to Rome.

The third section (Romans–Philemon) is known as the Pauline epistles. These thirteen books were written by Paul to churches in Rome, Corinth, the region of Galatia, Ephesus, Philippi, Colossae, and Thessalonica. Paul wrote these letters in response to certain issues taking place in these churches or to answer questions from the congregants. One letter, Romans (a church Paul had never visited), takes the form of a doctrinal treatise. Paul also corresponded with three individuals: Timothy and Titus, who were his coworkers; and Philemon, who was a respected member of the church in Colossae.

The fourth section (Hebrews–Jude) is known as the general epistles. These letters were written by apostles and leaders in the early church (James, Peter, John, Jude) to Jews and Gentiles alike, primarily to encourage the believers during a time of increasing persecution and to warn against false teachers. One letter, Hebrews, was penned by an unknown author to a predominantly Jewish audience.

The final section of the New Testament contains the prophetical book of Revelation. The title comes from the Greek *apokalupsis*, meaning "an uncovering," "an unveiling," or "a disclosure." Written by the disciple John, the last surviving apostle in the final decade of the first century (c. AD 94–96), it contains a record of a series of visions that John received while exiled on the isle of Patmos. John reveals what will happen during the "end times," including the final political setup of the world, the last battle of human history, the career and ultimate defeat of the Antichrist, the 1,000-year reign of Christ on earth (known as the Millennium), the final defeat of Satan, and the new heavens and new earth.

WEEK 28

JESUS IS THE PROMISED KING

MATTHEW 1–11

READING PLAN: **190** | Matthew 1–2 **191** | Matthew 3 **192** | Matthew 4 **193** | Matthew 5–6 **194** | Matthew 7 **195** | Matthew 8–9 **196** | Matthew 10–11

Matthew records, for a primarily Jewish audience, the good news about the most significant events in all of history—the birth, life, sacrificial death, and resurrection of Jesus of Nazareth. Israel's long-awaited Messiah and rightful King fulfilled dozens of Old Testament prophecies. But if Jesus was to be heralded and proclaimed King of the Jews, there would have to be proof that He came from the recognized royal family.

From the opening genealogy (revealing His descent from the royal line of David), to His miraculous conception, to the circumstances surrounding His birth—the homage of the magi, the murderous hatred of Herod, God's miraculous protection of the young Jesus, and God's appointment of a forerunner and herald named John—Jesus' kingship was shown. Following Christ's divine commissioning—His coronation—by baptism and anointing by the Spirit, He was greatly tested in the wilderness. Jesus' rejections of Satan's temptations further demonstrated His divine kingship and His absolute power over hell and sin. Jesus endured temptation to the very limit of Satan's power, and He resisted to that very limit.

Tested, tried, and triumphant, King Jesus inaugurated His public ministry. In one powerfully comprehensive yet compact message, the Lord set forth the foundational truths of the gospel of the kingdom He came to proclaim. This one continuous message of the Lord, traditionally called the Sermon on the Mount, delivered revolutionary truths to the minds of those Jewish religionists who heard them. Christ's pronouncements have continued to explode with great impact on the minds of readers for over 2,000 years.

Here was the manifesto of the new Monarch, who was ushering in a new age with a new message about true righteousness. Most Jews of Jesus' day expected the Messiah, the "Anointed One," to be, first of all, a military and political leader who would deliver them from the yoke of Rome and establish a prosperous Jewish kingdom that would lead the world. He would be greater than any king, leader, or prophet in their history. They saw the Messiah as the anticipated leader of a great welfare state in which even their routine physical needs would be provided. But Jesus would not allow Himself to be mistaken for that sort of king. His message and work as the promised King was, first and most importantly, internal and not external, spiritual and moral rather than physical and political.

Prior to this inaugural sermon, Jesus had been going about in Galilee, teaching in the synagogues and preaching the gospel of the kingdom. His legal qualification had been established through His genealogy, His prophetic qualification through the fulfillment of prophecy by His birth, His divine qualification by the Father's own attestation at His baptism, His spiritual qualification by His perfect resistance to Satan's temptations, and His theological qualification through the teaching of the Sermon on the Mount. Now another qualification was dramatically set forth: Jesus' divine power to heal. In performing these miracles, Jesus confirmed His deity and His claim to be the Savior of the world.

It is no wonder that Jesus' miracles brought such immediate and widespread attention. For people who seldom had means to alleviate even the symptoms of disease, the prospect of complete cure was almost too astounding to be believed. Even the rumor of such a thing would bring a multitude of the curious and hopeful. For a brief period of time, disease and other physical afflictions were virtually eliminated as Jesus went through the land, healing thousands.

Jesus said on several occasions that His miraculous works alone were more than enough reason to believe in Him. Such things had never happened before in the world and could only have a divine cause. This is what made the later rejection of the scribes, Pharisees, Sadducees, and others so self-condemnatory. No one could deny that Jesus performed the miracles. In the face of such overpowering evidence, those who would not believe in Jesus were indicted by every miracle that He performed.

As Jesus called and sent the twelve disciples, He did not do so on the basis of their innate worthiness, personal capabilities, or faithfulness, but solely on the basis of what He could make of them by His own power working through them. Among Christ's words to them in His second discourse were some warnings about how their ministry would be received and some concluding remarks about the cost of ministry. We then see the reactions of various individuals and groups to the evidence that Jesus presented about His divine identity. Often, these were negative responses of doubt, criticism, and indifference.

Yet even though the shadow of rejection never lifts from Jesus' story, the truth remains: He is the victorious King who will one day return with power and great glory.

REFLECTIONS

Jesus' life provides evidence of His supernatural birth. After Mary was betrothed to Joseph, "she was found with child of the Holy Spirit" (1:18). The supernatural birth of Jesus is the only way to account for the life that He lived. A skeptic who denied the virgin birth once asked a Christian, "If I told you that child over there was born without a human father, would you believe me?" The believer replied, "Yes, if he lived as Jesus lived." The greatest evidence of Jesus' supernatural birth and deity is His life.

Jesus shows us how to defeat Satan. Jesus' triumph over Satan shows us the way to victory. We can have victory over temptation by resisting in the same way Jesus resisted—by holding with complete obedience to God and His Word. We find help against temptation, just as we find help for everything else in the Christian life, by "looking unto Jesus, the author and finisher of our faith" (Hebrews 12:2). A hurdler soon learns that if he looks at the hurdles as he runs, he will trip and fall. So from start to finish he looks only at the goal, and by doing this, he clears the hurdles as they come. Keeping our eyes on Jesus is our only hope of conquering temptation and faithfully running "with endurance the race that is set before us" (verse 1).

We must experience the new birth. Jesus' teachings in the Sermon on the Mount reveal the necessity of the new birth offered by God. The standards of the Lord's righteousness are much too high and much too demanding to be met by human power. Only those who partake of the Lord's own nature through Jesus Christ can fulfill such demands. The standards that Jesus set forth in the Sermon on the Mount go far beyond those of Moses in the Law, demanding not only righteous actions but righteous attitudes—not just that people *do* right but also that they *be* right (see Matthew 5:17). No part of Scripture more clearly shows our plight and desperate situation without the Lord God.

HEROD'S TEMPLE

Herod the Great began making enhancements to the "Second Temple" in 20 BC, and by the time of Jesus' ministry, it was one of the most impressive structures in the world. The temple buildings were made of gleaming white marble, and the eastern wall of the large main structure was covered with gold plates that reflected the morning sun, making a spectacle that was visible for miles. The entire temple mount had been enlarged by Herod's engineers, with the large courtyard area atop the temple mount effectively doubled in size. The temple complex was magnificent by any standard.

STUDY QUESTIONS

1. What are some of the titles and descriptions used to describe Jesus in Matthew 1-2? How did Herod respond when he learned that a new King had been born in Bethlehem?

2. Why do you think it was necessary for Jesus to be baptized (see Matthew 3:13–17)? What was the significance of Jesus performing this act?

3. How would you describe the central message of the Beatitudes in Matthew 5:3–12? How do you think the people reacted when they heard of whom Jesus considered "blessed"?

4. How could you sum up Jesus' teaching in the Sermon on the Mount on prayer (see Matthew 6:5–15)? What does Jesus say we should and should not do when it comes to prayer?

5. What stands out to you in Jesus' parable of the wise and foolish builders in Matthew 7:24–29? What point was Jesus making about those who accept or reject His teachings?

6. How many different kinds of illnesses do you count in Matthew 8–9? What are some of the different types of miracles that Jesus performed?

7. Where was Matthew when Jesus called him to follow? What was the Pharisees' complaint when Jesus then shared a meal with Matthew at his home (see Matthew 9:9–13)?

8. What were Jesus' instructions to the Twelve before sending them out? What are some of the exciting and reassuring statements that He made to them in Matthew 10?

WEEK 29

JESUS IS THE GLORIOUS KING

MATTHEW 12–20

READING PLAN: **197** | Matthew 12 **198** | Matthew 13 **199** | Matthew 14
200 | Matthew 15–16 **201** | Matthew 17 **202** | Matthew 18–19 **203** | Matthew 20

The One foretold by the Old Testament prophets had arrived. Jesus had come to offer salvation and the kingdom of God to Israel. But it was apparent the Jewish leaders, as well as Jesus' own people, were rejecting His offer. Instead, the mounting unbelief was crystallizing into a determination on the part of the nation's religious leaders to destroy Christ. Did this mean God's plan was frustrated? What would be the nature of the kingdom now?

Jesus addressed these questions about the kingdom of God with a series of eight parables—a common form of Jewish teaching that used familiar objects to illuminate a spiritual truth. The underlying truth of these parables was that the final fulfillment of Christ's external, visible kingdom would be postponed until the time that Israel would believe in and receive her King. Nevertheless, the internal, spiritual kingdom of His saints had been established. Through their lives and testimony, He would now express His will on earth.

Jesus' prophetic parables also underscored the truth that some people will believe the gospel but many will not. A number of incidents in Jesus' life confirmed this spiritual law:

the hostility in His hometown of Nazareth, the hard-heartedness of King Herod, the superficial reception of the masses at the feeding of the five thousand, the worship of the twelve disciples after Jesus calmed the stormy sea, the desperate faith of a Canaanite woman, and the sinister plots of the Jewish leaders who sought to trap Him. Yet in the midst of this kingdom conflict, we see the true heart of Jesus for people as He performs more amazing miracles.

Jesus represented the compassionate heart of God. He was never coldly analytical concerning people's needs but was moved by the confusion, despair, and spiritual lostness of those around Him. Jesus experienced genuine anguish for the suffering of others—whether they were Jew or Gentile, man or woman, young or old, wealthy or poor. In His mercy, He extended compassion to self-centered thrill seekers and revealed the love of God even toward those whom He knew would reject Him.

This King wasn't only compassionate but also glorious. One day when Jesus was in the region of Caesarea Philippi, He gave His disciples a "final exam" of sorts, asking, "Who do you say that I am?" Peter professed that He was "the Christ, the Son of the living God" (Matthew 16:15–16).

Shortly after, Jesus went up a mountaintop with Peter, James, and John. There He underwent a dramatic change in appearance—a transfiguration—so the disciples could behold His glory. It would be hard to imagine what Jesus looked like at this moment, but the Gospel writers described His face as becoming bright like the sun and His clothes turning a dazzling white. In the Transfiguration, God showed that Jesus was His one and only Son, superior even to Moses and Elijah. The kingdom splendor of Christ revealed at this event was also a preview of His majesty to be manifested at His second coming.

Coming down from the mountain, Jesus was confronted with a petty argument among His disciples. They were likely at Peter's house when they began arguing about who was the greatest among them. Jesus responded by calling one of the children (who may have belonged to Peter's family) to come to Him. Jesus sat before them, holding this child in His arms, and said, "Assuredly, I say to you, unless you are converted and become as little children, you will by no means enter the kingdom of heaven" (Matthew 18:3). In this way, He taught the disciples profound lessons about being children of God.

It is no exaggeration to say that this single "sermon," delivered in such intimate surroundings, was the greatest discourse our Lord ever gave on life among the redeemed in His church. The first lesson in this masterful message was that everyone who enters the kingdom must do so as a child: with trust and without ambition for grandeur or greatness. Jesus went on to declare, "Therefore whoever humbles himself as this little child is the greatest in the kingdom of heaven" (Matthew 18:4).

Through Christ, those who believe in Him become God's own children, adopted through grace. Consequently, they bear the image of God's family and are joint heirs with Jesus of everything that God possesses. But there is another side to this theme of childlikeness: believers are also spiritual children with all the weaknesses that childhood implies. We are incomplete, dependent, undeveloped, unskilled, vulnerable, and immature. Thus, Jesus further taught that everyone in the kingdom must be treated as children, cared for as children, disciplined as children, and forgiven as children.

Later, in different settings and among various listeners (the Pharisees, His disciples, a rich young ruler), Jesus contrasted legalistic religion with the grace and truth of God and the values of earth with the realities of heaven. He spoke about a number of vitally important subjects—marriage and divorce, true greatness, the false promise of wealth, eternal life, and eternal judgment.

Most of those whom Jesus encountered wanted Him on their own terms. He was not a Messiah who came to offer a panacea of external peace in the world but the greater blessing of internal peace with God. And because He would not deliver them on their terms, they would not be delivered on His.

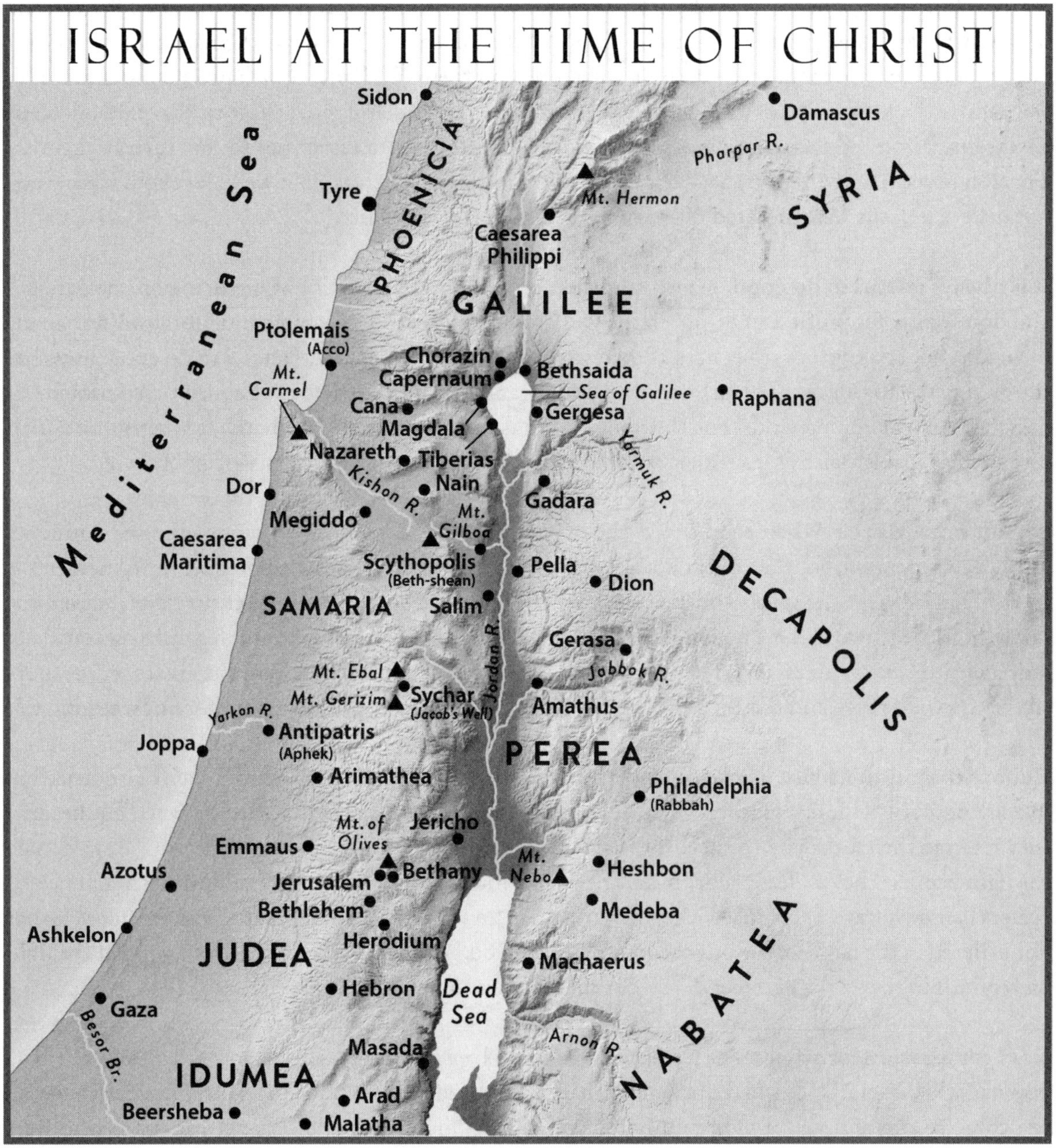

REFLECTIONS

We cannot be blind to what Jesus is doing in our midst. Jesus said on several occasions that His miraculous works should have been more than enough reason for the people of His day to believe in Him as the Messiah and the Son of God. For instance, on one occasion He said, "Believe Me that I am in the Father and the Father in Me, or else believe Me for the sake of the works themselves" (John 14:11). Such wonders had never happened on earth before, and they could only have had a divine cause. This is what made the rejection of the Jewish leaders of Jesus' day so self-condemnatory. No one could deny that Jesus performed the miracles, and only the most hard-hearted resistance to the truth could make a person reject His divinity in the face of such overpowering evidence. So it was that those who would not believe in Jesus were indicted by every miracle that He performed.

It is always lawful to do good. Jewish tradition prohibited the practice of medicine on the Sabbath and doing labor for profit. But no law in the Old Testament forbade plucking grain for food, nor giving medicine, nor healing, nor other acts of mercy on the Sabbath. It is always lawful to do good. Jesus has the prerogative to rule over not only man-made Sabbatarian rules but also the Sabbath itself, which was designed for worshiping God. "For the Son of Man is Lord even of the Sabbath" (Matthew 12:8) This was an inescapable claim of Jesus' deity—and, as such, prompted the Pharisees' violent outrage.

Do not reject Christ. When people have the opportunity to hear God's Word and even see it miraculously demonstrated, but then reject it, their guilt is intensified. It is far better to have heard nothing of Christ than to hear the truth and yet reject Him! "For if we sin willfully after we have received the knowledge of the truth, there no longer remains a sacrifice for sins, but a certain fearful expectation of judgment" (Hebrews 10:26–27). The greater the privilege that people are given, the greater the responsibility on their part—and the greater the light given, the greater the punishment for not receiving it.

Choose the way of Christ. Those who heard and saw Jesus did not reject Him for lack of evidence but in spite of overwhelming evidence. They did not reject Him because they lacked the truth but because they rejected the truth. They refused forgiveness because they wanted to keep their sins. They denied the light because they preferred darkness. The reason for rejecting the Lord has always been that people prefer their own way to His. "He who does not believe [in Christ] is condemned already, because he has not believed in the name of the only begotten Son of God. And this is the condemnation, that the light has come into the world, and men loved darkness rather than light" (John 3:18–19).

Have compassion for others. The Greek verb translated *compassion* literally means "to be moved in one's bowels," which is the place where ancient cultures considered the emotions to reside. Christ represented the compassionate heart of God and had this kind of "moving in the bowels" for those who were suffering, confused, in despair, and spiritually lost. Jesus felt pain and experienced genuine anguish for the suffering of *all* people. In His great mercy, Christ extended His compassion even to those who flocked to Him just to see Him perform miracles and do other signs. He revealed the loving heart of God toward even those who would not understand or believe and who would ultimately reject Him.

Bear good fruit. True followers of Jesus not only hear and understand the message of Christ but also bear fruit. Spiritual fruit is the inevitable product of spiritual life. There is the "spiritual fruit" of attitude, as described by Paul: "The fruit of the Spirit is love, joy, peace, longsuffering, kindness, goodness, faithfulness, gentleness, self-control" (Galatians 5:22–23). Genuine believers also bear "fruit" of behavior, which Paul referred to as "the fruits of righteousness which are by Jesus Christ, to the glory and praise of God" (Philippians 1:11). Fruit is the evidence of the Holy Spirit's work in the lives of God's children. Jesus declared that true and false branches—those who are genuinely related to Him and those who only seem to be—are distinguished by their bearing or not bearing fruit (see John 15:2–5). We are not saved by bearing fruit or by any other good work, because we cannot bear spiritual fruit or do any truly good work until after we are saved, but we are saved for fruit bearing.

Believers are like children. As Jesus explained, to be converted requires becoming like children. A child is dependent, unaffected, unpretentious, and unambitious. Children are not sinless or unselfish—they display their fallen nature from the earliest age—but they are nevertheless naive and unassuming, trusting of others and without ambition for greatness. It is the person who humbles himself as this child, Jesus declared, who is greatest in the kingdom of heaven. In God's eyes, the one who lowers himself is the one who is elevated; the one who genuinely considers himself to be the least is the one God considers to be the greatest. "The greatest among you shall be your servant," Jesus told the self-righteous Pharisees. "And whoever exalts himself will be humbled, and he who humbles himself will be exalted" (Matthew 23:11–12). The person who is not willing to humble himself as Jesus "humbled Himself" (Philippians 2:8) will have no place in Jesus' kingdom. For self-righteous Jews who exalted themselves so highly as to think God was pleased with them for their goodness, this was a shattering blow.

THE MEANING OF "CHRIST" (MATTHEW 16)

The term *Christ* literally means "the Anointed One." *Messiah*, the Hebrew equivalent for Christ, refers in the Old Testament to prophets (see 1 Kings 19:16), priests (see Leviticus 4:5, 16), and kings (see 1 Samuel 24:6, 10), in the sense that all of them were anointed with oil. This anointing symbolized a consecration for ministry by God. Jesus Christ, as the Anointed One, would be the ultimate Prophet, Priest, and King (see Isaiah 61:1). Peter, with his dramatic confession of, "You are the Christ, the Son of the living God" (Matthew 16:16), was declaring his faith in Jesus as the promised Messiah.

STUDY QUESTIONS

1. What was the source of the conflicts between Jesus and the religious leaders in Matthew 12:1–13? What conclusions did the Pharisees make about Christ?

2. What are the lessons contained in the parable of the soils (see Matthew 13:1–17)? What was Jesus' explanation of the parable of the tares (see verses 24–30)?

3. The feeding of the five thousand, as told in Matthew 14:13–21, is recorded in all four of the Gospels. What are the significant details of this work of Christ?

4. For what violations of the Mosaic law did Jesus take the Pharisees to task in Matthew 15:1–11? How did Jesus respond when He learned that the Pharisees were offended at His words?

5. What happened when Jesus quizzed His disciples as to His "reputation" in Matthew 16:13–20? What do you think was the significance of this moment?

6. What did the Transfiguration reveal about Jesus (see Matthew 17:1–13)? Why do you think the disciples who witnessed this event were not forever altered by it?

7. How did Jesus teach His bickering disciples a lesson by calling a small child? What does Jesus say about a believer who leads others into sin (see Matthew 18:1–9)?

8. How did Jesus respond to the rich young man? What did Jesus say about the disciples who had left everything to follow Him (see Matthew 19:16–30)?

WEEK 30

JESUS IS THE VICTORIOUS KING

MATTHEW 21–28

READING PLAN: **204** | Matthew 21 **205** | Matthew 22–23 **206** | Matthew 24
207 | Matthew 25 **208** | Matthew 26 **209** | Matthew 27 **210** | Matthew 28

Back in ancient times, the coronation of a monarch involved a display of great splendor and pageantry. The soon-to-be-crowned king would be dressed in the most expensive robes and jewels and would be driven through his capital city in an ornate carriage drawn by stately horses. Accompanying him would be his courtiers and foreign dignitaries, and following them would be a large retinue of the nation's finest soldiers. At the climax of these events, the king would be presented with a scepter or would participate in some other ritual signifying the transfer of power into his hands. Every part of the ceremony was designed to highlight the majesty, glory, and dignity of the king.

Jesus' entry into Jerusalem on a donkey portrays the most significant coronation the world has yet seen, yet it was one in marked contrast to the usual kind. Jesus was affirmed as King and was, in a sense, inaugurated into His kingship. But there was no pomp and only a brief sort of pageantry. *Brief* in that, only a few days later, the same multitude would reject and denounce Him, calling for His death when He did not come through as expected.

Before Jesus went to the cross, He would deliver His final message—commonly known as the Olivet Discourse—to His disciples on the Mount of Olives. Three times in recent days He had foretold His death to them. This time, He spoke of His second coming and the amazing events associated with it, when He would return to establish His millennial kingdom on earth.

The message had been prompted by the disciples' question, "Tell us . . . what will be the sign of Your coming, and of the end of the age?" (Matthew 24:3). The answer Jesus gave is the longest given to any question asked in the New Testament. Yet His purpose was to give them clarity and encouragement, not complexity and anxiety. The disciples were not learned men, and the truths Jesus communicated were essential for understanding His future return to earth in glory at the end of the age.

Even on the night before Jesus' crucifixion, He again reminded His disciples that He would one day return. First, though, He would have to suffer and die. The order and timing of events occurred exactly as God had planned. The appropriate time for Jesus to die was *now*, at Passover. This is when the sacrificial lambs were slain, and that celebration pointed to the Lamb of God who, as John the Baptist had proclaimed, takes away the sins of the world (see John 1:29). The sacrifices of all the other lambs were but faint symbols of what the true Lamb was about to accomplish.

There had been many times in the past when people sought to kill Jesus but were unable to do so. The first attempt on Jesus' life was made shortly after He was born, when Herod massacred all the male infants in the vicinity of Bethlehem. God sent an angel to warn Joseph to take Jesus and His mother to Egypt until the danger was over. On an occasion in His hometown of Nazareth, the people became incensed by His claim to be fulfilling Isaiah's prophecy. They succeeded in leading Him to the edge of a high cliff on the outskirts of the city, but before they could throw Him to His death, He miraculously passed through their midst and went His way. The Jewish religious leaders had then begun plotting His death soon after He began His public ministry, but they were not able to fulfill that intention.

The attempts to kill Jesus had failed because it was not God's time or His way for His Son to die. Only the sovereign grace of God could have brought Jesus to the cross. No human power could have accomplished it apart from God's will, and no human power could now prevent it, because it was God's plan. Everything prior to this moment had been a prologue in the sacred story of God's redemptive plan.

Everything in that story centers on the cross of Christ. It is the culmination of the Bible and redemptive history—the only eternal hope of fallen humanity. It is through the cross of Christ alone that the Lord provided the way for sinners to be saved and united with Him, the holy God. There is no salvation, no gospel, no biblical Christianity, apart from the cross of Christ.

As the King of heaven moved toward the hour of His suffering and death, the hostility of the Jewish leaders grew. Opposition among His own people increased. His disciples turned fearful. Jesus went the Garden of Gethsemane, where He prayed, "O My Father, if it is possible, let this cup pass from Me; nevertheless, not as I will, but as You will" (Matthew 26:39). Soon after, Jesus was arrested and forced to stand trial. This was followed by a sentence of death from the Roman governor Pontius Pilate.

Jesus was led to the cross, executed, and buried. Then we see the Lord's resurrection and hear His final, triumphant instructions to His disciples, where He issues His supreme command for them to go and make disciples of all nations. Every event and conversation in those final days of Jesus' ministry afforded Him one more opportunity to shine the light of God's truth into the world's darkness.

Across the pages of history, Israel's true King had journeyed from a manger in Bethlehem to a cross just outside of Jerusalem with one purpose: not to be crowned but to be crucified. However, one day, He will be crowned in a way that is perfectly befitting. One day, he will return on the clouds of heaven with power and great glory. On that day, Satan will be forever defeated, the curse lifted, the creation liberated and restored, sin and death conquered, the saints glorified, and Christ worshiped as the victorious King.

REFLECTIONS

We come to Jesus on *His* terms. As noted previously, most of the people we read about in Matthew's Gospel wanted Jesus on their own terms. They would not bow to a king who was not of their liking, even though He was the Son of God. They wanted Jesus to destroy Rome but not their cherished sins or their hypocritical and superficial religion. However, Jesus would not deliver them on their terms. Many people today are likewise open to a Jesus whom they think will give them wealth, health, success, happiness, and the worldly things they want. Like the multitude at the triumphal entry, they will loudly acclaim Jesus as long as they believe that He will satisfy their selfish desires. But like the same multitude a few days later, they will reject and denounce Him when He does not deliver as expected. When they are confronted with their sin and their need of a Savior, they curse Him and turn away. The words of the multitude were right, but their hearts were not. In any case, Jesus had come at that time not to be crowned but to be crucified. He will be crowned one day in a way that is perfectly befitting.

We are to look forward to Jesus' return. The theme of Christ's second coming permeates the pages of the New Testament and is the great anticipatory reality of Christian living. The Lord's return will be as real and as historical an event as was His first coming to this world. Believers look back to the moment of their saving faith in Christ, when their souls were redeemed. But they also look forward to the return of Christ, when their bodies will be redeemed and they will enter into the promised fullness of salvation. In that day Satan will be defeated, the curse will be lifted, Christ will be worshiped, the creation will be liberated and restored, sin and death will be conquered, and the saints will be glorified.

We are to make disciples for Christ. The Great Commission is a command to bring unbelievers to a saving knowledge of Jesus Christ. True converts are *disciples*—those who have accepted and submitted themselves to Jesus. Truly converted people are filled with the Holy Spirit and given a new nature that yearns to obey and worship the Lord. Even when they are disobedient, they know they are living against the grain of their new nature, which is to honor and please the Lord. Jesus' supreme command, therefore, is for those who are His disciples to become His instruments for making disciples of all nations. Jesus' own earthly ministry was to make disciples for Himself, and that is the ministry of His people.

STUDY QUESTIONS

1. What are the events that transpired when Jesus first arrived in Jerusalem (Matthew 21:1–17)? What do these events signify about who Jesus was?

2. What point was Jesus making by telling the parable of the marriage feast (see Matthew 22:1–14)? What was Jesus saying about those who are invited into God's kingdom?

3. Take a moment to reread what Jesus said was the greatest commandment (see Matthew 22:37–39). How can a person know when he or she is being obedient to this command?

4. What does Jesus' lament over the city of Jerusalem suggest about the heart of God (see Matthew 23:37–39)? What does it suggest about the heart of man?

5. How did Jesus describe the Tribulation that will occur at the end of the age? What did Jesus say about His second coming (see Matthew 24:29–31)?

6. What was the primary lesson in Jesus' parable of the ten virgins (see Matthew 25:1–13)? How does this lesson apply to Christ's return?

7. The parable of the fig tree is extremely brief (see Matthew 24:32–35). What message was Jesus conveying to the people through these few words?

8. What details about Jesus' arrest, trial, and crucifixion did you notice for the first time in your reading this week (see Matthew 26:47–56; 27:11–26, 32–56)?

WEEK 31

JESUS IS THE SUFFERING SERVANT

MARK 1–16

READING PLAN:	**211** | Mark 1–3	**212** | Mark 4–5	**213** | Mark 6–8
214 | Mark 9–10	**215** | Mark 11–12	**216** | Mark 13–14	**217** | Mark 15–16

When Jesus ministered on earth, He did more than just teach people. He was a man of *action*. He was more than a messenger of the gospel . . . He *was* the gospel. The good news of God was present in His life, His teaching, His death, and His resurrection. By His humility and His humanity, His service and His sacrifice, Jesus proved Himself as the ultimate Servant.

The action-oriented record of Jesus' life we find in Mark's Gospel briefly introduces John the Baptist as the Messiah's forerunner and then turns the spotlight on God's Servant. Immediately after Jesus' baptism and temptation, He arrives in Galilee, where He calls His first disciples—Peter, Andrew, James, and John—and embarks on a preaching and miracle-working tour that must have lasted for weeks. What follows next sets the stage for all that is to come: a series of controversies (or "conflict" episodes) with the Jewish leaders, beginning with the incident involving the disciples of Jesus picking grain on the Sabbath.

The contrast between Jesus' reception by His true disciples and the opposition to Him among the "religious" of His day was evident early on. Israel's religious leaders consisted of four different sects—the Pharisees, the Sadducees, the scribes, and the teachers of the Law—each of whom envied Jesus' popularity with the people. The Jewish religious establishment also resented Jesus for exposing their hypocrisy and self-righteousness. His claims to be the Messiah and the Son of God—claims that in their eyes were blatant blasphemy—incensed them.

The increasing tensions between Jesus and the Jewish leaders foreshadow a deadly showdown. Specifically, it is the last of the conflict episodes, when Jesus heals a man's withered hand on the Sabbath, that prompts the legalistic Pharisees to begin plotting together on how to destroy Jesus. Their tradition prohibited practicing medicine on this day of worship and rest except in life-threatening situations. But no actual law in the Old Testament forbade healing or any other acts of mercy on the Sabbath.

> The SABBATH was made for man, and not man for the SABBATH. Therefore the Son of Man is also Lord of the SABBATH.
>
> MARK 2:27–28

Christ's prerogative to rule over not only man-made sabbatarian rules but also over the Sabbath itself was another inescapable claim of His deity and, as such, resulted in the Pharisees' outrage. This, in turn, led to Christ's withdrawal to the Sea of Galilee with a great multitude from many places, where He named the rest of His disciples.

The Bible clearly states that Jesus—being the man of action that He was—"did not come to be served, but to serve, and to give His life as a ransom for many" (Mark 10:45). One way Jesus served those whom He came to save was by delivering God's truth to a world shrouded in darkness. Jesus taught the people, often using parables in His teaching, such as the parables of the sower, the lamp, the seed, and the mustard seed. These short, simple, earthbound stories communicated eternal truths to reveal previously unknown mysteries about the kingdom of God to believers and to conceal its truth from unbelievers.

Another way Jesus served was by delivering people from certain temporal trials. In all of Old Testament history, there had never been a person who exhibited such extensive healing power as Jesus. Physical healings were rare in the Old Testament, but Christ chose to display His deity by healing, raising the dead, and liberating people from demons. This not only showed the Messiah's power over the physical and spiritual realms but also demonstrated God's compassion toward those affected by sin, adding to an already-convincing presentation of Jesus as the Servant-Messiah sent by God.

In spite of Jesus' amazing works, His own family and friends misunderstood His message and ministry. The backlash that Jesus received in His final visit to an unbelieving Nazareth prompted Him to redefine what it means to be part of God's family. At this stage in His ministry, Jesus began to train the twelve disciples to join Him as fellow workers rather than as observers. Christ also broadened His ministry to the irreligious Gentiles in the area, healing and performing amazing miracles in Tyre, Sidon, Decapolis, and Bethsaida, where many religious outcasts willingly trusted and obeyed Him.

To the casual reader, some of the reports of Jesus' ministry may seem to be a collection of unrelated incidents, but ultimately, He was deliberately moving toward Jerusalem, the site of His final confrontation with the Jewish religious leaders. Jesus, knowing the time was short, set about teaching and modeling for His disciples a number of important kingdom truths, such as defining kingdom greatness, identifying true spiritual fruit, and warning those who would be stumbling blocks.

In the final week of Jesus' earthly life, the Son of Man entered Jerusalem to the glad shouts of the masses but also to the consternation of the Jewish religious leaders. Jesus then drove the money changers and merchants from the temple and publicly rebuked the scribes and Pharisees, which set Him on a collision course with the cross. Yet there were still lessons to be taught, so Jesus seized the opportunity in a sermon He delivered from the Mount of Olives just east of the temple. His prediction of the future destruction of the temple in Jerusalem prompted a question from the disciples about the character of the end times. Jesus responded by describing His second coming.

All the while, those who hated Jesus were moving to destroy Him. Jesus' followers, perhaps sensing trouble, reacted with everything from worship to abandonment. Finally, Christ was brought to two trials—the first one Jewish and religious; the other Roman and secular—and was sentenced to death.

God's redeeming work through His Son culminated in the cross, where Jesus bore the sins of the world. In Christ's atonement, God restored unity between Himself and sinful human beings, reinstating sinners to a relationship of "at-one-ment" with Him. This supreme revelation of God's gracious love was followed by the greatest event in history: the resurrection of Jesus Christ. The Son of God willingly came to earth to preach, die, and be raised for the very purpose of saving humankind eternally from sin.

REFLECTIONS

Consider the soil. Jesus appeals to those considering His claims to think about the kind of soil that represents their heart. If it is hard-packed and beaten down by neglect of God, He calls us to allow His Spirit to break up the ground and make it receptive to His Word. If the soil is shallow and superficial, He calls us to allow the Spirit to remove the rocky resistance that lies beneath the surface of our seeming acceptance of the gospel. If the soil is infested with the weedy cares of the world, He asks us to allow the Spirit to cleanse us of worldliness and to receive Him with no competing loyalties.

The cross before the crown. To come to Jesus Christ is to receive and keep on receiving. Yet Jesus and the authors of the New Testament make it clear there must be a cross before the crown, suffering before glory, and sacrifice before reward. The heart of Christian discipleship is giving before gaining.

The gospel is not self-focused. Christian discipleship strikes a death blow to self-centered false gospels. It leaves no room for the gospel of *getting*, where God is considered a type of genie who jumps to provide our every whim. It closes the door to the gospel of *health and wealth*, which asserts that if we are not healthy and prosperous, we have not exercised our divine rights—or do not have enough faith to claim our blessings. It undermines the gospel of improper *self-esteem*, which appeals to our narcissism and prostitutes the spirit of humble brokenness and repentance that marks the gospel of the cross.

STUDY QUESTIONS

1. Looking back through Mark 1–2, what happened when word of Jesus' miraculous power began to spread? How did the Jewish scribes react to Jesus' early ministry?

2. What was the job description of the twelve men chosen by Christ to be His disciples? How did Jesus respond when His own family members came to see Him (see Mark 3:13–19)?

3. How did the disciples respond when they found themselves being tossed about in a storm on the Sea of Galilee? What did they do after Jesus calmed the storm (see Mark 4:35–41)?

4. What happened when Jesus returned to Nazareth, His hometown, and taught in the synagogue (see Mark 6:1–6)? What lessons might the disciples have learned from this incident?

5. What effect did the Transfiguration have on the disciples Peter, James, and John? What did this event reveal about the identity of Christ (see Mark 9:2–13)?

6. What did Jesus do to cleanse the temple (see Mark 11:15–19)? Why do you think that Jesus was so angered by what He saw there?

7. According to Jesus, what worldwide events will happen during the Tribulation? What can followers of Christ expect during that time (see Mark 13:4–31)?

8. The Jewish rulers had already tried Christ before the Sanhedrin. In Mark 15:1–15, Jesus is also tried before Pilate. How were the two trials similar? How were they different?

WEEK 32

JESUS IS THE PROMISED MESSIAH

LUKE 1–9

READING PLAN:	**218** | Luke 1–2	**219** | Luke 3	**220** | Luke 4
221 | Luke 5–6	**222** | Luke 7	**223** | Luke 8	**224** | Luke 9

Try to imagine what it must have been like when Jesus, the promised Messiah, came into the world. Although His birth was attended by great heavenly fanfare, it generated little notice or interest among men. Only a few obscure witnesses—"shepherds living out in the fields" (Luke 2:8)—celebrated the blessed arrival of the Savior into our sin-scarred world.

Beginning with the unusual circumstances surrounding the birth of John the Baptist (who was Jesus' cousin), the events of the nativity in Luke's Gospel unfold: the announcement of Jesus' birth to Mary (the "annunciation"), His humble birth, the angelic visitation to the shepherds, and the Spirit-led responses of Simeon and Anna when Jesus was presented at the temple. Then, in the primary story that the Bible provides from His childhood, we see Jesus encountering the teachers at the temple when He was twelve.

Luke, a meticulous historian, drew on written sources and the eyewitness reports to present a carefully constructed and comprehensive account that reveals Jesus (whose name literally means "The Lord shall save") to be the long-awaited Messiah of the Jews—the one anointed by God and empowered by God's Spirit to deliver His people and establish His kingdom. In Christian thought, the term "Messiah" refers to Jesus' role as a spiritual deliverer—the One who sets His people free from sin and death. But in Jewish thought, the Messiah was believed to a political leader who would defeat their enemies and bring in a golden era of peace and prosperity.

Matthew traced Jesus' lineage from the royal line of David. But Luke's genealogy moves backward from Jesus to Adam, revealing Mary's part of the family tree. Thus we see the royal line passed through Jesus' legal father, Joseph—descended from Abraham—and physically through His mother's ancestral lineage to David. Another purpose of Luke's work was to highlight the universal scope of the gospel invitation: Jesus was not only the Jewish Messiah but also the Savior of non-Jews. Before Christ's earthly ministry is over, we will see exactly this—the Son of Man rejected by Israel and then offered to the world.

The beginning of Jesus' kingdom work was heralded by John the Baptist. This is significant because, in those days, monarchs who traveled in wilderness regions would have crews of workmen go ahead of them to make sure the road was clear of potholes, debris, obstructions, and other hazards that might make their journey difficult. In a spiritual sense, John paved the way for the Messiah, calling the people of Israel to prepare their hearts for His arrival.

John's admonitions to be baptized as part of their preparation seemed strange to Jewish ears. They were accustomed to Gentile proselytes seeking him out to be immersed in the Jordan. But the kind of baptism John spoke of—a baptism for the Jews—was new to them. John was calling them to be baptized as a public renunciation of their old way of life and to symbolize their spiritual readiness for the Messiah. Years later, Paul would connect baptism with the believers' identification with Christ, saying, "Therefore we were buried with Him through baptism into death, that just as Christ was raised from the dead by the glory of the Father, even so we also should walk in newness of life" (Romans 6:4).

After Jesus' baptism, He encountered opposition from the devil during His forty-day temptation in the wilderness. Then came the inauguration of His ministry. Jesus taught in the synagogue of Capernaum, healed many (including Peter's mother-in-law), toured Galilee with Peter and others, and cleansed a leper—which was followed by much (unwelcome) publicity. He also forgave and healed a paralytic, ate with "sinners," and opposed the Pharisees regarding their Sabbath rules. As Christ preached, healed, and taught the people throughout Galilee, Israel's promised Messiah displayed His sovereign authority over nature, disease and defilement, sin and its consequences, and religious tradition.

Just before Jesus delivered a sermon from a level place on a mountainside (probably near Capernaum), He demonstrated His authority over men by prayerfully choosing the twelve who would be His disciples. Jesus had many disciples, but He specifically commissioned this group with special authority to deliver the good news of the gospel on His behalf. These individuals would later be known as apostles ("messengers, sent ones")—the human leaders of the worldwide entity known as the church.

This was also the point in Jesus' ministry when He began to speak to the masses only in parables. Prior to choosing His disciples, Jesus had employed many analogies in His teaching, with meanings that were fairly clear in their context. Parables, however, required more explanation, and Jesus used them to obscure the truth from unbelievers while making it clearer to the twelve disciples. This veiling of truth from unbelievers was both an act of judgment and an act of mercy on Jesus' part. It was "judgment" because it kept them in the darkness that they loved, and it was "mercy" because they had already rejected the light, so any exposure to more truth would only increase their condemnation.

Although Jesus' ministry outside of Jerusalem was coming to an end, His training of the disciples was beginning in earnest. The propagation of the gospel and founding of the church would hinge on these chosen few, and their time to be trained by Christ would be measured in months—not years.

So Jesus taught them the Scriptures and theology. He guided them in the ways of godly living. He gave them moral instruction. He spoke to them of things to come. He performed numerous miracles in their presence. He was also transfigured in the sight of three of these men, His inner circle. And He employed all twelve disciples as His instruments to heal the sick, cast out demons, and do other miraculous works ahead of His final journey toward Jerusalem.

REFLECTIONS

Jesus was an actual person. Some people doubt whether Jesus actually existed, but many historians have written about Christ. Around AD 114, Tacitus wrote that Jesus was the founder of the Christian religion and was put to death by Pontius Pilate. Pliny the Younger wrote a letter to Emperor Trajan on the subject of Christ. In AD 90, the Jewish historian Josephus also penned a biographical note on Jesus. Likewise, the Talmud refers to Jesus of Nazareth. Jesus *was* a man in history—and His claims were true.

God's strength is made perfect in our weakness. From our human perspective, the propagation of the gospel and founding of the church hinged on a group of men whose most outstanding characteristic was their ordinariness. These individuals were chosen by Christ and trained for a time that is best measured in months, not years. Jesus taught them the Scriptures and theology. He discipled them in the ways of godly living—teaching them and showing them how to pray, how to forgive, and how to serve one another with humility. He gave them moral instruction. He spoke to them of things to come. And He employed them as His instruments to heal the sick, cast out demons, and do other miraculous works. These ordinary men, empowered by the Holy Spirit on the Day of Pentecost, valiantly undertook the task to which Jesus had called them. The work they subsequently began continues to this day, some 2,000 years later. The disciples of Jesus are proof that God's strength is made perfect in our weakness.

We must understand the heart of Jesus. When the crowds sought Jesus, He said to His disciples, "I must preach the kingdom of God to the other cities also, because for this purpose I have been sent" (Luke 4:43). Jesus had a passion for the lost that compelled Him to move from place to place. We can enhance our own passion for the lost by studying His love, compassion, and mercy. We can also study great men and women in church history—but ultimately we must understand the heart of Christ. As John wrote, "He who says he abides in Him ought himself also to walk just as He walked" (1 John 2:6).

STUDY QUESTIONS

1. What unexpected events transpired when Joseph and Mary came to present Jesus to the Lord at the temple in Jerusalem (see Luke 2:22–38)?

2. How would you describe the personality of John the Baptist? What did John preach to the people and what did he tell them to expect was soon coming (see Luke 3:1–17)?

3. What happened when Jesus called Simon (Peter), Andrew, James, and John to be His disciples (see Luke 5:1–11)? What did Jesus ask Peter to do, and what was his response?

4. Why would the events of Luke 5:27–32 have raised eyebrows and stirred up the Jewish religious leaders? How do Jesus' actions go against what the leaders would have taught?

5. What was Jesus saying and revealing about Himself through the healing of the man who was paralyzed (see Luke 5:17–26)? What was the Pharisees' complaint against Him?

6. Review Jesus' teachings in Luke 6:17–38. What are five kingdom truths or principles that you see in these verses? What are the main themes in this teaching?

7. How did Jesus define or describe the true cost of being His disciple in Luke 9:23–26? How could this "cost" apply to your own life?

8. Three would-be followers of Jesus approached Him in Luke 9:57–62. How would you describe Jesus' responses to each of these individuals?

WEEK 33

JESUS IS THE GREAT PHYSICIAN

LUKE 10–17

READING PLAN: **225** | Luke 10 **226** | Luke 11 **227** | Luke 12–13
228 | Luke 14 **229** | Luke 15 **230** | Luke 16 **231** | Luke 17

The Son of Man's destination was now Jerusalem, where He would die for the sins of the world. The biblical narrative in Luke's Gospel—much of it unique to his orderly, historical account of the life of Christ—now becomes a travelogue of that long journey to the cross.

From this point forward, Galilee is no longer Jesus' base of operation. We know from a comparison of the Gospels that Jesus made short visits to Jerusalem to celebrate feasts (see Mark 10:1; John 2:13; 5:1; 7:10; 10:22)—but those brief visits were only interludes in this period of ministry that would culminate in a final journey to Jerusalem. This turning point in Luke's Gospel is dramatically underscored by Jesus' focused determination to complete His mission of going to the cross, which we see in full force as He departs Samaria.

Jesus sent seventy disciples to every city and place across Judea (and possibly to Perea) that He was about to visit. He also visited the home of Mary, Martha, and their brother, Lazarus, in the village of Bethany, located about two miles from Jerusalem. Around this time, a lawyer (scribe) inquired, "What shall I do to inherit eternal life?" (Luke 10:25). Jesus, knowing the man was seeking to justify himself, answered with the parable of the Good Samaritan—which to this supposed expert in the law of God would have been a contradiction in terms.

We have already seen how much of Jesus' ministry was to the Gentiles. In fact, when Jesus inaugurated His public ministry by teaching in the synagogue in Nazareth, He recounted Elijah's ministry to the widow of Zarephath and Naaman the Syrian (see Luke 4:24–27), two Gentiles to whom God had determined to demonstrate His grace. Jesus was communicating that God's concern was not for the Jews alone but for all people, Jews and Gentiles alike.

This was a running theme of Christ's ministry: His compassion for the pariahs of society—Gentiles, Samaritans, women, children, tax collectors, sinners, and others regarded as outcasts in Israel. Repeatedly, those individuals on the fringe of society found grace in His eyes. In fact, after calling Matthew (also known as Levi), a tax collector, to be one of His disciples, Jesus attended a celebratory banquet at Matthew's house. This feast was attended by a number of other tax collectors and "sinners," as the Pharisees described them. Why did Jesus decide to eat and drink with such people? As he said to the Pharisees, "Those who are well have no need of a physician, but those who are sick. I have not come to call the righteous, but sinners, to repentance" (Luke 5:31–32).

JESUS' SERMONS IN LUKE'S GOSPEL

Sermon given in the synagogue (4:17–27)

Sermon given on the plain (6:17–49)

Sermon given in His parables (8:4–21)

Sermon given on the lost (15:1–32)

Sermon on God's kingdom (17:20–37)

Sermons on various themes (20:1–21:38)

Yet Jesus did not ignore the salvation of those who were rich and respectable either. From the outset of His public ministry to His final words on the cross, He showed Himself to be the Great Physician, eager to minister to those who were most aware of their need. The high value that Jesus accorded to women is especially significant. From the prominence of Mary, Elizabeth, and Anna in the nativity account to the events that occurred on resurrection morning, women played a central and visible role in the life and ministry of our Lord.

As Jesus continued His itinerant ministry, He healed a man on the Sabbath, providing Him with another opportunity to challenge the religious externalism of Israel's leaders. Knowing He was headed for a showdown with these false shepherds, which would end with His crucifixion, Jesus instructed His followers concerning a number of important subjects, including some strong words of discipleship.

Here the master storyteller used several parables, including that of the prodigal son, to teach kingdom truths, mainly that the salvation of people brings great joy to heaven! Jesus concluded with the parable of the unjust steward, directed to Christ's disciples, and the story of the rich man and Lazarus, told for the Pharisees. Jesus' point in presenting this grim account of heaven and hell was to show that unbelief is at heart a moral problem, not an intellectual problem. This was surely another reason why Israel's leaders were opposed to His teaching; it was not only that they felt threatened by Christ's popularity and authority. Meanwhile, the masses, enamored with the supernatural power of Jesus, were content to enjoy His blessings without committing to His high standards of discipleship.

In contrast, Jesus declared that He was bringing in an altogether different kind of kingdom, which was manifest through the rule of God in men's hearts by faith in Him. This kingdom was neither confined to a particular geographical location nor visible to human eyes. Neither was Jesus suggesting that the Old Testament promises of an earthly kingdom were hereby nullified. Rather, He was announcing that the earthly, visible manifestation of the kingdom was yet to come. And when it does come, it will appear quietly, invisibly, and without the normal pomp and splendor associated with a king's arrival.

Jesus' message was, above all, a call for people to repent. He was urging Jews and Gentiles, the religious and the outcasts, the physically sick and the spiritually sick, to turn from sin—to change their orientation and seek a new way. (The Greek word for *repent* literally means "a change of perception." To repent, therefore, is to change the way a person looks at sin and the way he looks at righteousness.) Repentance was, and is, the first demand of the gospel, the first requirement of salvation, and—as the Great Physician has always known—the first element of the saving work of God in the soul.

WOMEN IN THE GOSPELS AND ACTS

Mary	The mother of Jesus	Luke 1:26-56
Elizabeth	The mother of John the Baptist	Luke 1:5-25; 39–45
Anna	Prophetess who recognized Jesus as the Messiah	Luke 2:36-38
Joanna	Provided financial support for Jesus' ministry	Luke 8:3
Susanna	Provided financial support for Jesus' ministry	Luke 8:3
Martha and Mary	Sisters of Lazarus and friends of Jesus	Luke 10:38–42
Herodius	Queen who demanded John the Baptist's execution	Matthew 14:3–10
Salome	The mother of Jesus' disciples James and John	Matthew 20:20–24
Mary Magdalene	Among the first to witness Jesus' resurrection	Mark 16:9
Sapphira	Held back money from the early church	Acts 5:1–11
Candace	A queen of the Ethiopians	Acts 8:27
Dorcas (Tabitha)	Woman in Joppa who was raised from the dead	Acts 9:36–43
Lydia	Converted during Paul's ministry in Philippi	Acts 16:14
Priscilla	Wife of Aquila and coworker with Paul	Acts 18:2, 18
Bernice	Sister of King Agrippa before whom Paul appeared	Acts 25:13

REFLECTIONS

Jesus calls the ordinary to be His followers. Luke reports that Jesus "appointed seventy others also, and sent them out two by two before His face into every city and place where He Himself was about to go" (10:1). We know nothing else from the Bible about the identity of these seventy, but suffice it to say, they were ordinary men and women just like all of us. However, what they were able to achieve for Christ was *extra*ordinary: "Then the seventy returned with joy, saying, 'Lord, even the demons are subject to us in Your name'" (verse 17). Men and women like the seventy are simply those who confess Jesus as Lord and Savior, believe that God has raised Him from the dead, declare this belief publicly, and seek to make other disciples of Christ. They are not some sort of "upper-level" Christians—but what they can achieve for God when they submit to the authority of Christ is "upper level." As Jesus said, "Behold, I give you the authority to trample on serpents and scorpions, and over all the power of the enemy" (verse 19).

Recognize that discipleship is costly. Paul wrote, "For by grace you have been saved through faith, and that not of yourselves; it is the gift of God, not of works, lest anyone should boast" (Ephesians 2:8–9). We pay *nothing* to earn salvation—it is a free gift from the Lord. Yet living for Christ is a serious matter of discipleship that comes at a cost. To be a Christian means to rely on Christ's power rather than our own strength and to be willing to forsake our way to follow the path that He has established for us. Being a Christian can mean facing persecution, ridicule, and tribulation. As Peter wrote to the church, "Beloved, do not think it strange concerning the fiery trial which is to try you, as though some strange thing happened to you; but rejoice to the extent that you partake in Christ's sufferings" (1 Peter 4:12–13). Jesus likewise forewarned His disciples, "If they persecuted Me, they will also persecute you" (John 15:20). However, with this warning about the cost of discipleship, the Lord also promised, "Your heart will rejoice, and your joy no one will take from you" (John 16:22). Christ furthermore told His followers, "These things I have spoken to you, that in Me you may have peace. In the world you will have tribulation; but be of good cheer, I have overcome the world" (John 16:33). None of us can escape the difficulties of discipleship, but we have the promise from Jesus that He will enable us to handle them.

> He said to them all, "If ANYONE desires to come after Me, let him DENY himself, and take up his CROSS daily, and follow Me."
>
> LUKE 9:23

Heaven rejoices when a sinner repents. A *parable* can be defined as a long analogy often cast in the form of a simple story. Such stories were a common form of teaching in Judaism—and they became the primary method that Jesus employed to teach the people of His day. The parable of the prodigal son is perhaps the most familiar and beloved of all Christ's parables. However, unlike most of the others, it has more than one lesson. The prodigal is an example of sound repentance. The elder brother illustrates the wickedness of the Pharisees' self-righteousness, prejudice, and indifference toward repenting sinners. And the father pictures God, who is eager to forgive and longing for the return of the sinner. The main feature, however—as is true of the other two parables found in Luke 15—is the joy of God and the celebrations that fill heaven when a sinner repents.

We must adopt an attitude of dependence on God. As discussed previously, when Jesus was speaking of genuine salvation, He made a comparison to the characteristics of children: "I say to you, whoever does not receive the kingdom of God as a little child will by no means enter it" (Luke 18:17). For us to be saved, we must come to Christ with the dependent attitude and outlook of a little child: simple, helpless, trusting, unaffected, unpretentious, and unambitious. Of course, this is not to say that children are without sin; rather, they are naive and unassuming, dependent on others, and free from selfish claims to grandeur. They submit to the care of their parents and other loved ones, relying on them to meet all their needs. This is the kind of humble and dependent attitude anyone must have who seeks to enter the kingdom of God.

> Trust in the LORD with all your heart, and LEAN NOT on your own understanding; in all your ways ACKNOWLEDGE Him, and He shall direct your paths.
>
> PROVERBS 3:5–6

We cannot serve two masters. Jesus taught, "No servant can serve two masters; for either he will hate the one and love the other, or else he will be loyal to the one and despise the other." Jesus was speaking specifically about the love of money (or *mammon* in the Greek), saying, "You cannot serve God and [money]" (Luke 16:13). God desires for us to have a heart that is completely devoted to Him and not divided—to love and serve Him with all our heart, with all our soul, with all our strength, and with all our mind (see Luke 10:27). As Jesus said to the Pharisees who overheard Him, "You are those who justify yourselves before men, but God knows your hearts" (Luke 16:15). God knows our hearts, and He will not share the throne of our affections with anyone or anything else.

We enter into salvation through the "narrow gate." Jesus instructed, "Strive to enter through the narrow gate, for many, I say to you, will seek to enter and will not be able. When once the Master of the house has risen up and shut the door, and you begin to stand outside and knock at the door, saying, 'Lord, Lord, open for us,' and He will answer and say to you, 'I do not know you, where you are from'" (Luke 13:24–25). Our salvation does not come by confirmation, communion, baptism, church membership, church attendance, trying to keep the Ten Commandments, or by living out Jesus' teachings in the Sermon on the Mount. It does not come by giving to charity or even by believing there is a God! It does not come by simply being moral and leading a respectable life. Rather, salvation comes only when we enter through "the narrow gate" and receive by faith the gift of God's grace. Hell will be full of people who tried to reach heaven some other way. As the pastor and theologian Donald Grey Barnhouse once said, "Love that goes upward is worship; love that goes outward is affection; love that stoops is grace." God has stooped to give us grace. The question is whether we will receive it.

STUDY QUESTIONS

1. In Luke 10:1–24, we find an account of an evangelistic mission involving seventy other disciples of Jesus. What was the result of their ministry effort?

2. How did Jesus respond to the differences between the sisters Mary and Martha (see Luke 10:38–42)? How do you relate to Martha's reaction to Jesus in her home?

3. Jesus often had harsh words for the Pharisees (and also the scribes and teachers of the law). What were His primary criticisms against the Pharisees in Luke 11:37–54?

4. Review Jesus' warnings and words of comfort to His followers given in Luke 12:1–12. How do Jesus' words ring true for you in your life and your situation today?

5. Consider the two parables Jesus told in Luke 14:7–24. What are the dominant themes of those parables? What truths does Jesus seem to be emphasizing here?

6. Jesus relates the parable of the shrewd manager in Luke 16:1–13. What point was Jesus making in telling this particular story? How does His message this apply to the world today?

7. For whom did Jesus give the parable of the rich man and Lazarus (see Luke 16:19–31)? What was the point of Jesus' story? How is His message still pertinent today?

8. How did Jesus respond to the disciples' request to increase their faith? How does this relate to His teaching on forgiveness (see Luke 17:1–10)?

WEEK 34

JESUS IS THE GREAT REDEEMER

LUKE 18–24

READING PLAN: **232** | Luke 18 **233** | Luke 19 **234** | Luke 20 **235** | Luke 21 **236** | Luke 22 **237** | Luke 23 **238** | Luke 24

In Jesus' relentless progression toward the cross, we see the purpose for which Christ came to earth. The saving of sinners was His entire mission, and He would not be deterred.

While still ministering in the region of Perea, Jesus revealed a final round of lessons and parables to all who were open to receiving His truths. One of the many things Jesus taught was that nothing happens without faith in God. Like the widow and the humble publican in His parables, we must have persistent, prayerful, childlike, committed faith. This is not faith in ourselves, nor in riches, but faith in the righteousness of Christ the Redeemer.

True faith, however, is rare. "When the Son of Man comes," Jesus said, "will He really find faith on the earth?" (Luke 18:8). True faith means to relinquish trust in oneself and transfer that trust to someone or something else. True faith, according to the definition of Christ, always involves surrender to the will of God. What Jesus was teaching was nothing like positive-thinking psychology. He was saying that both the source and the object of all genuine faith is found only in God. And with God nothing will be impossible (see Luke 1:37).

The parable of the Pharisee and the publican perfectly illustrates how a sinner who is utterly devoid of personal righteousness can be declared righteous before God through an act of repentant faith in Christ the Redeemer. In contrast, the confidence of the Pharisees, who trusted in their own righteousness, was nothing but a damning hope. Human righteousness—even the righteousness of the most fastidious Pharisee who tried his best to follow the law—always falls short of the divine standard. As Paul would later write, "By the deeds of the law no flesh will be justified in His sight" (Romans 3:20).

Another individual who fell short was the rich young ruler. When this young man approached Jesus concerning salvation, our Lord immediately tested his willingness to deny all and follow Him. The ruler's unwillingness to heed Jesus' words revealed a deeper problem within: an unwillingness to submit to the lordship of Christ. Saving faith counts the cost and humbly cries out to God, as did the tax collector in Jesus' parable who said, "God, be merciful to me a sinner!" (Luke 18:13).

We see different aspects of our Lord in a succession of scenes as Jesus draws near to Jerusalem. After He healed blind Bartimaeus, Christ showed kindness to Zacchaeus, a tax collector in Jericho. This was Christ, the Friend of sinners, coming to seek and to save the lost. Through the parable of the ten minas, we meet Christ, the Judge of all the earth. Then, on the Sunday of Passion Week, we meet Christ, the King of kings, when Jesus entered Jerusalem on a donkey colt, to the wild cheers of the masses.

In rapid-fire fashion, the week's sobering events unfold. On Monday, Jesus went to the temple, cleansing it of the merchants and money changers. On Tuesday, He walked into the heart of enemy territory and clashed with the religious leaders who questioned His authority. He then taught the crowds who had made the holy pilgrimage to Jerusalem (and the temple) to celebrate the Passover feast.

Christ's teaching at this time included a stinging parable about wicked vinedressers—an obvious indictment of the Jewish rulers. His teaching also included a brilliant dialogue with the various religious leaders who were trying to trap Him with different theological and political questions in a series of carefully coordinated attacks. While in the temple that day, Christ noticed a poor woman making a sacrificial gift. He said of her, "This poor widow has put in more than all; for all these out of their abundance have put in offerings for God, but she out of her poverty put in all the livelihood that she had" (Luke 21:3–4). Jesus then prophesied the destruction of Jerusalem and taught about the end times.

Likely sometime between Tuesday and Wednesday, Judas, one of Jesus' disciples, joined the Jewish leaders' wicked conspiracy against Christ. On the Thursday of Passion Week, the Son of Man and His followers celebrated the Passover. There, in a rented upper room, Jesus instituted a simple meal that we call the Lord's Supper, which was intended to commemorate the new covenant in His blood.

The Passover was a special feast day in Israel's religious calendar and was inextricably linked to the Exodus, marking the day of the Israelites' redemption from Egypt. Passover began with the slaying of the Passover lamb, which had to be a lamb without blemish. According to the ancient historian Josephus, it was customary to slay the lamb at about three o'clock in the afternoon. This was the time of day that Jesus, the true Passover Lamb, would die.

At the Last Supper, Jesus predicted His betrayal by Judas. He also prophesized Peter's denial of Him after the disciple proclaimed, "Lord, I am ready to go with You, both to prison and to death" (Luke

22:33). Jesus then led His entourage to the Garden of Gethsemane. There, late on Thursday night, He agonized in prayer before being arrested. Then the tragic ending comes. The forsaken Son of Man was mocked, beaten, and dragged before the Sanhedrin. Lacking the legal authority to pronounce a death sentence on Christ, the Jewish council took Him to the Roman governor, Pilate, for a civil trial.

Jesus there was sentenced to death and led away for public execution at a place called the Skull. "As they led Him away, they laid hold of a certain man, Simon a Cyrenian . . . and on him they laid the cross that he might bear it after Jesus" (Luke 23:26). Jesus was nailed to a wooden cross, with criminals on the crosses to His right and His left. One criminal mocked Him, but the other asked Jesus to remember Him. Jesus assured the man that he would—that very day—reside with Him in paradise.

But the redemption story is not over. The final chapter of Jesus' experience on earth concludes with His victory over the grave! The women who went to Jesus' tomb on Sunday morning found it empty—a fact confirmed by Peter. Jesus then appeared to two disciples on the road to Emmaus, opening their minds to everything the Old Testament had said about Himself. Following this, Jesus appeared to the disciples in person, and commissioned them to take His message to the rest of the world.

In doing this, Jesus proclaimed that the good news of salvation should be preached to all nations; that is, His disciples were to publicly make the message known to the world. Preaching is the proclamation of certainties, not the suggestion of possibilities. As faithful preachers and devoted followers, they would proclaim God's truth with His delegated authority and under His divine commission.

REFLECTIONS

We are to be distinct from the world. "The chief priests and the scribes sought how they might kill Him, for they feared the people" (Luke 22:2). If your life is Christlike, you will bear some of the reproach that He bore. Christianity confronts the system of the world by being distinct from it. It exposes sin so it can disclose the remedy. If we are committed to Christ, our lives will be distinct from the world.

Our hope is the resurrection. The resurrection of Jesus is the greatest event in history. It is so foundational to Christianity that no one who denies it can be a true Christian. Without the resurrection there is no Christian faith, salvation, or hope. The foundation of all our hope is expressed in Jesus' words: "I am the resurrection and the life. He who believes in Me, though he may die, he shall live" (John 11:25).

The cross is the focal point of our faith. Jesus evokes different images in people's minds. Some picture Him as a baby in a manger. Many picture Him as a compassionate healer who restored the sick and raised the dead. Others picture a fiery preacher speaking the Word of God to great crowds. Yet the one image of Christ that surpasses the rest is Jesus on the cross. To know Christ crucified is to know Him as the author and finisher of your faith. Christ's suffering on the cross is the focal point of the Christian faith. It is where His deity, His humanity, His work, and His suffering are most clearly seen.

STUDY QUESTIONS

1. What happened as Jesus approached Jericho? Who was Zacchaeus and what was his story (see Luke 19:1–4)? Is there a modern comparison to Zacchaeus today?

2. How did Zacchaeus respond after his encounter with Jesus (see Luke 19:5–10)? How was this a lesson to those watching the event unfold?

3. How would you describe Jesus' actions as He entered Jerusalem (see Luke 19:28–44)? What were His instructions to the disciples? What was the reaction of the crowd?

4. Why did Jesus say that the poor widow's offering was pleasing to God (see Luke 21:1–4)? Who was Jesus' message directed toward?

5. What surprising event took place immediately following the first Lord's Supper (see Luke 22:7–38)? What did Jesus want to teach the disciples?

6. Review the scene that took place in the Garden of Gethsemane in Luke 22:39–46. What details stand out? What was Jesus' warning to the disciples?

7. In Luke's account of the crucifixion, what does Jesus say and do (see Luke 23:26–46)? What were His actions, and how did they impact those witnessing the event?

8. How did Jesus reassure His disciples after His resurrection that He was not a "spirit"? What instructions did He give them before returning to heaven (see Luke 24:36–49)?

WEEK 35

JESUS IS THE WORD MADE FLESH

JOHN 1-11

READING PLAN:	**239** | John 1-2	**240** | John 3	**241** | John 4
242 | John 5-6	**243** | John 7-8	**244** | John 9-10	**245** | John 11

What has been true for centuries is still true now: there are many opinions about who Jesus is. However, for John the apostle—the disciple who was closest to Jesus and an eyewitness to His earthly ministry—there was no dispute. Jesus was the Christ, the Son of God. In fact, as John stated near the end of his Gospel, the main reason he wrote a record centering on the person and work of Christ was so people would "believe that Jesus is the Christ, the Son of God," and that by believing they "may have life in His name" (John 20:31).

John was concerned with providing reasons for *saving faith*. First and foremost, he wanted to convince his readers of Jesus' true identity as the Word made flesh, the God-man whose divine and human natures were perfectly united into one person, the prophesied Messiah and Savior of the world. John accomplished this purpose in part by organizing his entire account of Jesus' life around eight "signs," or proofs, that reinforced His deity.

Incarnation is the theological term for Jesus, the Son of God, coming to earth as a human. Although the term is not used in the Bible, it is based on clear references in the New

Testament to Jesus as a person "in the flesh." For those who spoke Greek, "the Word" emphasized that Jesus had the essence or attributes of deity. Jesus, the Messiah, was fully God. He also became fully man, except that He took only the outward appearance of sinful flesh, because He was completely without sin. What did this mean then? What does it mean now? Simply put, *to know Jesus is to know God.*

John also wanted to assure that believers would receive the gift of eternal life—a term that refers not only to the eternal *quantity* but also divine *quality* of life. It literally means "life of the age to come," a reference to resurrection and heavenly existence in perfect glory and holiness. This life in the Lord Jesus is experienced even before heaven is reached. Although it will not fully manifest until the resurrection, it is the life of God in all believers as they participate in the life of the Living Word: Jesus Christ.

John provides many witnesses who prove that Jesus is the Messiah and Son of God. First, John the Baptist gave testimony on three different days to three different audiences. These events took place in AD 26–27, just a few months after Jesus' baptism. Next, Jesus worked His first public miracle (the first sign) of changing water into wine at a wedding in Cana of Galilee—an astounding sign that unmistakably pointed to Jesus' divine identity. Finally, when Christ cleansed the temple in righteous indignation, telling the merchants and money changers, "Do not make My Father's house a house of merchandise!" (John 2:16), it demonstrated His zeal for God's house and His promised power of resurrection.

Following these events, Jesus engaged in a nighttime dialogue with Nicodemus, a member of the Sanhedrin, gently confronting him with his need for regeneration. The conversation reinforced not only that Jesus was God's messenger but also that He had come to offer salvation. Jesus' subsequent conversation with the Samaritan woman revealed to her that He was the promised Messiah—and all previous distinctions between true and false worship based on location disappeared. True worshipers are all those who worship God "in spirit and truth" (John 4:23) through the Son, from the heart.

> For God so LOVED the world that He GAVE His only begotten Son, that whoever BELIEVES in Him should not PERISH but have everlasting LIFE.
>
> JOHN 3:16

Also important in this story was Jesus' demonstration of love for humankind, which knew no boundaries. This Samaritan woman was a social outcast, yet despite the ethnic, cultural, historical, and theological tensions between the Samaritans and Jews, Jesus exhibited the character of divine love that is all-encompassing and does not discriminate.

Christ performed two more healings—the second and third signs. First, Jesus performed a long-distance healing of a nobleman's son who was sick in Capernaum. Next, He healed a man who had been paralyzed for thirty-eight years. It was this healing that caused a shift among the religious elite from reservation toward Him to outright rejection. The opposition centered around the controversy regarding Jesus' healing the man on the Sabbath and Jesus' clear statements about His deity.

Jesus then fed the five thousand (the fourth sign) and exerted His power over nature by walking on the Sea of Galilee (the fifth sign). These miracles set the stage for His controversial discourse about being the "bread of life" (John 6:35), and many followers turned away. This smoldering dislike of Christ would erupt into an inferno of hatred at the Feast of Tabernacles in Jerusalem several months later.

This feast was known for water-drawing and lamp-lighting rites. Jesus referenced both themes by first inviting the thirsty to come to Him and then, the next day, by calling Himself the light of the world. Upon hearing this, the Jews took up stones to kill Him, but because Jesus was on a divine time-table and His hour had not yet come, He was able to escape.

Jesus' next act, healing a man with congenital blindness (the sixth sign), emphasized the blindness of the hyper-religious Jews. We see in them characteristics of callous unbelief, from its false standards, biased research, and rejection of obvious fact to its self-centeredness and never-ending demand for more evidence. The drama heightened even further when Christ addressed these false shepherds leading the nation astray and declared Himself to be "the good shepherd" (John 10:11). This ultimately prompted the Jews to take up stones to try to execute Him, but Jesus escaped from enemy hands once again.

Jesus' brief time in the area beyond the Jordan ended, and He moved back into the area of Jerusalem. His death on the cross was now only a few days away, and the scene in John's Gospel changes from hatred and rejection to an unmistakable witness of the glory of Christ. All the rejection and hatred of the Jews could not dim Jesus' glory as displayed through the resurrection of Lazarus. This seventh sign was the capstone of Jesus' public ministry. As such, it evidenced His glory, for not only did it point clearly to His deity and strengthen the faith of His disciples, but it also led Him directly to the cross.

REFLECTIONS

Jesus came to save us from spiritual death. If Jesus had been the military Messiah the people expected, He would have brought an army into Jerusalem and attacked the Romans. Instead, He went after a group of His fellow countrymen who were profaning the temple. The supreme issue for Jesus was not Rome's army but God's temple. The Messiah did not come as a military, economic, political, or social savior from injustice and oppression, but as a spiritual Savior to rescue people from sin and death.

We must be born again. Jesus told Nicodemus, "Unless one is born again, he cannot see the kingdom of God" (John 3:3). Those who are spiritually dead have no life by which they can respond to spiritual things, much less live a spiritual life. Those who are apart from God are "spiritual zombies"—the walking dead who do not know they are dead. They go through the motions of life, but they do not possess it. A dead person needs to be made *alive*. This is what salvation gives—spiritual life.

Jesus is the only way to salvation. When we witness that Jesus is the only way to God, we are not proclaiming our view of right religion but God's revelation of truth. We do not proclaim that Jesus is the only "door" to salvation simply because we are already saved, or because it suits our temperament, or because we are bigoted and exclusive. Rather, we proclaim it because *God* has proclaimed in His Word that Jesus is the only way for people to find salvation and eternal life. We proclaim a narrow gospel because Jesus said, "I am the door. If anyone enters by Me, he will be saved" (John 10:9).

STUDY QUESTIONS

1. What descriptions (titles and terms) does John the Baptist use to introduce the person of Jesus Christ to the world (see John 1:29–38)?

2. Jesus told Nicodemus that he had to be "born again" to see the kingdom of God (see John 3:1–21). What does this concept mean? How would you explain it in your own words?

3. What was John the Baptist's attitude as Jesus became more prominent and popular (see John 3:27–36)? How did John's followers react to these developments?

4. How would you describe the woman whom Jesus met at the well in Samaria (see John 4:7–20)? What do you observe about her that impresses you?

5. How did Jesus describe God, the heavenly Father, in the conversation with the Samaritan woman (see John 4:21–24)? What are the implications of this truth?

6. What was the crowd's response to Jesus' teaching when He traveled to Jerusalem (see John 7:1–24)? How did Jesus characterize His own teaching?

7. What type of freedom was Jesus talking about in his conversation with the "Jews who believed Him" in John 8:31–36? What did they say about Jesus in verses 48–53?

8. In what ways was Jesus' raising of Lazarus a foreshadow of future events (see John 11:43–44)? How do you think the crowd reacted to Jesus performing this miracle?

WEEK 36

JESUS IS THE LIGHT OF THE WORLD

JOHN 12–21

READING PLAN: **246** | John 12 **247** | John 13–14 **248** | John 15–16
249 | John 17–18 **250** | John 19 **251** | John 20 **252** | John 21

Love. Hate. Belief. Rejection. Everywhere Jesus went in Jerusalem during that final week leading up the cross, the reactions to Him were different.

The Sanhedrin and other Jewish leaders wanted Jesus dead—but He was popular with the multitudes, and they feared stirring them up if they had Jesus killed during Passover time. Others, such as Mary, demonstrated their love. Mary poured out her soul and her perfume in an act of unmeasured adoration for her Lord, anointing His feet just before His triumphal entry into Jerusalem. In that testimony of love and honor, she offered her most expensive earthly possession in effusive worship. This was significant because, by this action, Jesus presented Himself officially to the nation as the Messiah and Son of God.

In spite of the Jewish leaders' intentions, Jesus entered the city according to His own timeframe. In so doing, He forced the issue of His arrest so that His crucifixion might happen exactly on the Passover day, when the lambs were being sacrificed. In God's perfect timing, at the precise time foreordained from eternity, Jesus presented Himself to die. And with the cross looming,

Jesus completely shifted from public ministry before the masses to private ministry before a few faithful followers, devoting Himself to His disciples.

Up to this point, John has centered on the rejection of Jesus by the nation. Now, on the night of what would be Jesus' betrayal and arrest, John centers on the handful of people who did receive Him and the farewell words and works of Christ. These final acts and conversations comprise Jesus' legacy to His followers.

Only hours before Jesus' arrest, when He gathered His disciples in an upper room to share one last meal, Jesus took a towel and basin of water and washed His disciples' feet. This shocked and embarrassed them, because while the dusty conditions of the region necessitated the need for foot washing, the act was left to the lowliest of servants. Jesus was thus demonstrating the depth of His love for these men. He was also teaching the lesson of selfless service that would be supremely exemplified by His death on the cross. Furthermore, Christ's actions served as a symbol of spiritual cleansing and a model of Christian humility.

Jesus even washed the feet of Judas, saying afterward, "Assuredly, I say to you, one of you will betray Me" (John 13:21). The men were perplexed by this, even though Jesus identified the betrayer by dipping a piece of the bread into the wine and handing it to Judas. Jesus then said to him, "What you do, do quickly" (verse 27). Judas then departed in order to betray Jesus to the Jewish leaders later that evening.

JERUSALEM IN JESUS' TIME

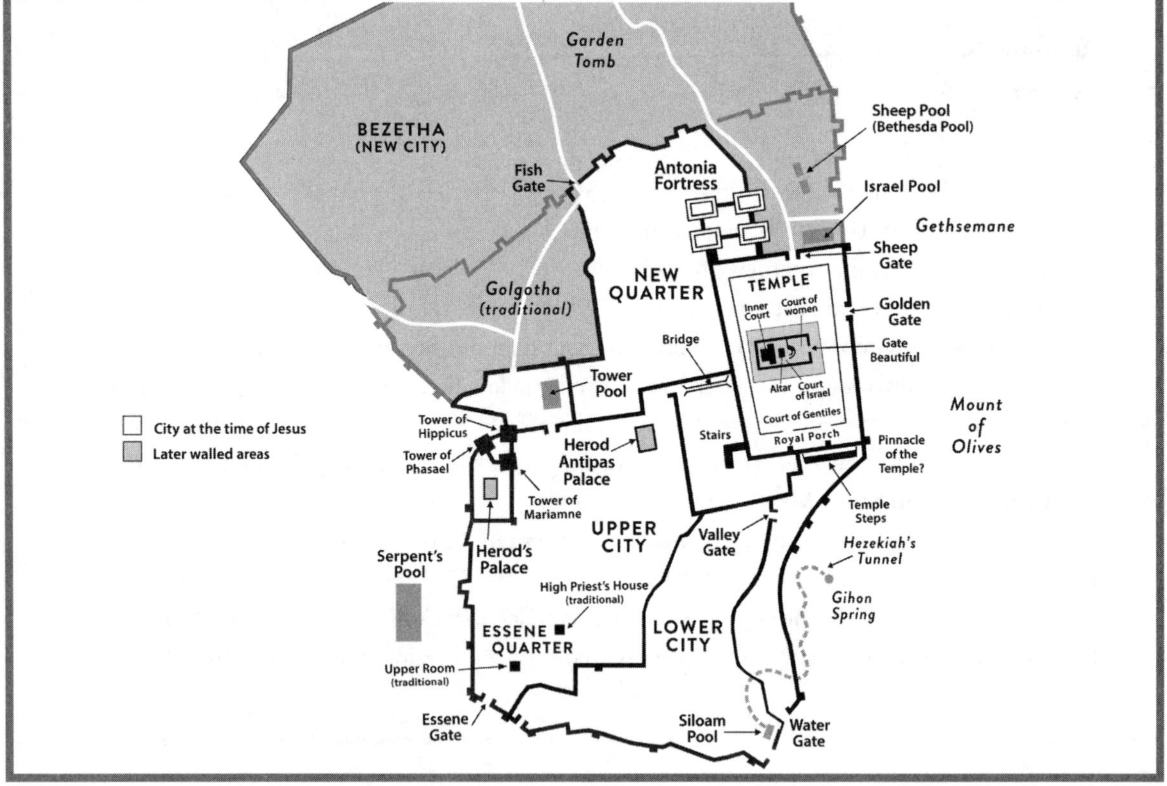

Jesus then gave His valedictory address, promising to send the eleven disciples "the Spirit of truth" (John 14:17) and telling them, "A little while longer and the world will see Me no more" (verse 19). Little did the disciples understand their world was about to be shattered. They would be bewildered, confused, and riddled with anxiety by the events that would transpire. Jesus, anticipating their devastation, spoke words of comfort to them, emphasizing the promise that He was the One who gives believers comfort, not only by virtue of His future return but also in the present, via the powerful ministry of the Holy Spirit.

Jesus also presented an extended metaphor from agricultural life—that of a vine and its branches. Jesus stated that He was the vine, His Father was the vinedresser, and the disciples were the branches. Jesus used this illustration because the vine and the branches perfectly picture the necessity of fruitfulness in a believer's life and the impossibility of such an experience without a rich, deep, vital, and ongoing relationship with Christ. Those who live such a fruitful life, Christ warned, would encounter the world's hatred, just as He had. But the disciples were not to panic. The Spirit of God would come, not only as their Helper and Comforter, but also as the Convicter of all who are antagonistic to the gospel.

> I AM the true vine, and My FATHER is the vinedresser. Every BRANCH in Me that does NOT BEAR FRUIT He takes away; and every branch that BEARS FRUIT He prunes, that it may bear MORE FRUIT.
>
> JOHN 15:1–2

Jesus then prayed for His followers. This prayer both revealed the genuine face-to-face communion that the Son had with His heavenly Father and also provided a detailed account of the content of the communication between God the Father and God the Son. The prayer also formed a sort of transition, marking the end of Jesus' earthly ministry and the beginning of His intercessory ministry for believers.

From there, John followed the logical flow of events: Jesus' rejection, arrest, trials, and execution. However, rather than detracting from Jesus' mission, all the debasing and shameful acts that were directed toward Christ actually constituted evidence that confirmed who Jesus actually is and the reason for which He had come to earth. In the crucifixion of Christ is both the climax of redemptive history and the apex of humanity's wickedness. The execution of the Savior was the utter depth of man's depravity, yet the vilest expression of evil in human history could not permanently extinguish the Light of the World. Jesus rose from the dead, appearing to Mary Magdalene outside the tomb, and then to His followers in different settings—including Peter and several other disciples who had returned to fishing. It was at this time that Jesus restored Peter, instructing Him, "Tend My sheep" (John 21:16).

With the later exception of Paul, the resurrected Christ did not appear to unbelievers, because He knew the evidence of His resurrection would not convince them if His other miracles had not. Therefore, He appeared exclusively to His own in order to confirm their faith in the living Christ. Such appearances were so profound they transformed the disciples from cowardly men hiding in fear to bold witnesses for Jesus. In the end, this was John's purpose in recording these post-resurrection appearances: to offer crowning proof that Jesus truly was the Messiah and Son of God who laid down His life for His own.

REFLECTIONS

God will one day end the curse. Jesus said to Martha, "I am the resurrection and the life. He who believes in Me, though he may die, he shall live. And whoever lives and believes in Me shall never die" (John 11:25–26). Ever since Adam and Eve sinned in the garden of Eden, there has been a curse on the earth (see Genesis 3:14–19), and that curse has sent the earth and all of its inhabitants careening into disasters, tears, sickness, and the grave. Sin was not God's purpose for humankind. All things in the world were created for the good and blessing of humanity, but sin corrupted that goodness and blessing and brought about a curse instead. Jesus came to bring life, and one day—in God's time—sin will one day have run its course and be forever destroyed. As the apostle Paul proclaimed, "'O Death, where is your sting? O Hades, where is your victory?' The sting of death is sin, and the strength of sin is the law. But thanks be to God, who gives us the victory through our Lord Jesus Christ" (1 Corinthians 15:55–57).

We should be generous in our worship. In an act of unmeasured love, "Mary took a pound of very costly oil of spikenard, anointed the feet of Jesus, and wiped His feet with her hair" (John 12:3). In that adoring testimony of honor, Mary poured out her soul in worship even as she poured out the perfume, losing all sense of restraint and economy in her adoration of her Lord. Mary did not offer that valuable possession to support a program or ministry but offered it to Jesus Himself. She did not selfishly seek a tangible result from her generosity but without hesitation offered her most expensive possession to the Lord in an act of effusive worship. In the same way, God desires our adoration and worship: "Oh come, let us worship and bow down; let us kneel before the LORD our Maker. For He is our God, and we are the people of His pasture, and the sheep of His hand" (Psalm 95:6–7).

Jesus calls us to put others before ourselves. The dusty conditions of Judea necessitated the need for foot washing. Although the disciples most likely would have been happy to wash Jesus' feet, they could not conceive of washing each other's feet. This was because at the time, foot washing was reserved for the lowliest of menial servants. Peers did not wash one another's feet, except very rarely and as a mark of great love. In Luke 22:24, we read that the disciples were so busy arguing about who was the greatest among them that none of them stopped to wash their feet—so Jesus performed the task. When Jesus did this, they were all shocked. Peter even protested Christ's action, saying, "You shall never wash my feet!" To this, Jesus replied, "If I do not wash you, you have no part with Me" (John 13:8). Jesus was modeling what loving and serving others looks like in the kingdom of God: "If I then, your Lord and Teacher, have washed your feet, you also ought to wash one another's feet" (verse 14). Jesus' act of washing His disciples' feet also serves as a symbol of spiritual cleansing and a model of Christian humility.

We must abide in Christ. Jesus said to His disciples, "I am the vine, you are the branches. He who abides in Me, and I in him, bears much fruit; for without Me you can do nothing" (John 15:5). Jesus used the vine illustration for three reasons. First, His disciples would recognize the analogy immediately, because Israel was often referred to as a vine in the Old Testament Scriptures. Second, grapevines grew everywhere in Palestine. When Jesus spoke of pruning procedures, He was describing exactly what vinedressers did to produce good crops of grapes. Third, the vine and branches perfectly illustrate the kind of relationship that must exist between Jesus and anyone who wants to be His disciple. This analogy is for all Christians. For anyone to know life and bear fruit, that person must be connected to Jesus Christ.

Our work is an extension of Christ's work. Jesus said to His heavenly Father, "I have glorified You on the earth. I have finished the work which You have given Me to do" (John 17:4). In Jesus' incarnation—His act of becoming a flesh-and-blood human being on earth while also being fully God—He glorified His heavenly Father by accomplishing His mission of reconciling fallen and sinful people to their Creator and providing eternal life to those who determine to trust in Him. Jesus' supreme purpose on this earth was "to seek and to save that which was lost" (Luke 19:10), and this is also the supreme mission of Christ's church. The work of the church is an extension of the work of her Lord. "As You sent Me into the world, I also have sent them into the world" (John 17:18).

Jesus endured the shame of the cross for us. "[Jesus], bearing His cross, went out to a place called the Place of a Skull . . . where they crucified Him" (John 19:17–18). The victim of a crucifixion was typically nailed or tied to a wooden stake and left to die. Crucifixion was used by many nations of the ancient world, including Assyria, Media, and Persia. (Alexander the Great crucified 2,000 inhabitants of Tyre when he captured the city.) Crucifixion was the Romans' most severe form of execution, so it was reserved only for slaves and criminals—no Roman citizen could be crucified. In the crucifixion of Christ, the wickedness of humankind reached its apex. The execution of the Savior was the vilest expression of evil in human history . . . the utter depth of man's depravity. In fact, Christians in the early church are reported to have begged God's forgiveness for the unknown sufferings that they caused Jesus, realizing they could not conceive of the full extent of the pain He endured at men's hands—a pain to which they knew their own sins had contributed. Yet Jesus, for our sake, "endured the cross, despising the shame, and has sat down at the right hand of the throne of God" (Hebrews 12:2).

JESUS' HIGH PRIESTLY PRAYER

For Himself: Affirms the glory of the cross, expresses the essence of eternal life, and rejoices in the shared glory of the Father.	John 17:1–5
For His disciples: Prays for their knowledge, their perseverance, their joy, their sanctification, and for their mission on the earth.	John 17:6–19
For future believers: Prays for their oneness, their perfect unity, their future presence with Him, and for their mutual love for one another.	John 17:20–26

STUDY QUESTIONS

1. Jesus and His disciples had a meal in the home of Martha, Mary, and Lazarus (see John 12:1–7). How did Mary's attitudes and behavior contrast with that of Judas?

2. How did Jesus attempt to comfort His confused disciples during the final hours before His death (see John 14:1–4)? What assurances did He give them?

3. In your own words, summarize the main ideas of what Christ taught in His metaphor of the vine and branches (see John 15:1–17).

4. What sobering words about the world's treatment of Christians did Jesus give His followers (see John 15:18–25)? Have you ever experienced this kind of treatment?

5. How did Jesus demonstrate His deity at the time of His arrest in the Garden of Gethsemane (see John 18:2–14)? Why did these acts only intensify the guilt of Jesus' enemies?

6. Compare Peter's response in the Garden of Gethsemane with his response at Jesus' trial (see John 18:10–27). Why do you think there was such a change in him?

7. How did Jesus deal with Thomas's doubt after the resurrection (see John 20:24–29)? What is the difference between honest doubt and hard-hearted skepticism?

8. What reason or purpose does John provide for writing his Gospel (see John 20:30–31)? How effectively has this purpose been served in your life?

WEEK 37

THE CHURCH HAS A MISSION

ACTS 1–14

READING PLAN: **253** | Acts 1–2 **254** | Acts 2–4 **255** | Acts 5–6 **256** | Acts 7–8 **257** | Acts 9–10 **258** | Acts 11–12 **259** | Acts 13–14

At the end of Luke's Gospel, the risen Christ commissioned His disciples to preach to all nations in His name, beginning in Jerusalem. This is exactly where we find Jesus' followers as Luke continues his carefully documented account of the founding of Christianity. The apostles and Jesus' other disciples are in Jerusalem for the feast of Pentecost.

Following Christ's ascension into heaven, the time had come for the fulfillment of His promise of the indwelling Spirit. This miraculous outpouring of God would birth the church and empower the believers to take the life-changing message of the gospel to the world. It came about on the Day of Pentecost when the believers (about 120 in total) gathered together in an upper room. Suddenly, "there appeared to them divided tongues, as of fire, and one sat upon each of them" and they "were all filled with the Holy Spirit" (Acts 2:3–4).

Peter then preached a sermon that led to 3,000 conversions, launching the church in its mission. He and John were the first leaders of this new entity. A healing at the temple gave them an open door to declare that Jesus, crucified and risen, was the prophesied Messiah.

Their preaching, however, made them a target of the Sanhedrin—the same authorities who had arrested Jesus. Undaunted by the threats, the believers prayed for courage, the apostles kept preaching, and everyone continued caring for one another so extravagantly that those outside the church were startled.

The offended Jewish authorities, led by the high priest, soon arrested and jailed Peter and his colleagues. However, God miraculously freed His spokesmen, and the apostles marched back to the temple to resume preaching. After this, "daily in the temple, and in every house, they did not cease teaching and preaching Jesus as the Christ" (Acts 5:42).

The rapid growth of the church meant an influx of people. More people meant more needs and new ministries. Soon, administrative and logistical problems threatened to consume all the apostles' time. Rather than neglect prayer and the teaching of God's Word, they commissioned a group of men to attend to the pressing needs of the body.

A man named Stephen was one of these newly appointed "deacons." He ministered powerfully among the people until the day he encountered a group of argumentative Jews who lied about him to the Jewish authorities. Standing before the high priest and powerful council of the Jews after his arrest, Stephen gave a concise review of Jewish history and then accused the council of murdering the Messiah. This blunt sermon enraged the Jews, and Stephen became the first martyr in church history.

Stephen's death seemed to escalate the Jews' persecution of the followers of Christ. From a human perspective, this was an awful turn of events. However, from a divine perspective, everything resulted in a greater good, for the persecution forced the Christians to scatter to the surrounding regions of Judea and Samaria. Thus, in the midst of terrible persecution, the church actually grew.

The ministry of the disciple Philip extended beyond Samaria. Luke reveals that Philip, during this time of intense persecution of the church, was sovereignly instructed to go south into the desert. On the way, he met an official from the court of the queen of Ethiopia. Philip's conversation and evangelization of the Ethiopian eunuch reveal a marvelous truth: the message of Christ was—and is—a worldwide gospel. All nations and languages would be invited and included in the kingdom of God.

What happened next proved to be another monumental event in the history of the church. A man named Saul of Tarsus had risen to the forefront of the Jewish persecutions against the church. He would eventually be responsible for the spread of Christianity throughout the Roman Empire—but before Christ could use this talented man, He first had to transform him. The change in Saul from his dramatic encounter with Christ on the Damascus road was instantaneous. In less than one week, he went from "breathing threats and murder against the disciples of the Lord" (Acts 9:1) to preaching Jesus as the Son of God in the synagogues. The church was understandably suspicious at first, but Saul's powerful and persistent preaching, coupled with efforts by the Jewish authorities to kill him, convinced the apostles that his conversion was genuine, and he was accepted as one of them.

Another watershed moment occurred when the Holy Spirit arranged for a Gentile army officer named Cornelius to visit Peter. In a vision, Peter was instructed, "What God has cleansed you must not call common" (Acts 10:15). God was telling Peter that He would show no partiality between Jews and Gentiles when it came to acceptance into His kingdom. Cornelius, in turn, invited Peter to visit his home in Caesarea. When he, his family, and his friends received the word of God through Peter's preaching, they had the same experience of the Holy Spirit as the Jewish believers at Pentecost.

The Jewish believers accompanying Peter were amazed. This evangelistic encounter was not a fluke; God had confirmed His acceptance of the Gentiles as heirs of His grace. The Roman authorities, realizing they were unable to stop the masses from embracing this new faith, launched a direct attack on the leaders of the Christians. No more mere threats and warnings—Herod had James executed and Peter arrested. It appeared Peter would be killed as well, but God sent an angel to free him from prison.

The Holy Spirit then selected Saul (now called Paul) and Barnabas as messengers in the church's missionary movement. Paul, Barnabas, and John Mark (who was Barnabas's cousin) set sail, stopping on Cyprus, where they confronted a false prophet. The mission then moved to Perga. For an unknown reason, John Mark left and returned to Jerusalem, while Paul and Barnabas continued to Antioch.

The initial reaction to Paul's preaching was favorable, but jealous Jewish leaders in the audience tried to discredit him and his message. The assembled Gentiles nevertheless embraced the gospel. This further incited the Jewish leaders, who stirred up a mob that ran Paul and Barnabas out of town. These events serve as a microcosm of Paul's ministry: stiff opposition from most Jews and acceptance of the gospel by many Gentiles. The apostle's perseverance in the face of persecution, as well as the growth of the church despite many challenges, is testimony to the power of the Holy Spirit. Yet the rising number of Gentile converts in a previously all-Jewish church would set the stage for a coming controversy.

REFLECTIONS

We are to preach the gospel. The church today often emphasizes many different programs, methods, and approaches to ministry—and many of these are helpful to believers. Yet what is often sacrificed in these activities is the priority of preaching. The first event in church history, following the coming of the Holy Spirit, was Peter's sermon. It led to 3,000 conversions and launched the church. The book of Acts is largely the record of apostolic preaching. Preaching has always been *central* to the church's mission.

The Holy Spirit can sanctify a life. The Holy Spirit transformed Saul in two fundamental ways. First, He took Saul's natural strengths—his gifts as a leader, a man of conviction, a profound thinker—and refined those traits. Second, He eliminated undesirable characteristics in Paul, replacing his cruel hatred with love, his aggressive spirit with peace, his hard-nosed treatment of people with gentleness, and his pride with humility. Only the Spirit of God can so thoroughly sanctify a life!

All are welcome in the church. The world expresses its intolerance and bigotry at every level, from silent prejudice to outright war. The church is not immune to this tendency. Those who belong to other cultures, races, social positions, or levels of income often find themselves unwelcome in the church. Such intolerant exclusivism grieves the heart of the Father, "who desires all men to be saved" (1 Timothy 2:4).

STUDY QUESTIONS

1. What words and phrases does Luke use in his opening paragraph (see Acts 1:1–5) to drive home the truth of Christ's resurrection?

2. What did the believers do following the ascension of Jesus into heaven? What are we told about the identity of this group (see Acts 1:12–26)?

3. What are some of the names for Jesus that Peter used in his preaching (see Acts 3:12–26; 4:8–12; 5:29–31)? How had the disciples' view of Christ expanded?

4. Luke includes a story in Acts 5:1–11 that contains a sobering warning against sin in the church. What are the implications of this event for the church today?

5. What were the requirements for the men chosen to lead the church in serving ministries (see Acts 6:1–7)? Why would these qualities be needed?

6. What happened immediately following Stephen's death (see Acts 8:1–3)? Why do you think Stephen's murder did not placate those who were opposed to the gospel?

7. Review the parable of the soils that Jesus told in Matthew 13:3–8, 18–23. How does this illustrate the varying reactions to the gospel that are reported in Acts 8?

8. What happened to Saul as he made his way to Damascus to round up more Christians? How did his traveling companions react (see Acts 9:1–9)?

WEEK 38

THE CHURCH MUST ACT ON ITS MISSION

ACTS 15–28

READING PLAN:	**260** | Acts 15–16	**261** | Acts 17–18	**262** | Acts 19–20
263 | Acts 21–22	**264** | Acts 23–24	**265** | Acts 25–26	**266** | Acts 27–28

The Gentile believers flooding into the church uncovered underlying attitudes of pride and prejudice. Some legalistic Jews even demanded the new converts be circumcised. Fierce arguing among the parties prompted a convening of the first church council, where the apostles and elders considered the relationship between the Mosaic Law and the gospel of grace.

This ecumenical council would establish the answer to the most vital doctrinal question of all: "What must a person do to be saved?" The Jerusalem Council (as it was later called) concluded that Gentiles were equal partners with the Jews in God's eternal plan and that salvation depended solely on belief in Jesus—not on keeping the law of Moses.

When it was time for a second missionary journey, Barnabas and Paul disagreed concerning John Mark. Barnabas wanted to take his cousin, but Paul refused, citing his desertion during their first evangelistic endeavor. Thus, in the sovereignty of God, two missionary teams were formed: Paul and Silas, and Barnabas and Mark. The two teams departed Antioch in two directions, with Paul and Silas returning to the churches of Asia Minor.

At Lystra, Paul met Timothy, who became a beloved colleague. Forbidden by the Holy Spirit to go into the provinces of Asia and Bithynia, Paul and his companions were directed instead to the city of Troas. There, Paul had a divine vision instructing him to go to Macedonia.

At Philippi, they encountered a group of God-fearing women. Paul and Silas then went to Thessalonica—and saw a typical response to the gospel: revival among the Greeks and rioting at the hands of the Jewish leaders. The ruckus pushed Paul and Silas to Berea. But before long, hostile Jews from Thessalonica attacked Paul's work in that city. This succeeded in getting the great evangelist to Athens.

At Mars Hill, Paul powerfully preached the gospel of the resurrected Christ by using concepts and terms the Athenian philosophers could easily grasp. Some scoffed at his message; others wanted to hear more. Moving on to Corinth, Paul met Priscilla and Aquila, a married couple who proved to be faithful gospel partners. After stops in Syria and Ephesus, he arrived back at the church at Jerusalem to report on his activity. This marked the end of his second missionary journey.

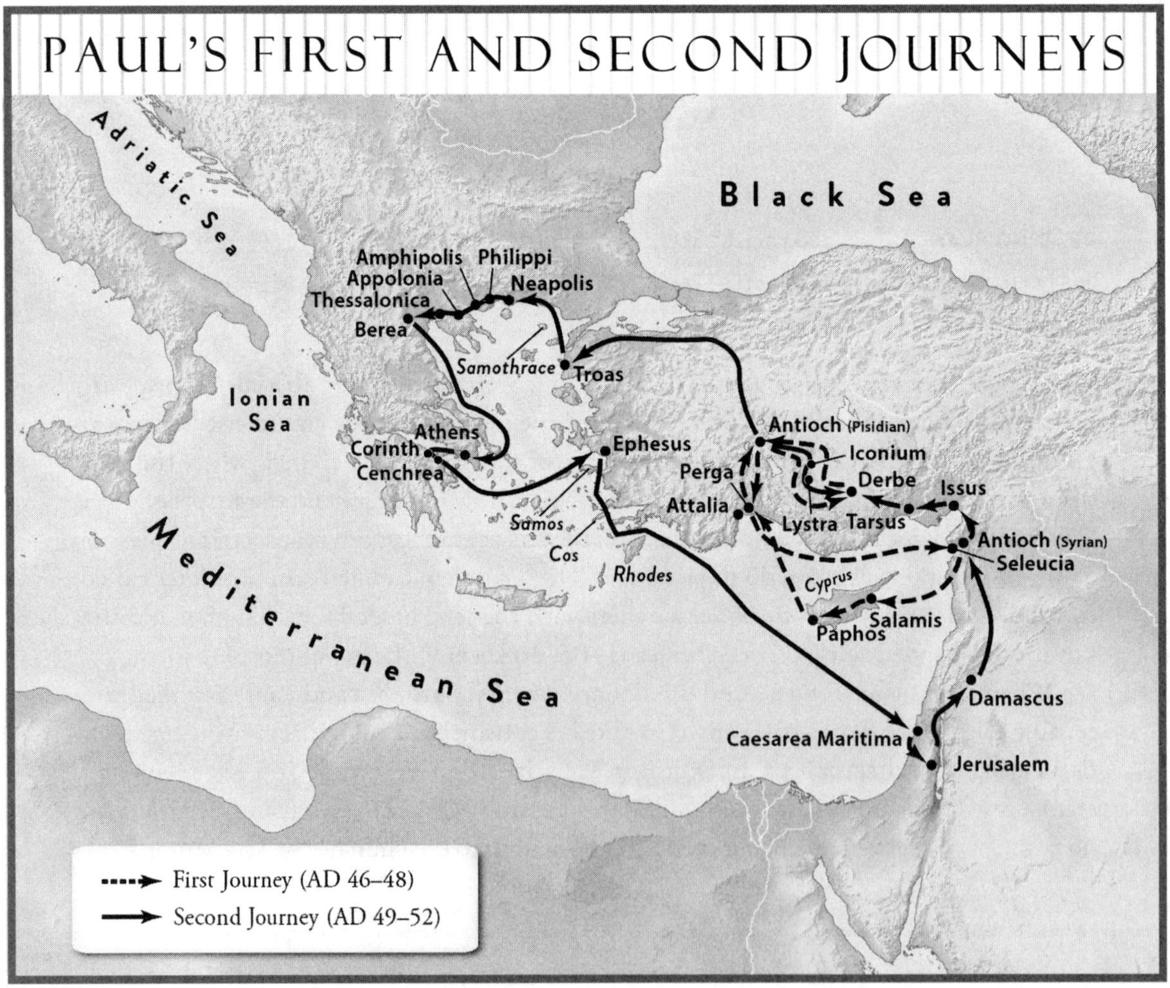

It is believed that Paul launched his third missionary trip in an attempt to undo the damage caused among the churches by opponents of the gospel. Beginning at Antioch, the great apostle journeyed through Galatia and Phrygia to Ephesus. His ministry there lasted more than two years until area tradesmen, who sold idols of the goddess Diana, instigated a riot, claiming the spread of Christianity was threatening their livelihood.

From Ephesus, Paul ventured into Achaia. In Athens, he was again divinely protected from a murderous Jewish plot. Arriving at Miletus, the apostle summoned the elders of the Ephesian church to bid them an emotional farewell. This scene revealed the presence of a well-trained group of disciples who would carry the message of Christ throughout Asia.

As Paul visited Tyre and Caesarea, prophecies were given that warned him of imprisonment if he continued to Jerusalem. Yet Paul determined to complete his mission even if it meant dying in the name of Christ. When he arrived at Jerusalem, he was welcomed by believers. However, due to the strong Jewish animosity toward him, James and the elders encouraged him to participate in a public Jewish ceremony of purification at the temple, hoping to quell the false rumors that Paul was undermining Mosaic Law.

This attempt to placate the enemies of the gospel proved to be an utter failure, with a group of Jews from Asia making false and highly inflammatory accusations against the apostle. Only the quick action of a detachment of Roman soldiers saved Paul from being beaten to death by an angry mob. Paul then addressed the crowd, presenting his credentials as a devout Jew trained under the highly respected rabbi Gamaliel. He even described his unlikely encounter with the risen Christ on the Damascus road. But when he mentioned Jesus' command to go to the Gentiles, the mob erupted in anger.

Paul, barely escaping a flogging, was brought before the Jewish high council. The atmosphere was highly charged, and the high priest ordered Paul slapped after he uttered the first sentence of his defense! Paul also underwent three trials. The first was before Felix, the Roman governor in Caesarea. The second was two years later before a new governor, Festus. At this point, Paul used his rights as a Roman citizen to request a hearing before Caesar. Paul's third trial was before Festus and King Agrippa, who was in Caesarea for a political visit. The two men became embroiled in a controversy over Paul's testimony, with Festus declaring, "Much learning is driving you mad!" (Acts 26:24), and Agrippa saying to him, "You almost persuade me to become a Christian" (verse 28). Although it was decided that Paul had done nothing to deserve death or chains, he and other prisoners were sent to Italy.

Bad weather on the Mediterranean Sea made for rough sailing. At the height of a storm, Paul gathered the ship's crew together and said that God had guaranteed him safe arrival in Rome and that everyone sailing with him would be protected from harm. The ship did run aground and break apart off the coast of Malta, but all 276 people on board swam safely to shore.

During Paul's three-month stay there, the forces of hell attempted to keep him from reaching Rome, yet he was showered with hospitality. Finally reaching Italy, Paul was warmly received by some believers and granted house arrest rather than imprisonment in a Roman penal facility. The binding effect of his appeal to be heard by Caesar had brought him to the capital city of the Roman Empire as a prisoner, where he awaited trial. Soon, Paul would begin ministering in the most influential city in the world.

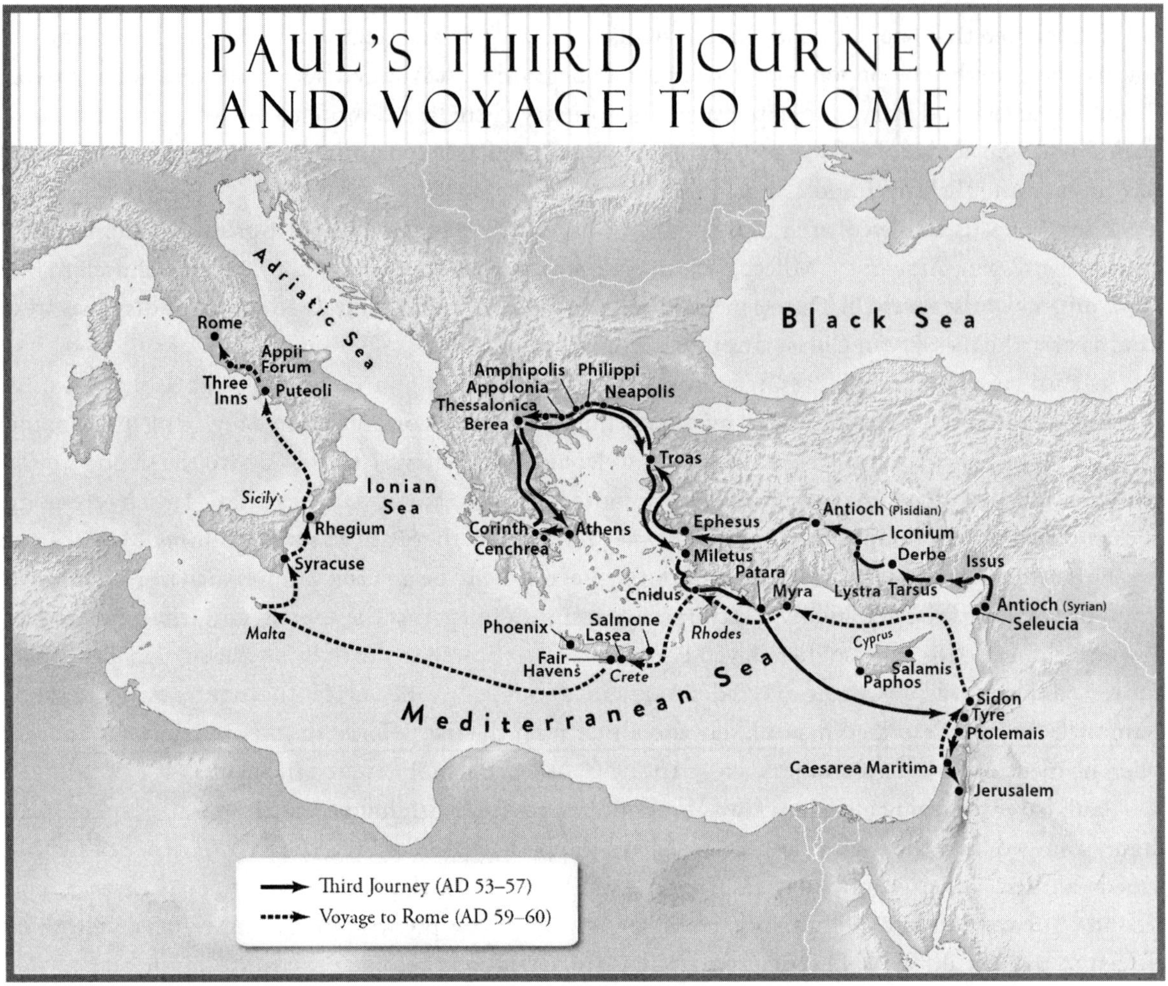

REFLECTIONS

Salvation comes through faith in Christ alone. Historians point to seven ecumenical councils in the church's early history, especially noting the Councils of Nicea (AD 325) and Chalcedon (AD 451). Yet the most important council was the first one—the Jerusalem Council—because it established the answer to the vital doctrinal question of *what a person must do to be saved*. The apostles and the elders defied efforts to impose legalism and ritualism as necessary prerequisites for salvation, with James—the leader of the Jerusalem church—saying, "I judge that we should not trouble those from among the Gentiles who are turning to God, but that we write to them to abstain from things polluted by idols, from sexual immorality, from things strangled, and from blood" (Acts 15:19–20). In this way, the apostles and elders forever affirmed that salvation is totally by grace through faith in Christ alone.

Conflict will occur when the gospel is preached. "The Jews who were not persuaded, becoming envious, took some of the evil men from the marketplace, and gathering a mob, set all the city in an uproar and attacked the house of Jason" (Acts 17:5). Conflict will often occur when the true gospel is preached. The gospel does not gather everyone together, nor is it a generally tolerable opinion that nonbelievers can take or leave. Instead, it splits people, dividing the penitent from the hard-hearted, the saved from the unsaved, the righteous from the reprobate, and those who love its truth from those who reject it.

Believers shake the world. The mob who assaulted Jason's home had this complaint against Paul and his coworkers: "These [men] have turned the world upside down" (Acts 17:6). Courage must be coupled with the proper content if believers are to shake the world in this way. To have the right message, but not the boldness to proclaim it, renders it useless. But to boldly proclaim error, as the cults do, causes even greater harm. Proclaiming the *truth* with boldness, as Paul did, cannot help but change the world.

We wield the sword of the Spirit. The weapon Christians are to wield in their battle with Satan is "the sword of the Spirit, which is the word of God" (Ephesians 6:17). Even the book of Acts, which records the apostles' evangelistic ministry, emphasizes the preaching of the Word over signs, wonders, miracles, and exorcisms. In fact, early in the book, the apostles defined the priorities of their ministry in the church: "We will give ourselves continually to prayer and to the ministry of the word" (Acts 6:4). As the apostle Paul would later write, "Woe is me if I do not preach the gospel!" (1 Corinthians 9:16).

God gives us opportunities to share the gospel. Near the end of the book of Acts, we read that Paul was in a dire situation when he returned to the city of Jerusalem. "All the city was disturbed; and the people ran together, seized Paul, and dragged him out of the temple; and immediately the doors were shut" (Acts 21:30). The crowd had not gathered to hear Paul preach but to beat and kill him right there on the spot. The apostle Paul, however, used this occasion to proclaim to the Jewish people how God's saving power had transformed his life. "Paul stood on the stairs and motioned with his hand to the people. And when there was a great silence, he spoke to them in the Hebrew language, saying, 'Brethren and fathers, hear my defense before you now'" (21:40–22:1). God gives us opportunities to share the message of salvation. The question is whether we will *act* when He does.

We are each called to do our part for Christ. The book of Acts ends with this line: "Paul dwelt two whole years in his own rented house, and received all who came to him, preaching the kingdom of God" (28:30–31). The church in Acts had been faithful in carrying out the charge that Jesus had given to them when He was departing from this world: "You shall be witnesses to Me in Jerusalem, and in all Judea and Samaria, and to the end of the earth" (1:8). The church has since passed down the baton over the centuries through many different hands to us today. As the apostle Peter wrote, "Always be ready to give a defense to everyone who asks you a reason for the hope that is in you" (1 Peter 3:15). Will the future generations that follow us find that we ran our segment of the race carefully?

STUDY QUESTIONS

1. What specific issue threatened to tear apart the early church? What did the first-century believers do to try and resolve this bitter debate (see Acts 15:1–6)?

2. What principles for resolving conflicts among believers do you find in the decisions made by the Jerusalem Council (see Acts 15:6–21)? Which of these can you use this week?

3. How did Paul and his team end up in Philippi, and what significant events happened there (see Acts 16:11–40)? What does this reveal about Paul's character?

4. What evidence suggests that the men Paul encountered in Acts 19:1–7 were not yet saved? What happened after Paul spoke with them about Christ?

5. What are some possible reasons as to why Luke included the story of Eutychus in his record (see Acts 20:7–12)? What do you learn from this incident?

6. What happened when Paul returned to Jerusalem and went to the temple to undergo ritual purification (see Acts 21:17–26)? Why did Paul feel the need to submit to this Jewish rite?

7. What subject caused an uproar during Paul's address to the Sanhedrin (see Acts 22:20–24)? What two factions in the Jewish council began bickering (see 23:6–10)?

8. In what ways was the voyage to Rome an ill-advised decision (see Acts 27:1–38)? How did Paul demonstrate the qualities of a leader during the harrowing voyage?

WEEK 39

BELIEVERS ARE JUSTIFIED BY FAITH

ROMANS 1–8

READING PLAN:	**267** | Romans 1–2	**268** | Romans 3	**269** | Romans 4
270 | Romans 5	**271** | Romans 6	**272** | Romans 7	**273** | Romans 8

As God's apostle to the Gentiles, it was Paul who led the church in spreading Christianity throughout the Roman Empire. He made three missionary journeys to much of the Mediterranean world, tirelessly preaching the gospel that he once had sought to destroy. Toward the close of his third missions trip, he wrote this letter to the Romans from Corinth.

Unlike Paul's letters to other churches, he was not writing the Romans to correct aberrant theology or rebuke ungodly living. This church—which was likely founded by some who were converted on the Day of Pentecost—was doctrinally sound. Yet, like all churches, these believers were in need of rich doctrinal and practical instruction.

As much as Paul longed to meet these Christians, he had thus far been prevented from visiting them. However, in God's providence, the apostle's inability to visit Rome gave the world this divinely inspired masterpiece of Christian doctrine that later became the New Testament book of Romans. The overarching theme of the book is the righteousness that comes from God. God justifies guilty and condemned sinners by grace alone—and through faith in Jesus alone. Paul first presents the theological truths of this theme and then details its practical outworking in the lives of individual believers and the life of the church.

The entire thrust of Paul's letter is distilled in its opening paragraphs. The bad news is that a destructive power has gripped human beings at the core of their being—*sin*. However, the good news of the gospel is that a righteous God makes sinners righteous through faith. In Christ, sin can be forgiven, selfishness can be overcome, guilt can be removed, and people can indeed have hope and eternal glory.

The wages of sin is DEATH, but the gift of God is ETERNAL LIFE in Christ Jesus.

ROMANS 6:23

Paul understood his readers could not fully understand the wonder of God's grace until they comprehended God's righteous anger against sin. So, in the first part of his letter, he expounds on the wretchedness of the human heart and the divine wrath elicited by this rebelliousness. He is determined for the believers to understand we are *all* sinners under God's wrath—and the consequences of sin are eternal. We are also without excuse, writes Paul, because God has made Himself evident to all people in the marvels of nature and in the human conscience. But instead of acknowledging and worshiping God in response to this revelation of Himself, fallen humanity has rejected Him and increased in sin.

As a result of humanity's God-less choice, the Lord gave them over to a depraved mind. A mind that finds God worthless becomes worthless itself. It is debauched, deceived, and deserving only of divine wrath. The final verdict, then, is that unredeemed humankind is guilty of all charges, with no grounds for acquittal. This is the verdict Paul proclaims: "All have sinned and fall short of the glory of God" (Romans 3:23). This divine indictment silences every mouth and quells every argument to the contrary. There can be no defense—humanity is incapable of saving themselves. There is only one way to be right with God, and it is not through works. Righteousness comes only by faith in response to God's grace.

This is where Paul reveals that "bad" news is necessarily part of the "good" news. Paul, having shown that God is a holy judge, now reveals the God of love who reaches out with open arms to lost, wayward, sinful people. Sinners are saved, Paul explains, by turning to God for the righteousness that He alone provides. God "justifies" (or declares repentant sinners righteous) solely on the merits of Christ's righteousness. Jesus' death on the cross has provided the way of salvation for everyone who comes to God in faith. Christ's perfect righteousness, which is the only standard God accepts, is now imputed to the believer's account. This act of Christ provides a pardon from the guilt and penalty of sin.

Paul, the consummate theologian, knew that after his readers heard this, they would have questions. *How complete or secure is this salvation in Christ? How can what one man did at one time in history have such an impact on humankind? If the old self is dead, why is there continually a struggle with sin?* So Paul sets out to demonstrate the practical ramifications of salvation for those who have been justified.

He declares that the gospel doesn't stop at the miracle of justification. It includes *sanctification*, the process by which God makes redeemed sinners holy, transforming them into the very likeness of Christ. Believers are able to live in obedience to God's Word through the power of His Spirit, whose work Paul now highlights. It is the Spirit who frees the redeemed from sin and death, changes their nature, empowers them to overcome the desires of their unredeemed flesh, confirms their adoption as God's children, and guarantees their eternal glory. There can be no success or progress in the Christian life apart from an utter dependence on the third Person of the Trinity.

Paul punctuates this part of his letter with profound teaching about the believer's absolute security. Not only are we saved by the blood of Christ and indwelt by the Spirit, but we are also safe in the Father's love. God, who graciously saved us from sin and death and began the process of transformation in us, will never let us go. Paul, also giving thought to the concerns of his Jewish readers, explains how the Old Testament law given to Moses relates to their faith in Christ. After discussing the purpose and the limitations of the law, which Paul knew well as a former Pharisee, he assures his fellow Jews (and everyone else) that they are no longer under the jurisdiction or penalties of this law but are under grace.

REFLECTIONS

We are *saved* by Christ. Paul writes, "I am not ashamed of the gospel of Christ, for it is the power of God to salvation for everyone who believes" (Romans 1:16). Some object to terms such as *salvation* and being *saved*, claiming the ideas they convey are out of date in modern society. But salvation is God's term, and there is no better one to describe what He offers fallen humanity through the sacrifice of His Son. Through Christ and Christ alone, we can be *saved* from sin, Satan, judgment, wrath, and spiritual death.

All humanity is guilty of sin. "All have sinned and fall short of the glory of God" (Romans 3:23). *All* means *all*—everyone except Christ, the only sinless human. Unredeemed humankind has no defense and is guilty of all charges. The defense must rest, as it were, before it can say anything, because the omniscient God has demonstrated the impossibility of any grounds for acquittal. Absolute silence is the only possible response, just as there will be utter silence in heaven when Jesus one day breaks the seventh seal and releases the seven trumpet judgments upon the condemned earth (see Revelation 8:1–6).

Jesus' act of redemption is permanent. Jesus broke the power of sin and death, but the converse is not true. Sin and death cannot break the power of Christ! The condemnation of Adam's sin is reversible; the redemption of Christ is not. The effect of Adam's act is permanent only if not nullified by Christ. The effect of Jesus' act, however, is permanent for believing individuals and not subject to reversal or nullification. We have the great assurance that once we are in Jesus Christ, we are in Him forever.

Jesus calls us to transformation. Christ is not looking for those who want to add Him to their lives as an insurance against hell, or want to apply His high moral principles, or want only to be outwardly reformed by having their old nature improved. Jesus calls those who desire *an entirely new nature* created in His own holy likeness. He calls those who are willing to die with Him in order to be raised with Him. When we come to Him on His terms, He changes our destiny from eternal death to eternal life.

STUDY QUESTIONS

1. What does Paul reveal in the opening chapter of Romans about the *promise* of the good news and the *Person* of the good news (see Romans 1:1–7)?

2. Why does Paul argue that when it comes to a person's standing before God, no one has the right to boast or be filled with religious pride (see Romans 3:9–20)?

3. How does Paul refute the idea that we receive salvation by faith but must preserve it through good works? What evidence does he give that salvation is unconditional (see Romans 5:1–11)?

4. How would you summarize Paul's response to the idea that believers in Christ can continue to live as they did when they were unbelievers (see Romans 6:1–23)?

5. What illustration does Paul use to explain the manner in which believers are dead to the law (see Romans 7:1–6)? What stands out to you from this illustration?

6. In what areas are you frustrated by your sinful inclinations? Based on Romans 7:13–25, how effective is legalism in fighting against the inclinations of the flesh?

7. According to Paul's statements in Romans 8:1–17, what acts or ministries does the Holy Spirit perform in us, through us, and for us?

8. What does Paul mean by the references to "groaning" in Romans 8:18–25? What more do you learn in this passage about the Holy Spirit?

WEEK 40

BELIEVERS WALK IN RIGHTEOUSNESS

ROMANS 9–16

READING PLAN:	**274** | Romans 9	**275** | Romans 10	**276** | Romans 11
277 | Romans 12	**278** | Romans 13	**279** | Romans 14	**280** | Romans 15–16

Up to this point, Paul's letter to the church in Rome has been filled with essential doctrine for Jews and Gentiles alike. He is halfway through this letter, and already he has covered such universally applicable topics such as God's wrath against sinful humankind, the universality of sin, the security of salvation, and the process of sanctification, in addition to a remarkable exposition and defense of the doctrine of justification.

Now, this Jewish apostle to the Gentiles needs to clarify some important truths regarding Israel as well as contradict some prevailing falsehoods that many of the early Jewish believers accepted as truth. First, Paul addresses the question of whether, in light of Christ's offer of salvation to all Gentiles, the Jews have been forsaken by God as a people. Did they still have a unique place or purpose in God's plan of redemption?

Paul notes that Israel's sin had abrogated the Mosaic Covenant—the covenant of law given through Moses at Sinai—but had been replaced by the *new* covenant in Christ. This new covenant was eternal and unilateral, meaning that God's promise to accomplish something was based on His character and not on the response or actions of the beneficiary. Paul, with profound wisdom, demonstrates that while not all physical descendants of Abraham are true heirs of God's covenant with Abraham, Israel still has a future in God's plan. Those who come to God in repentance and faith are His children, His chosen people, the true spiritual seed of Abraham: "Brethren, my heart's desire and prayer to God for Israel is that they may be saved" (Romans 10:1). The sovereign God will be faithful to keep His promises to those of Israel who accept the sacrifice of His Son.

After penning pages of rich theological truth, Paul spends the rest of his letter explaining how these doctrines should look in a believer's daily life. For him, theology can never be divorced from life. It always has practical implications. So, he urges the Romans to faithfully walk in righteousness. The apostle's description here is nothing short of supernatural living! When we give ourselves fully to God as living sacrifices, then we, in the power of the Spirit, live out what is true of us theologically in Christ—and the result is staggering. We are transformed, not conformed; generous, not stingy; loving, not hypocritical and hateful; others-centered, not self-absorbed; forgiving, not vengeful.

Supernatural living and spiritual service go hand in hand. One of the ways the Spirit equips Christians for greater service is through spiritual gifting. A spiritual gift can be defined as a divine enablement for ministry that the Holy Spirit freely imparts to every believer. Such gifts cannot be earned, pursued, or worked up. They are merely received through the grace of God. Paul presents some of the categories of spiritual gifts here—"prophecy . . . ministry . . . teaching . . . exhortation . . . liberality [giving]" (Romans 12:6–8), in addition to leading and showing mercy. Each believer has at least one gift, or often a combination of gifts uniquely blended together. Spiritual gifts are not for the exaltation of the one with the gift but are to be used in loving concern for the benefit of others in the church.

What Paul reveals is that the miracle of salvation impacts every relationship of the believer—both in the church and the world. Our initial response to salvation should be to fully present our bodies as living, holy sacrifices acceptable to God. Paul's next concern is having right relationships in the church with brothers and sisters in Christ, and even with enemies. Paul then focuses on the need for right relationships in the world. First, we show respect for governing authorities; and second, we love our neighbors and live holy lives that will stand out against the dark backdrop of a world without God.

Paul then returns to the topic of the power of sin—only this time he forewarns the believers of sin's power to destroy the spiritual and moral character of a church. Blatant sin is not the only danger to a church's spiritual health and unity. Satan often works to create division between Christians over matters of personal preference and historic tradition. These are neither commanded nor forbidden in Scripture, yet when imposed on others, the attitudes and behaviors that accompany such matters inevitably cause confusion, strife, and ill will. Across church history, these differences have crippled the work, the witness, and the unity of countless congregations, destroying fellowship and fruitfulness.

In the church at Rome, the believers' unity was threatened when mature (strong) believers conflicted with immature (weak) believers. The strong Jewish believers understood their freedom in Christ and realized the requirements of the Mosaic Law were no longer binding. The mature Gentiles understood that idols were not gods and, therefore, they could eat meat that had been offered to idols. But in both cases, the consciences of their weaker brothers and sisters were troubled. These weaker believers were tempted to violate their consciences, become more legalistic under feelings of guilt, or even to sin. Knowing the mature Jews and Gentiles would be able to understand these struggles, Paul addresses most of his comments to them before concluding his letter.

Because Paul had spoken so forcefully on so many issues to a church he had never visited, he wanted to make sure, in his closing comments, that he did not seem insensitive or unloving. He commends the Romans for their involvement in the work of the gospel, shares information about his ministry and future plans, and then reiterates his heart's desire to minister in Rome and to fellowship with the church there.

Paul ends the letter by mentioning more than two dozen friends and coworkers, giving us a rare glimpse into his own relationships and gratitude for those who had been such a help and encouragement to him in life and ministry. As the faces of these redeemed and transformed Jews and Gentiles flash through Paul's mind, he closes his epistle with a hymn of praise: "Now to Him who is able to establish you according to my gospel and the preaching of Jesus Christ . . . to God, alone wise, be glory through Jesus Christ forever. Amen" (Romans 16:25, 27).

> We then who are STRONG ought to bear with the scruples of the WEAK, and not to please ourselves.
>
> ROMANS 15:1

REFLECTIONS

We are to obey governing authorities. Paul writes, "Let every soul be subject to the governing authorities. For there is no authority except from God, and the authorities that exist are appointed by God" (Romans 13:1). Believers are to be model citizens—law-abiding rather than rabble-rousing, obedient rather than rebellious, respectful of government rather than demeaning of it. We must speak against sin, injustice, and immorality with fearful dedication, but we must do so within the framework of civil law and with respect for civil authorities. We are to be a godly society, doing good and living peaceably within an ungodly society, manifesting our transformed lives so the saving power of God is seen clearly.

We are an example of Jesus to the world. To accept one another as Christ accepted us is a sure mark of godliness. Failure to accept one another in love is an affront to the Savior who brought us into God's kingdom. A congregation that is divisive, quarrelsome, contentious, and judgmental gives the world reason to ridicule Christ's church and to reject the One who is their only hope of salvation.

God deserves the credit for what He accomplishes through us. The people God uses to accomplish His will are His instruments, so we should never take personal credit for what God does through us. Just as no brush takes the credit for a masterpiece it was used to paint, no Christian should deny or belittle what God does through him or her—for to do so is to deny and belittle God's own work.

STUDY QUESTIONS

1. What main characters and events in Israel's history does Paul mention in Romans 9:6–29? How does Paul argue that Israel's unbelief is consistent with God's plan?

2. What agricultural imagery does Paul use in Romans 11:16–24 to demonstrate that God's setting aside of Israel is not a permanent condition?

3. Paul calls believers in Christ to give themselves fully and completely—body, mind, and will—to God (see Romans 12:1–2). According to Paul, what is involved in doing this?

4. Paul outlines some of the spiritual gifts in Romans 12:3–8. What do you think your spiritual gifts are? How are you using these God-given abilities to serve the body of Christ?

5. How does Paul use some of the Ten Commandments in Romans 13:8–10 to demonstrate that love is the fulfillment of the law? What does Paul say about love?

6. Based on Romans 14:1–13, what was the situation in the church in Rome? Why do you think there was so much judging of each other?

7. In areas where the Scripture neither prescribes nor prohibits behavior, what counsel does Paul give for determining a course of action (see Romans 15:1–6)?

8. Review the names Paul mentions in Romans 16:1–16. What insights into the work of the first-century church can you glean from Paul's personal greetings?

WEEK 41

BELIEVERS ARE UNITED IN FAITH

1 CORINTHIANS 1–11

READING PLAN: **281** | 1 Corinthians 1–2 **282** | 1 Corinthians 3–4 **283** | 1 Corinthians 5 **284** | 1 Corinthians 6–7 **285** | 1 Corinthians 8 **286** | 1 Corinthians 9–10 **287** | 1 Corinthians 11

Paul's association with the important commercial city of Corinth began during his second missionary journey, when he spent eighteen months ministering in the city. After leaving Corinth, he heard of immorality in the Corinthian church and wrote a letter (which has since been lost) to confront the congregation's sin. During his ministry in Ephesus, he then received further reports of trouble and divisions in the Corinthian church.

The Corinthians had written to Paul as well, asking for clarification of some issues. Paul planned on remaining at Ephesus a little longer and then wintering in Corinth, so he responded by writing the letter we know as 1 Corinthians. He sent the letter with Timothy, his coworker in the faith, anticipating his own departure for Corinth as he wrote.

Even by the pagan standards of its own culture, Corinth was known for its debauchery and depravity. The city's most prominent edifice was a temple dedicated to Aphrodite, the Greek goddess of love, that housed about 1,000 priestesses who were "religious" prostitutes. Within his letter, Paul lists some of the specific sins for which the city was noted. Tragically, some of the worst sins were still found among the church members. Such worldliness was the most serious problem of the Corinthian church. Most of the believers could not consistently divorce themselves from their old pagan ways. So it became necessary for Paul to write to correct this as well as to command the faithful Christians to break fellowship with unrepentant members and put them out of the church.

At the outset of this letter, Paul wanted to establish that what he had to say was said with God's authority. Given that his message was so corrective, this was of great necessity. One of the qualifications of an apostle was witnessing the risen Christ. Paul explained to the Corinthian church that he had witnessed the resurrected Christ in a unique way. He also lovingly reminded them that they belonged to God and to each other in a far-reaching fellowship. He summarized their position and their blessings as believers in Jesus Christ, as children of God, and as saints (or "set apart ones"). In so many words, Paul was saying, "Look at who you are! Look at what you have!" Only then did he say, "Now I plead with you, brethren, by the name of our Lord Jesus Christ . . ." (1 Corinthians 1:10).

The Corinthian believers had fallen short in many ways, but the first thing for which Paul called them to task was quarreling. Before Jesus' crucifixion, He had prayed that His church would be one (see John 17:20–23). Immediately after Pentecost, the newly empowered believers were in harmony with each

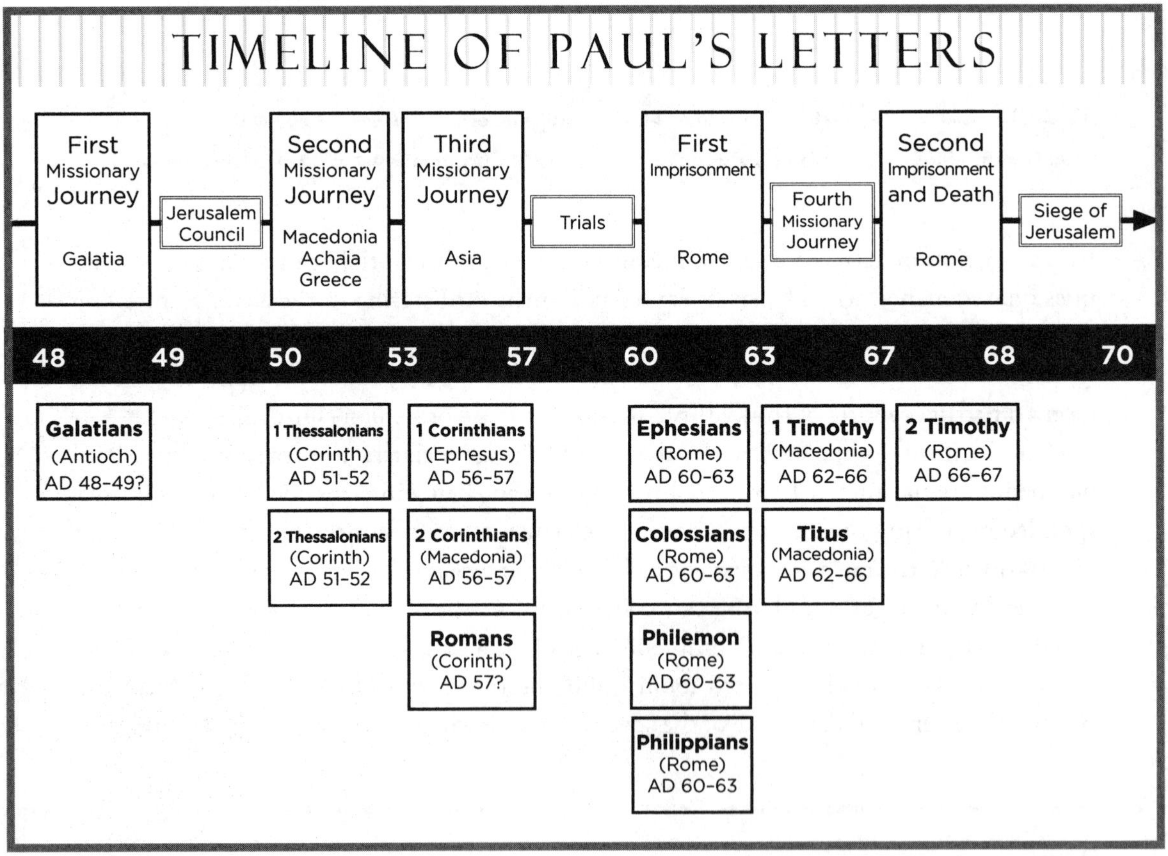

other—sharing, rejoicing, worshiping, and witnessing together (see Acts 4:32–35). Their unity bore great fruit in their ministry to each other and in their witness to the world.

The Corinthian church needed that sort of harmony. These immature believers, enamored by high-profile Christian personalities, had established cliques loyal to those who had ministered to them—such as Apollos, Peter (Cephas), and even Paul. Still another group pledged allegiance to Christ alone. Paul made a plea for repenting of their factions, for doctrinal agreement, and for remembering the great priority of the church: *preaching the gospel.* Paul also took the opportunity to focus on the true nature and practice of godly servant-leaders . . . a leadership style embodied by Christ and modeled in His willingness to lay down His life for His followers. Christian ministers, wrote Paul, are to be stewards (or managers) of the mysteries of God, caring spiritual fathers, and, above all else, servants of Christ.

> GOD has chosen the FOOLISH things of the world to put to SHAME the wise.
>
> 1 CORINTHIANS 1:27

Paul then forged ahead to address sexual sin in the church. As serious as this immorality was in itself, the church's tolerance of it was even worse. Not only did Paul command that persistently sinning church members be disciplined, but he also presented the method, the reason, and the sphere of that discipline. He discussed two other sinful carryovers from before the Corinthians were saved: their tendency toward litigation and marriage problems.

Much of the marital difficulty in the church reflected the pagan culture from which they had not fully separated. In Greek and Roman societies, most women were little more than slaves, the possessions of their husbands, who often virtually bought and traded their wives at will. In many Jewish communities, the woman's situation was not much better. Divorce had become easy and commonplace and was almost always the man's prerogative. Paul gave counsel for Christian marriages as well as believers married to unbelievers, calling for lifetime commitment. Paul also taught on the subject of singleness, maintaining that celibacy is good and a gift from God—thought not superior to marriage.

Paul also touched on the roles of women in the church. The Corinthians had asked about women's submission and head coverings. Paul responded there was nothing inherently spiritual about wearing a covering. He further clarified that in Christ, male and female believers are equal in the world, in the church, and before God. Their roles in His work are different in function but not in importance.

A gray area of Christian living for these believers was the questionable practice of eating food that had been offered to idols. After conversion, many believers resented eating food bought out of idol markets because it reminded them (and sensitive Gentile believers) of their previous pagan lives. So Paul offered highly practical answers on principles for Christian liberty, what Christian liberty means, and when believers should voluntarily limit their freedom for the sake of "weaker" believers.

In further discussions of how the Corinthians should relate to one other, Paul called them away from gluttonous revelry around their special fellowship meals. He called them to unity and purity in their preparation for and observance of the Lord's Supper, reminding them, "For as often as you eat this bread and drink this cup, you proclaim the Lord's death till He comes" (1 Corinthians 11:26).

REFLECTIONS

We must remember our position before God. Paul writes that the believers in Corinth were "sanctified in Christ Jesus, called to be saints, with all who . . . call on the name of Jesus Christ our Lord" (1 Corinthians 1:2). He also writes, "God is faithful, by whom you were called into the fellowship of His Son, Jesus Christ" (verse 9). As Christians, one of the strongest rebukes we can have when we sin is to be reminded of who our Father is. And reminding ourselves of whose we are should be one of our strongest deterrents to sin. Remembering our position can compel us to improve our practice.

The Bible is the supreme authority. Paul states, "I plead with you, brethren, by the name of our Lord Jesus Christ, that you all speak the same thing, and that there be no divisions among you" (1 Corinthians 1:10). When the Word of God is not the supreme authority, division is inevitable. Such happens even in churches today, when pastors and other leaders begin substituting their ideas for the truths of Scripture. The substitution is seldom intentional, but it will always happen when the Bible is neglected. A Bible that is not studied carefully cannot be followed carefully. And where it is not followed there will be division, because there will be no common ground for beliefs. When the truth of Scripture is not the sole authority, men's varied opinions become the authority.

Ministers must serve the Lord rightly. Christian ministers are called to serve their congregations in Christ's name, but they cannot serve others rightly unless they serve their Lord rightly. And they cannot serve Him rightly unless they see themselves rightly: not "puffed up" (1 Corinthians 4:18) but as His servants. Ministers who become so occupied with counseling and helping their congregation that they spend little time in the Word of God are unable to meet those people's deepest needs because they have neglected their greatest resource for correctly knowing and adequately meeting those needs. This usually leads to compromising God's truth for the sake of peoples' desires. Before all else, ministers must be servants of Jesus Christ—"serving the Lord with all humility" (Acts 20:19). Then, and only then, can they best serve other people.

WASHED, SANCTIFIED, JUSTIFIED
(1 CORINTHIANS 6:11)

Washed: This refers to new life through spiritual cleansing and regeneration.

Sanctified: Results in new behavior brought about by a transformed life. Sin's dominion is broken and replaced by a new pattern of holiness.

Justified: Refers to a new standing before God. In Jesus' death, believers' sins were put to His account so that His righteousness could be put to theirs.

We are to stay out of patterns of sin. Paul, referring to a member of the Corinthian church who "has his father's wife," instructs the congregation to "purge out the old leaven" and remove him from their fellowship (1 Corinthians 5:1, 7). It is not that everyone in the church must be perfect, for that is impossible. Everyone falls into sin and has shortcomings. The church is in some ways a hospital for those who know they are sick. They have trusted in Christ as Savior and want to follow Him as Lord—to be what God wants them to be. No, it is not the ones who recognize their sin and hunger for righteousness who are to be put out of fellowship but those who *persistently* and *unrepentantly* continue in a pattern of sin about which they have been counseled and warned. We should continue to love them and pray for them, so that they repent and return to a pure life. And if they do repent we are to gladly and joyfully "forgive and comfort" them and welcome them back into fellowship (2 Corinthians 2:7).

Spirituality is not determined by marital status. In 1 Corinthians 7:1–40, Paul instructs the Corinthians on matters related to singleness and marriage. Marriage was instituted by God and is the norm for man-woman relationships (see Matthew 19:5–6), and it is a great blessing to humankind. But it is not required for believers or for anyone else. Paul's point is that if you are single that is good—and if you are married or get married, stay married and retain normal marital relations, for that is of God.

Obedience to God honors God. God is dishonored when anyone sins, but He is especially dishonored when His own people sin. Because the Lord has specially honored us by bestowing on us His forgiving grace, we especially dishonor Him by our sin. When in justice He is forced to chastise us, He is further dishonored by unbelievers who accuse—as did the nations around Israel and Judah—that He does not even take care of His own people. Sin of any sort takes glory from God. In the same way, God is honored when His people are faithful and obedient. Just as our sin reflects against His honor, so our obedience reflects to His honor. When we forsake sin, we glorify our heavenly Father. And when we use our Christian liberty for His sake and for the sake of His other children, we glorify Him still more.

CHRISTIAN LIBERTY (1 CORINTHIANS 8:1–13)

The Greeks and Romans believed that evil spirits could invade humans by attaching themselves to food before it was eaten and that they could only be removed by the food's being sacrificed to a god. The sacrifice was meant not only to gain favor with the god but also to cleanse the meat from demonic contamination. Paul and mature believers knew better than to be bothered by such food offered to idols and sold in the marketplace. They knew the deities didn't exist and that evil spirits did not contaminate the food. However, some of the newer converts still imagined that idols were real and their consciences were accusing them strongly with regard to eating food that had been offered to them. Paul understood these believers could fall back into old sins by getting involved in food offered to idols, so he cautioned the mature believers to "beware lest somehow this liberty of yours become a stumbling block to those who are weak" (1 Corinthians 8:9). Paul then gave them a warning: "When you thus sin against the brethren, and wound their weak conscience, you sin against Christ" (verse 12).

STUDY QUESTIONS

1. What are some of the specific things in the lives of the Corinthians for which Paul thanked the Lord? In what ways had the Corinthians been enriched by Christ (see 1 Corinthians 1:4–9)?

2. What specific situation in 1 Corinthians 1:10–17 had created disharmony in the Corinthian church? How did Paul exhort the congregation to pursue unity?

3. What was the centerpiece of Paul's message to the believers according to his words in 1 Corinthians 2:1–5? How would this message apply to a church today?

4. How did Paul describe his life as an apostle (see 1 Corinthians 4:1–13)? Why do you think he talked about these things? What does it reveal about his heart?

5. What immoral situation did the Corinthians allow—and why (see 1 Corinthians 5:1–13)? What apostolic command does Paul give to the church regarding this sinning brother?

6. What broad truths about marriage and divorce does Paul teach in 1 Corinthians 7:1–40? What does the apostle say about celibacy?

7. What counsel does Paul give the believers regarding food sacrificed to idols (see 1 Corinthians 8:4–13)? When should a Christian voluntarily limit his or her liberty?

8. How does Jesus' willing submission to the Father serve as an example of how it is never demeaning to live out our God-appointed roles (see 1 Corinthians 11:1–12)?

WEEK 42

BELIEVERS SERVE ONE ANOTHER

1 CORINTHIANS 12–2 CORINTHIANS 6

READING PLAN: **288** | 1 Corinthians 12–13 **289** | 1 Corinthians 14 **290** | 1 Corinthians 15–16 **291** | 2 Corinthians 1 **292** | 2 Corinthians 2–3 **293** | 2 Corinthians 4–5 **294** | 2 Corinthians 6

The misunderstanding, misuse, and counterfeiting of spiritual gifts was an issue seriously affecting the church at Corinth. Some of these believers recognized the problem and wrote to Paul. So, in 1 Corinthians 12–14, the apostle answers their questions, providing practical guidance on the purpose, assignment, discernment, and use of these gifts.

Paul helped his readers distinguish God-given, Spirit-controlled, Christ-glorifying gifts (intended for serving one another in the building up of the church) from the mystical experiences called *ecstasy* and *enthusiasm* found in the pagan religions of Corinth. Paul also wrote about the root cause of the Corinthians' immature abuse of spiritual gifts: their failure to love. In what we know as the "love chapter" of the Bible (1 Corinthians 13), Paul set forth the proper attitude and atmosphere for the exercise of spiritual gifts in the church.

The Corinthians were also confused about the bodily resurrection of believers. Paul laid the foundation that one day they would be raised with Christ to eternal life by reviewing the evidence for Jesus' physical resurrection and showing the implications of denying it: "But if there is no resurrection of the dead, then Christ is not risen. And if Christ is not risen, then our preaching is empty and your faith is also empty" (1 Corinthians 15:13–14). He then discusses the question of how a general resurrection could be possible and how "we shall all be changed" (verse 51).

Paul's closing "victory song" in 1 Corinthians 15 has been put to music in such masterpieces as Handel's "Messiah" and Brahms's "Requiem." Praising God in anticipation of resurrection, Paul proclaims the great transformation, triumph, and thanksgiving that the raising of God's saints will bring. He finishes with an exhortation for holy living in the present until that day comes through the stewardship of giving, doing the Lord's work the Lord's way, and love within the Christian fellowship.

However, this would not be Paul's final word to these believers. Not long after writing the letter of 1 Corinthians, he was informed of more difficulties in Corinth: a group of self-appointed apostles had infiltrated the church, intent on ruining Paul's ministry so they could step in and control the people with their wrong ideas. In order to create their platform, they had convinced the Corinthian believers to turn from Paul—and Paul's reputation took a severe beating.

The apostle responded by going to Corinth. This so-called "painful visit" was not successful from Paul's perspective. Someone in the Corinthian church (possibly one of the false apostles) even openly insulted him. A saddened Paul then returned to Ephesus and wrote a harsh follow-up to 1 Corinthians (known as the "severe" letter) that is not in the Bible and sent it with Titus to Corinth.

To Paul's relief, the majority of the Corinthians who heard that letter repented of their rebellion against him. The apostle, wise enough to know that some rebellious attitudes still smoldered, then wrote the letter that we call 2 Corinthians. His main concerns were to defend his apostleship, to exhort the Corinthians to resume preparations for the collection for the poor at Jerusalem, and to again confront head-on the false teachers that had opposed him and the gospel of Christ that he preached.

Paul opens by identifying himself as an apostle of Jesus Christ by the will of God and by defending himself against the charge that his trials were God's punishment for his sin. The apostle's life was indeed an amazing juxtaposition of affliction and comfort. Yet Paul makes the point that God has been comforting him in his suffering, not chastening him. As he explained to the believers, "For as the sufferings of Christ abound in us, so our consolation also abounds through Christ" (2 Corinthians 1:5).

Next, Paul defends his integrity and replies to the specific charge that he was dishonest, unfaithful, and fickle for having changed his travel plans. Rather than engage in a battle of "he said / they said," Paul elevates the entire discussion to the motives and attitudes of his heart. By this, he provides a priceless look at a noble man of God—even urging the Corinthian believers to forgive someone who had evidently assaulted him (verbally and publicly) during the apostle's "painful visit."

Paul does admit his discouragement over the Corinthians' suspicions toward him, but he also declares the encouragement he has found in Christ. Turning his thoughts and his pen toward the permanence of the new covenant, he rejoices in the relationship believers can have with God because of the complete salvation brought by Christ. As he writes, "Therefore we do not lose heart. Even though our outward man is perishing, yet the inward man is being renewed day by day" (2 Corinthians 4:16). The false teachers had charged him with being weak and imperfect in his ministry. Instead of denying those charges, he embraced them and focused all the more on the glory of Christ, declaring that the priceless truth of the gospel can flourish and shine only in humble containers.

Paul's consuming passion in life was to please the Lord. His activities were motivated not by the fear of death (he actually longed for heaven!) but by the sobering reality of the judgment seat of Christ, where every believer's earthly deeds will be judged and their good works rewarded. The tireless apostle shares that he would gladly suffer in this world if it means gaining a reward in the world to come.

In the tension between genuine faith and unbelief we find in this letter, Paul speaks of a triumphant kind of patience that bears up under hard labor and remains hopeful—despite persecution, accusations, or even death—in anticipation of future glory. God has reconciled with repentant sinners, offering friendship to them through the cross of Christ. Furthermore, discussing the realities of ministry, he states his heart is joyful because many of the Corinthians had believed the gospel. Yet the congregation also contained imposters, masquerading as Christians, who caused Paul much heartache.

Another preposterous allegation was that Paul had no affection for the Corinthians and was abusive, manipulative, and dictatorial. What could God's servant do other than remind the believers of his love for them? On the basis of his track record of unconditional love, Paul exhorted the Corinthians to open their hearts to him and to separate themselves from intimate association with unbelievers.

REFLECTIONS

The resurrection is our hope. The coming resurrection is the hope of the church and all believers. Whatever happens to our present bodies—whether they are healthy or unhealthy, beautiful or plain, short-lived or long-lived—they are not our permanent bodies, and we should not hold them too dearly. Our blessed hope and assurance is that these created natural bodies one day will be recreated as spiritual bodies. "The body is sown in corruption, it is raised in incorruption" (1 Corinthians 15:42).

We look to Christ in times of trial. How do believers find triumph in the midst of troubles? By gazing at the glory of God revealed in Jesus Christ in the mirror of Scripture. Nowhere is God's glory more clearly manifest than in the Person of His Son. Therefore, the only way to successfully live the Christian life is by "beholding . . . the glory of the Lord" (2 Corinthians 3:18) and by "looking unto Jesus, the author and finisher of our faith, who for the joy that was set before Him endured the cross" (Hebrews 12:2).

We cling to Christ in times of trial. Some people come to church, profess Christ, and even get baptized. Yet when trouble comes, they leave—and never come back. Maybe they encountered a broken relationship, the death of a loved one, or some other struggle, and the circumstances were so overpowering they blamed God and walked away, convinced that Christianity doesn't work. As believers, we may experience times of struggle and doubt, but our faith will never be destroyed. We cling to the Lord despite our trials because we love Him. That kind of loving perseverance results in true blessing.

STUDY QUESTIONS

1. According to Paul's teaching in 1 Corinthians 12:1–11, what is the source and purpose of spiritual gifts? Does this teaching still apply today? Why or why not?

2. How does Paul's analogy of the body demonstrate both the unity and diversity of gifts and abilities within the church (see 1 Corinthians 12:12–31)?

3. According to Paul, if Jesus had never risen from the dead, what would be the consequences for believers (see 1 Corinthians 15:13–19)?

4. How does the truth of the resurrection provide an incentive for both service and sanctification of believers (see 1 Corinthians 15:30–34)?

5. What amount of money does Paul stipulate believers must give (see 1 Corinthians 16:1–4)? How does this compare with Old Testament requirements under the law (see Leviticus 27:30–33)?

6. What are the dire circumstances to which Paul alludes in 2 Corinthians 1:8–11? What phrases does Paul use to describe this situation?

7. Paul uses imagery about a "triumph" in 2 Corinthians 2:12–17 that would have been understood by people in the Roman Empire. What does he say we have received in Christ?

8. What does the term "workers together with Him" (or "God's fellow workers") suggest (see 2 Corinthians 6:1–10)? How does Paul describe his life as a servant of God?

WEEK 43

BELIEVERS ARE FREED FROM THE LAW

2 CORINTHIANS 7–GALATIANS 6

READING PLAN: **295** | 2 Corinthians 7 **296** | 2 Corinthians 8–9 **297** | 2 Corinthians 10–11 **298** | 2 Corinthians 12–13 **299** | Galatians 1–2 **300** | Galatians 3–4 **301** | Galatians 5–6

Despite their blind spots and failings, Paul loved the Corinthian church deeply. This is seen in the apostle's expressions of joy and relief at their repentance after they received the letter carried by Titus: "Now I rejoice, not that you were made sorry, but that your sorrow led to repentance" (2 Corinthians 7:9). Next, Paul takes the opportunity to exhort them to excel in giving, with details on when, how, and why Christians should give.

Paul's desire in this was to motivate the believers to complete a collection for the needy believers in the Jerusalem church. In discussing the patterns of giving, Paul cited the generosity of the Macedonians, followed by the ultimate example of sacrifice, Jesus Christ. He assures them that the spiritual law of "sowing and reaping" furthers the kingdom of God and that, when done in the right spirit, giving is the path to true prosperity and joy.

Following this, in 2 Corinthians 10–13, there is a shift in tone. Paul now directly takes on the false apostles who have remained in the church and their unrepentant followers. In light of the Corinthian church's gullibility, Paul employs the forceful language of warfare to remind these Christians that the spiritual war they are in requires weapons from the heavenly arsenal. He also challenges the false apostles by reluctantly comparing himself to them.

Although Paul found defending himself to be distasteful, the issues facing the Corinthians were so critical that he could not permit these wolves in sheep's clothing to undermine his teaching of the gospel. So he conducts a short course for the Corinthians in how to distinguish a true messenger of God from a false one. In the process, he reveals the heavenly vision he had received and his sufferings for the gospel—demonstrating that, unlike the false apostles, he possesses genuine qualifications.

Paul, to further differentiate himself, contrasts his correct view of ministry with the faulty view of these opponents. He tells the Corinthians they will be able to distinguish true men of God by qualities such as faithfulness, sacrifice, honesty, and a desire to build others up rather than tear them down. In closing, he lays out a pattern of what it means to mature in Christ. His words form a wonderful discussion of the essential elements of spiritual growth.

The inclusion of 2 Corinthians in the New Testament canon suggests the Corinthians responded favorably. This letter, in which Paul poured out his heart, achieved its goal of reconciling this church to him. Paul's next letter, Galatians, was also written in response to an assault on the church by false apostles. These wolves were preying on the flock, so Paul also wrote to these churches he had helped establish in and around Galatia (modern-day Turkey) on his first missionary journey.

As recorded in the book of Acts, the early church began with converts from Jewish backgrounds steeped in Hebrew traditions and practices. However, large numbers of Gentiles also began embracing Jesus as the Messiah, most as a direct result of Paul's missionary journeys. Sadly, these Gentile churches were often targeted by Jewish legalists (called Judaizers) who, in essence, urged believers to embrace the tenets of Judaism—especially the rite of circumcision and a fanatical devotion to keeping the law of Moses. They also savagely attacked Paul's credibility as an apostle of Christ.

In the Galatian churches, the strategy seems to have worked. Many Galatian believers began to question Paul's authority, legitimacy, and motives. They also began to doubt his message. The result was confusion among the congregations and, ultimately, an angry apostle who once again had to defend his apostleship. Paul's consternation over their defection from the gospel of grace is evident from the sharpness of his words: "O foolish Galatians! Who has bewitched you?" (Galatians 3:1).

Paul's concern in this was not his own popularity but the integrity of the true gospel. So, he explains that he has been appointed by God and offers valuable information about his background—even recounting the details of his most significant trip to Jerusalem after his conversion. It was all to prove the message he proclaimed was identical to that of the other twelve apostles.

The eternal and theological implications of the Judaizers' teachings were grave, so the apostle went even further, communicating the distinctions between law and grace. In the Mosaic rituals and standards, the Galatian believers were drifting toward an impotent substitute. They had not lost their salvation, but they had lost its joy in their return to the bondage of a self-imposed legalism. Paul, drawing on Abraham and assorted Old Testament passages, reminds the Galatians that salvation has never come any other way than by grace through faith, wholly apart from human merit or work.

In the next portion, Paul does not so much preach to the Galatians as pour out his heart. Continuing to contrast grace and law, faith and works, he compares the two sons of Abraham, Ishmael and Isaac. Ishmael was the way of legalism, symbolizing those Jews who were only naturally birthed and trusted in their own works. Isaac was the way of grace, symbolizing anyone who had undergone spiritual birth by trusting in Jesus' work. Paul points his readers to the freedom all believers enjoy, the sonship they have through spiritual adoption, and the inheritance that is theirs because of God's sovereign grace.

The final section of Galatians is a portrait of the Spirit-filled life. Genuine faith is more than belief in divine truth; it is also the bearing of divine fruit under the direction and by the power of the Spirit. So Paul tells the Galatian believers, "Walk in the Spirit . . . [be] led by the Spirit" (Galatians 5:16, 18). It is the Holy Spirit who makes the life of faith work.

Paul closes by comparing those who glory in the flesh with those who glory in the cross. His conclusion—a parting salvo against the Judaizers—condemns their religious pride and hypocrisy. Paul then celebrates the cross of Christ as the source of every believer's righteousness and acceptance before God.

REFLECTIONS

We must identify false teachers. Three principles can be distilled from Paul's contrast of himself with the false apostles. First, we must not be taken in by smooth, clever, seemingly spiritual oratory. Such speech may mask lies and deception. Second, we must go beyond teachers' words and examine their lives. Those consumed with accumulating wealth and power are not true servants of Christ. Finally, we must not make tolerance a virtue. Tolerance is the supreme virtue only to those who lack strong convictions. To discern true from false spiritual leaders is vital to the health of the church. To fail to exercise discernment is to open wide the door to the sheepfold and allow Satan to ravage God's flock.

Remember the true foundation. The "pillars" of the gospel are the grace of God and the death of Christ. Those are the pillars that, by its very nature, legalism destroys. Those who insist they can somehow earn salvation by their own efforts undermine the very foundation of Christianity and nullify the precious death of Christ on their behalf.

> You are no longer a SLAVE but a son, and if a SON, then an HEIR of God through Christ.
>
> GALATIANS 4:7

Motives matter to God. The validity of good works in God's sight depends on whose power they are done in and for whose glory. When good works are done in the power of the Spirit and for His glory, they are accepted by our heavenly Father. But when they are done in the power of the flesh and for the sake of personal recognition or merit, they are rejected by Him. Legalism is separated from true obedience by a person's attitude and the condition of his or her heart. One is a rotten smell in God's nostrils, whereas the other is a sweet savor.

STUDY QUESTIONS

1. What surprises you about Paul's description of the Macedonians' generosity in 2 Corinthians 8:1–7? What phrases does he use? What was their situation?

2. How does Paul describe his own demeanor, attitude, and tone where the Corinthians are concerned (see 2 Corinthians 10:1–16)?

3. According to Paul, what is more important than feeling good about oneself or commending oneself (see 2 Corinthians 10:12–18)?

4. Paul emphasized that he did not take money from the Corinthian believers (see 2 Corinthians 11:7–12). Why would he choose to make this point?

5. Despite his obvious misgivings, Paul elected to tell the Corinthians about his vision of paradise (see 2 Corinthians 12:1–10). How did he describe his experience?

6. What does Paul reveal as the driving force behind his actions in the past (see Galatians 1:10–24)? How does that compare with his current motivation?

7. How does Paul contrast the law and faith in Galatians 3:10–18? What does Paul say is the destiny of the person who fails to completely keep to the law?

8. Paul contrasts the works of the flesh with the fruit of the Spirit (see Galatians 5:19–26). Is he arguing that those who commit are not really Christians? Why or why not?

WEEK 44

BELIEVERS FIGHT AGAINST THE ENEMY

EPHESIANS 1–PHILIPPIANS 4

READING PLAN: **302** | Ephesians 1–2 **303** | Ephesians 3 **304** | Ephesians 4–5 **305** | Ephesians 6 **306** | Philippians 1–2 **307** | Philippians 3 **308** | Philippians 4

No one would think to look for gratitude and joy in a prison. Yet it is believed that is exactly where the apostle Paul was when he wrote Ephesians and Philippians.

During the three years Paul spent pastoring the church in Ephesus, he probably taught them all the great truths contained within this biblical epistle. Yet Paul wanted his brothers and sisters in the faith to be thankful for their immeasurable blessings in Christ *and* to live in a manner worthy of those blessings. So he began this correspondence with a refresher course in theology, ultimately giving a panoramic view of God's perfect plan of redemption from eternity past. That God would so graciously and lovingly choose every believer, Jew or Gentile, for salvation moved the apostle to prayers of praise to God and to passionately intercede for the Ephesians to be filled with all the fullness of God.

Those who have been saved by faith, wrote the apostle, are new creations being transformed into Christ's image and likeness. "We are His workmanship, created in Christ Jesus for good works, which God prepared beforehand that we should walk in them" (Ephesians

2:10). The old ways are gone; as new people, God has gifted us to live together in an entity called the church. In unity and love—with Christ as the head of this body, and with each member doing his or her part to build it up through the gifts of the Spirit—we are to live to the glory of God.

Paul notes that conformity to Christ should *contrast* with conformity to the world. The Ephesians lived in a spiritually dark and pagan city, but they had been saved out of that darkness, and now they were to live in the light. God ordained humble submission as a key aspect of transformed living, especially in relationships of authority: wives to husbands, children to parents, employees to employers. But believers' primary concern should not be about who they are *over* but about who they should be *under*.

These descriptions of the faithful Christian life led Paul to the topic of spiritual warfare. If the believers are walking worthy of their calling—in humility rather than pride, unity rather than divisiveness, the new self rather than the old, light rather than darkness—they will experience opposition from the enemy. Yet God does not leave His saints unprotected in this cosmic conflict. The Lord provides all the necessary armor for them to combat and thwart the adversary. Paul's closing passage in Ephesians serves as a heartening reminder that, in Christ, not only can believers *withstand* the devil's assaults, but we can also *defeat* the diabolical forces arrayed against God and the church.

Paul had firsthand knowledge of these kinds of spiritual attacks. In his next letter, he is writing to the church at Philippi, informing the believers about his house arrest in Rome (the place from which he composed the letter). Paul writes to exhort them to unity and the pursuit of Christlikeness. He tells them why he has decided to send home one of the helpers they had sent to him. He warns them against false teachers and expresses his thanks for the Philippians' financial gift.

> Let each of you LOOK OUT not only for his OWN interests, but also for the interests of OTHERS.
>
> PHILIPPIANS 2:4

The bond of love between Paul and these believers is so strong that their friendship and prayers have encouraged him again and again during his imprisonment. Paul assures the Philippians that his painful circumstances have actually caused his joy to increase. It does not matter that he is chained to a Roman guard day and night, maligned by detractors, or facing possible execution. As long as the saving gospel of Christ is being preached, he is fully confident the Lord's cause will triumph.

Paul then calls on the congregation to likewise conduct themselves as citizens of heaven. "For our citizenship is in heaven, from which we also eagerly wait for the Savior" (Philippians 3:20). This was a description he knew they would understand. Philippi had the distinction of being a Roman colony—a privileged status that was a source of civic pride. As responsible citizens, they were careful not to bring disrepute on their city. How much more then should they bring honor to the kingdom of Christ?

The apostle also pleads for them to be on guard against the discord that can be generated by only a few people. If they allow the supreme example of God's Son, who willingly condescended to come to earth in human form to provide redemption for fallen mankind, to serve as their motive, they will be united in humility. Paul thus commands the complainers in the congregation to stop their grumbling and disputing, presenting the example of three men who exhibit godly lives: himself, Timothy (Paul's son in the faith), and Epaphroditus (a Philippian native whom the church had sent to bring the gift and minister to Paul's needs). Paul states that he and these two men are passionately devoted to the Lord, not with their own interests. They have risked health, freedom, and life for the sake of Christ.

In Paul's compelling salvation testimony and the imagery of a footrace (representing the Christian life), we see his concern for spiritual growth. He had once sought to impress man and God in worthless ways. Now, like a sprinter, he is straining with all his might for the prize of spiritual perfection—and he wants other believers in Christ to follow his example.

The church at Philippi was facing many dangers, which Paul hints at throughout the letter: persecution, lack of unity, false teachers. But it is the dispute between two prominent women that threatens to split the church—a situation compounded by the failure of the elders and deacons to deal with it. So Paul instructs them to stand fast in the faith, holding their position like soldiers in the front line. He concludes by again expressing his gratitude for the financial gift they sent. Underlying his words of thanks are not only principles of contentment but also the picture of a man utterly content. Paul could rejoice in every situation because his heart was guarded by the peace of God and the God of peace.

REFLECTIONS

We are to engage in spiritual battle. It is far too easy for believers to become complacent to the seriousness of the spiritual battle raging around them. They are not interested in the "armor of God" because they are not engaged in war. Yet God gives no deferments or exemptions. His people are at war and will continue to be at war until He returns and takes charge of earth. A Christian who no longer has to struggle against the world, the flesh, and the devil is a Christian who has fallen into complacency. A Christian who has no conflict in life is a Christian who has retreated from the front lines of service.

We are to commit to holy living. Salvation has three time dimensions: past, present, and future. The past dimension is that of *justification*, when we placed our faith in Jesus and were redeemed. The present dimension is *sanctification*, the time between our justification and death (or, if still living, when Jesus returns). The future aspect is *glorification*, when salvation is completed and we receive our glorified bodies. Holy living, then, demands us to commit our lives to the service of Christ with every faculty we possess.

We are to pursue the prize. People who make an impact in the world have a single-minded commitment to reaching their goals. The same is true for Christians. There are no gimmicks or shortcuts to a life that makes an impact for the truth of Christ. Such lives are the direct result of a maximum effort to reach the spiritual goals of Christlikeness in life and ministry. Many noble servants of God have suffered much to reach those goals. Many even paid with their lives. All had one thing in common—their own comfort was less important than being like the Lord Jesus Christ in this world. They left their mark on the church through their undying devotion to Him and their untiring efforts for His gospel.

STUDY QUESTIONS

1. According to Paul, what are the past, present, and future aspects of God's work in our lives (see Ephesians 1:3–6, 7–12, 13–14)? Why do you think Paul takes such a broad view?

2. Paul provides the Bible's most concise statement of "salvation by grace through faith" in Ephesians 2:8–9. To what does the word *that* in verse 8 refer? What does it mean?

3. What obstacles can impede the spiritual growth and maturing of an individual Christian? What can impede the growth of a whole congregation (see Ephesians 4:1–16)?

4. What words of warning does Paul give to followers of Jesus in Ephesians 5:1–7? Why should we not participate in sinful deeds?

5. What protective (defensive) pieces of armor are children of God given in their ongoing struggle with the forces of evil? What offensive weapons are we given (see Ephesians 6:10–20)?

6. What words and phrases reveal the kind of deep relationship that existed between Paul and the church in Philippi (see Philippians 1:3–11)?

7. Instead of grumbling and arguing with God about their lot in life, Paul urged the Philippians to remember their mission. What exactly was their calling (see Philippians 2:12–18)?

8. Paul spells out the kind of thought life that leads to a stable Christian experience (see Philippians 4:4–9). What are the hallmarks of that way of thinking?

WEEK 45

BELIEVERS SET A GODLY EXAMPLE

COLOSSIANS 1–2 THESSALONIANS 3

READING PLAN:	**309** | Colossians 1–2	**310** | Colossians 3–4	**311** | 1 Thessalonians 1–2
312 | 1 Thessalonians 3–4	**313** | 1 Thessalonians 5	**314** | 2 Thessalonians 1–2	**315** | 2 Thessalonians 3

Several years after the Colossian church was founded (likely by Epaphras), a heresy arose that contained elements of what was called Gnosticism and aspects of Jewish legalism. So concerned was Epaphras about this heresy that he made the long journey from Colossae to Rome, where Paul was a prisoner. In the letter of Colossians, Paul teaches on several key areas of theology and refutes this heretical teaching that threatened the Colossian church.

These false teachers—the Gnostics—were telling Christians in the region of the Lycus River Valley (where Colossae was located) that Jesus was not sufficient—that they needed something more. They held that they were privy to a higher level of spiritual knowledge and secrets of spiritual illumination that were beyond Jesus Christ and the Word. These heretics formed an exclusive group that disdained "unenlightened" Christians. They had effectively beguiled some believers and drew them away from confidence in Christ alone.

Paul therefore wrote to the Colossians to present the absolute sufficiency of Jesus Christ for salvation and sanctification. The Colossians had Christ, and He was sufficient, so they did not need to be intimidated by the false teachers. Paul also declares the sufficiency of Christ over the false teachers' philosophy (what he equated as worthless deception) and over legalism.

Next, Paul calls his readers to simultaneously be preoccupied with heavenly realities *and* put sin to death in the here and now by yielding to the Holy Spirit. Christians must dress themselves spiritually in accordance with their new identity, "putting on" the lifestyle of the new man. Paul discusses the personal characteristics and the home life of this "new man," as well as how faith in Christ should affect the relationships between masters and slaves (comparable to employers and employees today). He then broadened the discussion to focus on prayer, walking in wisdom, and the gracious speech of believers.

Paul's parting passage features a number of Christians who helped in his ministry while he was imprisoned at Rome. The eight men named are not all well-known figures, but many of them had stuck with Paul for years, and each was special to him. Ultimately, Colossians presents a powerful case for the divinity of Jesus Christ. The theme of the book can perhaps best be summed up by Paul's words in Colossians 3:11: "Christ is all and in all." He is God, Creator, Savior, and head of the church.

The next letters from Paul are 1 and 2 Thessalonians, both of which have been called the "eschatological epistles." However, in light of their extensive focus on the church, they are better categorized as the "church epistles." Paul likely had many reasons for writing 1 Thessalonians—all coming out of his concern for the flock from which he had been forcefully separated (see Acts 17:1–9). The apostle carried an overwhelming burden of responsibility for all the churches, so it must have been refreshing for him to minister to the Thessalonian believers, whom he deemed worthy of commendation.

Some of Paul's purposes included encouraging the church and answering false allegations. He comforts those who are being persecuted, expresses joy in their faith, and reminds them of the importance of moral purity. He also condemns the sluggard lifestyle, corrects a wrong understanding of prophetic events, defuses tensions, and exhorts the believers in the basics of Christian living.

In 1 Thessalonians, Paul reveals the concerns of a pastor and the kind of spiritual care a leader must provide for his people. Paul understood that even a church as strong as the one in Thessalonica might be tempted to settle for the spiritual status quo, so he exhorts the believers throughout the letter to strive for spiritual excellence. Although the surrounding culture continually lowered its moral standards, the Thessalonians could not lower their standards.

These believers were living in expectation of the Savior's return—yet had questions. *What happens to the Christians who die before Jesus comes? Do they miss His return?* Paul's purpose in discussing the Day of the Lord is not primarily theological or eschatological but pastoral—to give them hope and comfort. In a closing challenge, he identifies the struggling sheep that are hindering the growth of the healthy sheep, instructing them on how to adequately deal with the members among their community.

After penning 1 Thessalonians, Paul remained appraised of the happenings in Thessalonica. He learned that the church had matured and expanded, but pressure and persecution had also increased. In addition, like in so many other congregations, the seeds of false doctrine concerning the Lord had been sown, and the people were behaving disorderly. So Paul wrote a second letter to this beloved flock who were becoming discouraged by persecution and needed incentive to persevere.

The letter of 2 Thessalonians is primarily pastoral in nature, though it contains much prophetic material. The main issue Paul addresses in the first two chapters stemmed from a misunderstanding in the church being generated by false teachers about the coming Day of the Lord. Paul reveals that this Day has not arrived and will not arrive until certain events occur. He then urges his readers to be ready for the end times by not being deceived, forgetful, ignorant, unbelieving, insecure, or weak.

In the rest of the letter, Paul requests prayer and issues a warning against those in the community who had remained idle. Paul reminds the believers of how he had acted when he was with them—working "with labor and toil night and day" (2 Thessalonians 3:8). Paul addresses these issues by offering comfort for the persecuted, correction for the falsely taught and frightened, and confrontation for the disobedient and undisciplined. He then closes with a prayerful benediction to God.

REFLECTIONS

Jesus is sufficient. One of the great tenets of Scripture is that Christ is completely sufficient for all matters of life and godliness. He is sufficient for creation, salvation, sanctification, and glorification. He is so pure that within Him there is no blemish, stain, defilement, corruption, or error. He is so complete that there is no other God besides Him. He is the only begotten Son and all the treasures of wisdom and knowledge are in Him. As Paul proclaims, "For in Him dwells all the fullness of the Godhead bodily; and you are complete in Him, who is the head of all principality and power" (Colossians 2:9–10).

We must practice what we preach. Paul states that he and his coworkers were "approved by God to be entrusted with the gospel" (1 Thessalonians 2:4). Paul knew he could be confident in God's power because he was committed to God's truth not only in his preaching but also in his living. Enemies of the truth will often try to destroy our ministry by persecution. When that does not work, they will try to undermine people's trust in our message or our personal integrity. For this reason, we must follow Paul's example and not only *preach* the truth of the gospel but also *live* out of that truth.

We have work to do in this world. Paul reminds the Thessalonians of a command that he gave when he was with them: "If anyone will not work, neither shall he eat" (2 Thessalonians 3:10). Our culture's work ethic has eroded, but the biblical work ethic remains constant. When we diligently pursue the vocation to which God has called us, we honor the Lord. Furthermore, the Bible says we have a responsibility to care for the poor: "Pure and undefiled religion before God and the Father is this: to visit orphans and widows in their trouble" (James 1:27). But neither the world nor the church owes a living to those too who purposefully choose to be lazy and not work. As Paul reminds the believers, "We were not disorderly among you; nor did we eat anyone's bread free of charge, but worked with labor and toil night and day, that we might not be a burden to any of you, not because we do not have authority, but to make ourselves an example of how you should follow us" (2 Thessalonians 3:7–9).

STUDY QUESTIONS

1. For what three things did Paul pray for the Colossians to be filled (see Colossians 1:9)? Why did Paul pray that the Colossians might have strength (see verses 10–14)?

2. Review the different commands that Paul lists in Colossians 3:1–11. What are believers in Christ to "put to death" or "put off" when it comes to their spiritual lives?

3. What instructions does Paul give about prayer in Colossians 4:2–4? What is the difference between simply praying and actually being a person who is *devoted* to prayer?

4. What outstanding qualities did Paul acknowledge and give thanks for in the lives of the Thessalonian believers (see 1 Thessalonians 1:3–10)? Why did he begin with these holy habits?

5. What metaphor does Paul use to picture his ministry "style" in 1 Thessalonians 2:7–9? What words and phrases does he use to elaborate on this image?

6. Paul wrote to inform and to comfort the believers in Thessalonica. What reassuring or encouraging truths do you find in 1 Thessalonians 4:13–18?

7. In 2 Thessalonians 1:9–12, Paul speaks of God being "glorified" by His people. What does this mean? How is this accomplished by believers in Christ?

8. What were some of the devices and tricks employed by the false teachers to confuse and upset the Thessalonian believers (see 2 Thessalonians 2:1–4)?

WEEK 46

BELIEVERS PREACH THE GOSPEL

1 TIMOTHY 1–2 TIMOTHY 4

READING PLAN: **316** | 1 Timothy 1–2 **317** | 1 Timothy 3 **318** | 1 Timothy 4–5
319 | 1 Timothy 6 **320** | 2 Timothy 1 **321** | 2 Timothy 2 **322** | 2 Timothy 3–4

First Timothy is one of two inspired letters that Paul wrote to his beloved son in the faith. In Acts 16:1–5, we learn that Timothy was from Lystra, a city in the Roman province of Galatia. Paul had led him to Christ, undoubtedly during his first missionary journey when he visited Lystra. When Paul revisited the city on his second missionary journey, he chose Timothy—who was probably in his late teens or early twenties—to accompany him.

Timothy was to be Paul's disciple, friend, and co-laborer for the rest of the apostle's life. Paul often sent him to churches as his representative, and 1 Timothy finds him on another assignment, serving as pastor of the church at Ephesus. Paul had great concern for the church in that city—the result of three years of personal ministry there. Despite its rich spiritual history, the Ephesian church had been targeted by false teachers. So Paul wrote this epistle to prepare Timothy for the onslaught of these enemies of the gospel.

Paul also urges Timothy to make praying for the lost a priority within the Ephesian church: "Therefore I exhort first of all that supplications, prayers, intercessions, and giving of thanks be made for all men" (1 Timothy 2:1). (The perverted gospel of the Judaizers in Ephesus, who taught salvation only for the elite, was certainly restricting the believers' evangelistic intercession.) Paul also instructs Timothy on the qualifications for pastors and deacons—as there is a link between the spiritual quality of a congregation and the godliness of its leaders. The character qualities Paul stresses stood in sharp contrast to the unqualified leaders that had assumed positions at Ephesus. Also, certain women had wrongly assumed power. All needed to be publicly rebuked.

Paul, after addressing the problems caused by the false teachers, goes on to deal directly with the false teachers themselves, focusing on their origin and content. He asserts that any tolerance of error dishonors the God of truth and anyone who champions ungodly ideas should be publicly rebuked. What Paul offers next is an array of Spirit-inspired counsel for Timothy in several areas of church business: the treatment of older men and women in the church; the care of widows; the church's obligations to honor, protect, rebuke, and select elders; and some identifying markers of corrupt teachers.

FIGHT the good fight of FAITH, lay hold on eternal LIFE, to which you were also CALLED.

1 TIMOTHY 6:12

Paul wraps up his instruction by counseling the young pastor what to teach those who are rich in material possessions. Paul also urges Timothy to resist temptation and cling to his divine calling. Timothy was God's man for the church at Ephesus. His effectiveness would depend on what he fought for, followed after, fled from, and was faithful to.

When Paul wrote to Timothy a second time, he was again in prison, apparently rearrested as part of Nero's persecution of Christians. This time, Paul had no hope for release. Previously, he had been under house arrest, where he could interact with people and minister. At this time—likely five to six years later—he was in a jail cell, in chains, abandoned by virtually all for fear of persecution, and facing imminent execution.

So Paul urges Timothy to hasten to Rome for one last visit. (Whether Timothy actually made it to the city of Rome before his mentor's execution is not known.) Furthermore, Paul was sensing the young pastor at Ephesus was in danger of weakening spiritually under the pressure of the church and the persecution of the world. His final words to Timothy contain many admonitions, including around twenty-five imperatives. Perhaps Timothy was questioning his gifts, his calling, or his likely success. Whatever the nature of his difficulties, Timothy was clearly discouraged.

Paul counsels Timothy that he does not need more from God; rather, he needs to appropriate all that God has already given him. He needs to be diligent, use his gifts, hold on to sound doctrine, put his confidence in Scripture, and resist the false teachers that had infiltrated the flock. Paul implores Timothy to be strong (the key exhortation of the first part of the letter) and to continue to preach the Word (the main admonition of the last part).

Using the vivid pictures of a teacher, a soldier, an athlete, and a farmer, Paul presents several important elements of a vibrant Christian life. Perhaps anticipating questions from Timothy, the apostle then offers some powerful motives for faithfulness. From there, Paul inspires and encourages the young pastor to be, first and foremost, a man of the Word.

TIMOTHY AND TITUS

Timothy, whose name means "honoring God," became Paul's chief disciple, having been well spoken of by the brethren in Derbe and Iconium. Since Paul speaks of him as "a true son in the faith" (1 Timothy 1:2), it is likely Timothy came to salvation during Paul's first missionary journey, even though he was raised by a godly mother and grandmother. Timothy's father was an unbelieving Greek (see Acts 16:1–3).

Timothy remained faithful to Paul from the beginning to the end. Paul dispatched him on the second journey to Thessalonica, on the third journey to Corinth, to Philippi during his first Roman house arrest, and to Ephesus during his final travels. He names Timothy in the salutation not only in both Thessalonian letters but also in 2 Corinthians, Philippians, Colossians, Philemon, and even in Romans 16:21. At some time, Timothy was imprisoned and later released (see Hebrews 13:23), presumably after Paul's death.

Titus is not mentioned by name in Acts, but it is likely he was led to faith in Christ by Paul before or during his first missionary journey. Later, Titus ministered with Paul on the island of Crete and was left behind to continue and strengthen the work there. After Artemas or Tychicus arrived to direct the ministry, Paul wanted Titus to join him in Nicopolis, in the province of Achaia in Greece, and stay through the winter.

Due to Titus's involvement with the church at Corinth during Paul's third missionary journey, he is mentioned nine times in 2 Corinthians (see 2:13; 7:6, 13, 14; 8:6, 16, 23; 12:18), where Paul refers to him as "my brother" (2:13) and "my partner and fellow worker" (8:23). The young elder was already familiar with Judaizers, false teachers in the church, who among other things insisted all Christians, Gentile as well as Jew, were bound by the Mosaic Law. Titus had accompanied Paul and Barnabas years earlier to the Council of Jerusalem, where that heresy was the subject (see Acts 15; Galatians 2:1–5).

In many ways, 2 Timothy is a spiritual inventory. Paul addresses Timothy's motives and character, concentrating on his internal condition rather than his external success. He also gives commands to avoid, expose, and battle spiritual impostors and heresy in the church. By pointing out his own example of faithfulness and reiterating their biblically based convictions, Paul instructs Timothy to "hold fast the pattern of sound words" that he has received from him (2 Timothy 1:13) and be a courageous defender of the faith. He reminds his young colleague of the rich resources he has in the Word of God.

As Paul neared the end of his life, he could look back without regret. In fact, his mood in 2 Timothy is one of triumph. (Most scholars believe this was the last letter Paul wrote.) In the final chapter, he examines his life from three perspectives: the present reality, for which he was ready; the past, when he had been faithful; and the future, as he anticipated his heavenly reward. Here we see into the heart of a man of God whose quest was to live to the glory of God by helping to build up the church of Jesus.

REFLECTIONS

Evangelism begins with evangelistic prayer. Paul writes to Timothy, "I exhort first of all that supplications, prayers, intercessions, and giving of thanks be made for all men" (1 Timothy 2:1). The greatest example of evangelistic praying is our Lord. Isaiah 53:12 tells us that He "made intercession for the transgressors." On the cross, He prayed, "Father, forgive them; for they do not know what they do" (Luke 23:34). God answered those prayers with 3,000 converts on the Day of Pentecost and countless more through the centuries. Do we pray for the lost like that? Do we have the passion that inspired John Knox to cry out, "Give me Scotland or I die"? Is our attitude that of George Whitefield, who prayed, "O Lord, give me souls or take my soul"? Can we, like Henry Martyn, say, "I cannot endure existence if Jesus is to be so dishonored"? God honors evangelistic prayer. Standing among those who killed Stephen was a young man named Saul of Tarsus. Could it be that the great apostle's salvation was in answer to Stephen's prayer, "Lord, do not hold this sin against them"? Evangelism begins with the evangelistic prayer.

Christian leaders have integrity. The most important qualities leaders can demonstrate are not intelligence, a forceful personality, glibness, diligence, vision, administrative skills, decisiveness, courage, humor, or any other similar natural attribute. Those all play a part, but the *most* desirable quality for any leader is integrity. While integrity is most desirable in secular leadership, its absence is absolutely fatal to spiritual leadership. Integrity is living what we teach and preach. This is why all the qualifications for leaders given in 1 Timothy 3:1–13 describe their moral character. It is not the typical list a corporate analyst might come up with, because the issue is not leadership skills but spiritual example. Those who lead people to Christlikeness must follow a pattern of godly behavior that others can follow. They must be above reproach in their moral life, home life, spiritual maturity, and public reputation.

We must lead others by our example. Paul writes to Timothy, "Let no one despise your youth, but be an example to the believers" (1 Timothy 4:12). The greatest tool of a leader is the power of an exemplary life. The Puritan writer Thomas Brooks said, "Example is the most powerful rhetoric." Setting an example of godly living that others can follow is the essential condition of excellence in ministry. When a pattern of godliness is missing, the power is drained out of preaching, leaving it an empty shell. Authoritative preaching is simply undermined if there is not a virtuous life backing it up.

We do everything for the glory of God. There is no aspect of life or conduct, however apparently insignificant, that should not be directed to the glory of God. Every legitimate job has intrinsic value because it is the arena in which we live out our Christian lives. Christianity is not an ideal but something that triumphs in the real world. As believers, we most commonly interact with that world in the workplace as we live out our faith on our jobs. We are to be a "city that is set on a hill" (Matthew 5:14). We must thus be concerned that our conduct on the job shows others the power of Christ to transform a life. Our work performance will bring either praise or blasphemy to the name of God.

Beware the signs of loving money. Paul writes, "Godliness with contentment is great gain . . . having food and clothing, with these we shall be content" (1 Timothy 6:6, 8). What are the signs that we have fallen into a love of money? First, those who love money are more concerned with making it than with honesty or giving a quality effort. We must pursue truth and excellence, for which money may be the reward. Second, those who love money never have enough. Like the leech's daughters of Proverbs 30:15, all they say is, "Give and give!" Such people stand in contrast to Paul, who wrote, "I have learned in whatever state I am, to be content" (Philippians 4:11). Third, those who love money tend to flaunt it. They derive an inordinate pleasure from wearing, driving, or living in what money buys. Fourth, those who love money resent giving it. They want to use it all for their own gratification. Finally, those who love money often sin to get it. They will cheat on their income tax or expense account, or pilfer from work. Those who compromise their principles for money betray a heart that loves money more than God, righteousness, and truth.

> For the love of MONEY is a root of all kinds of EVIL, for which some have strayed from the faith in their GREEDINESS.
>
> 1 TIMOTHY 6:10

Faithful ministry has a cost and a reward. Faithful ministry in God's service is bittersweet. It brings suffering and joy, disappointment and gratitude. Duty can bring the deepest pain or highest joy. Spiritual duty unfulfilled brings dissatisfaction, regret, and anguish, no matter how easy unfaithfulness may be. On the other hand, spiritual duty fulfilled brings satisfaction and happiness, whatever the cost of faithfulness. The Christian who is obedient to his duty under the Lord can say with Peter, "If anyone suffers as a Christian, let him not be ashamed, but let him glorify God in this matter" (1 Peter 4:16).

God provides the strength to get us "unstuck." Many years ago, engineers in New Jersey were building a bridge over the mouth of a river on the Atlantic Coast. As they were putting down pilings, they came across the hull of a ship buried in the sand. To keep the bridge on the planned route, the hull would have to be removed. The engineers tried every mechanical means they could think of to move the hull, but the ship remained firmly in place. Finally, a young engineer suggested placing several barges above the hull on either side, running cables underneath the hull, and attaching them tightly to the barges at low tide. When the tide rose, the hull was loosened. At the next low tide the cables were tightened again, and at high tide the ship was loosened some more. After several cycles of tides, the ship eventually was freed. What humanly devised mechanical force could not accomplish, the immeasurably greater forces of nature accomplished easily. Many Christians and churches today are like that hull, embedded in spiritual immobility. They recognize the problem and try every human means to extricate themselves, but to no avail. But what God's children cannot accomplish in their own strength, their heavenly Father can do by the power of His Spirit. As Paul advised his younger coworker in the faith, "You therefore, my son, be strong in the grace that is in Christ Jesus" (2 Timothy 2:1). We are to operate in the strength that our heavenly Father provides so we may endure "as a good soldier of Jesus Christ" (verse 3).

STUDY QUESTIONS

1. How does Paul describe what the false teachers had done (see 1 Timothy 1:3–7, 18–20)? How does Paul's personal testimony relate to his warning against false teachers?

2. What instructions concerning apparel does Paul give to Timothy for the women in his congregation (see 1 Timothy 2:8–10)? What reasons does Paul give for providing this instruction?

3. What do Paul's harsh words in 1 Timothy 4:1–5 about the purveyors of false teaching reveal to you about the importance of truth?

4. How were the widows to be cared for in the church (see 1 Timothy 5:3–16)? What distinctions were made? Who are the people in similar need in society today?

5. Why does Paul share with Timothy the contrasting actions of his ministry associates (see 2 Timothy 1:15–18)? How was Paul hoping to both challenge and encourage Timothy in this?

6. Paul uses three analogies in 2 Timothy 2:1–7 to highlight several indispensable qualities of a strong spiritual life. What is the main point of each analogy?

7. What do you learn about Paul's "mentoring" methods in 2 Timothy 3:10–14? How did Timothy carefully follow and model Paul's example?

8. According to 2 Timothy 4:1–5, why is preaching such a serious calling? What should the job description of the preacher encompass?

WEEK 47

BELIEVERS HAVE AN ANCHOR IN CHRIST

TITUS 1–HEBREWS 6

READING PLAN: **323** | Titus 1–2 **324** | Titus 3 **325** | Philemon 1
326 | Hebrews 1–2 **327** | Hebrews 3 **328** | Hebrews 4–5 **329** | Hebrews 6

Titus, just like Timothy, had become a beloved disciple of Paul and fellow worker in the gospel—most likely serving with Paul on his second and third missionary journeys. Paul's purpose in writing the letter of Titus was to encourage and strengthen this young pastor who had succeeded him in a difficult ministry.

Titus was the direct envoy of the apostle, sent to the island of Crete to strengthen the churches for effective evangelism in their pagan culture. Paul's central theme in the letter thus revolves around church leadership. He tells Titus that only those whose character meets divine standards should be allowed to enter or remain in ministry.

Titus was also to prepare the churches to counteract the false teaching and debauched living of certain leaders. Paul charges Titus—and, through him, the congregations in each city—not simply to denounce the behavior of these leaders but also to silence them and even remove them from their fellowships. For the people in the pew, their primary evangelistic preparation was to live godly lives. How they behaved toward governmental authorities and unbelievers was also crucial to their testimony. Additionally, Paul states, the preaching of sound doctrine produces relationships in the church marked with humility, submission, and love. God's purpose in calling out church elders and commanding His people to live reverently with one another is to bear witness to His plan of salvation. Paul urges Titus to speak with authority about these things.

Throughout the letter, it is clear Titus has a larger role than simply *maintaining* the church in Crete. His role is to bring more people to *faith* in Christ. Paul's closing remarks admonish Titus to remind believers of the importance of their attitude, testimony to the unsaved world, and relationships. A humble witness by a well-ordered body of believers will offer the most compelling message of the gospel.

The short letter of Philemon was written by Paul to a prominent member in the Colossian church. Paul sent the letter with a man named Tychicus, who was accompanying Philemon's runaway slave Onesimus as he went back to his master. Onesimus was not a believer at the time he stole money from Philemon and ran away—he met Paul in Rome and then became a Christian. The apostle grew to love Onesimus, for he was providing valuable service to Paul in his imprisonment. But by stealing and running away, Onesimus had both broken Roman law and defrauded his master. Paul knew those issues had to be dealt with, so he sent Onesimus back to Colossae, along with his beautiful personal letter, urging Philemon to forgive Onesimus and welcome him back to service as a brother in Christ.

Paul uses this real-life situation to teach the importance of forgiving others and the spiritual character of one who forgives. Paul does not appeal to law or principle but to love. He can do this because he knows Philemon to be a spiritually mature man whose heart is right with God.

The letter of Hebrews, penned by an unknown author, was primarily addressed to Christians from a Jewish background. Although these individuals were primarily converts to Christ, there were likely a number of unbelievers in their midst who were attracted by the message of salvation but had not yet made a commitment. This generation of Hebrew Christians had practiced the Levitical sacrifices at the temple in Jerusalem, yet they were an immature group who were tempted to hold on to the spiritually powerless traditions of Judaism. Furthermore, they were suffering persecution by fellow Jews.

The author's purpose in writing the letter is to emphasize the superiority of Christianity over Judaism and to give believers confidence in the preeminence of Christ. Jesus is higher than any angel and superior to any Old Testament hero the Jews held in high esteem. Christ is above any Old Testament institution, greater than any Old Testament ritual, and better than any Old Testament sacrifice.

JESUS BETTER THAN ANGELS

A precedent had been set in the Qumran community of messianic Jews living near the Dead Sea. They had dropped out of society, established a commune, and were including the worship of angels in their brand of reformed Judaism. They were even claiming the angel Michael was higher in status than the coming Messiah. These doctrinal aberrations could explain the emphasis in Hebrews 1 on the superiority of Christ over angels.

Hebrews delineates the differences between the unsaved Jew in Judaism and the redeemed Jew in Christianity. The author warns those Jews within the community who knew the basic truths of the gospel but still did not trust in Christ alone to accept Jesus not just intellectually but with their whole heart. The writer summarizes this warning with this statement from Israel's history: "Do not harden your hearts as in the rebellion, in the day of trial in the wilderness" (Hebrews 3:8).

Some of the unbelieving Jews had likely made a shallow profession of faith without believing in Christ fully. Apart from entering into the blessing of the New Covenant, they could not have eternal life. The genuine believers, on the other hand, were reminded of the certainties of God's promises—the divine assurance that all who come to God through His Son will be saved. God has never reneged on His promises and never will. Thus, it is impossible for anyone who trusts in Christ to lose their salvation.

The positive side of the gospel is that salvation does immeasurably more than deliver sinners from spiritual death; it produces spiritual life. Salvation should be sought not only because of the terrible consequences of *rejecting* it but also because of what is gained when people *embrace* it. Believers enter into God's perfect rest because of the beauty and grace of their merciful High Priest.

The heart of Hebrews focuses on the high priesthood of Jesus. He alone has done what the priests of the old order could never have done. In one perfect and final act of sacrifice, He opened the way to God permanently. As a result, anyone at any time may, by faith in Christ, enter into God's presence.

REFLECTIONS

The work of the church is a team effort. Paul stresses in Titus that all believers have a role to play in the church. It is not possible for a pastor, or even a team of pastors in a large church, to meet all the needs of a congregation. Not only is there not enough time for one person to do it all, but other believers invariably have spiritual gifts and abilities the pastor does not have, by which good deeds can be accomplished and the needs of believers met. Beyond that, a harmonious, loving, and serving church also will be a beacon to the world, attracting unbelievers to the light of salvation through trust in Christ.

True believers stay with Christ. The author of Hebrews writes, "We have become partakers of Christ if we hold the beginning of our confidence steadfast to the end" (3:14). If we really believe the gospel, then at the end of the day, the end of the year, and the end of life, our commitment to Him will still stand. The greatest proof of salvation is continuance in the Christian life. Staying true to the Lord marks the difference between *profession* of faith and *possession* of faith.

God came to us. In sending Jesus, God entered the world and felt everything we will ever feel. If God had not done this, He never could have been a high priest, a mediator, or an intercessor. He never could have offered the perfect and absolute sacrifice for the sins of His people, which divine justice required. The Incarnation was not an option; it was an absolute necessity. It was imperative if humanity was to be saved. God had to come down to where we are in order to bring us back to Himself.

STUDY QUESTIONS

1. Paul's opening salutation in Titus 1:1–4 is packed with truth. What does Paul say about his own calling? What does he reveal about the character of God?

2. To which specific groups of people does Paul give instructions in Titus 2:1–10? What are the specific exhortations given to each group?

3. What does Paul teach in Titus 3:1–8 about the miracle of salvation? What does he teach in this passage about the gift of God's grace on humanity?

4. Paul reveals much about his situation and history with Philemon (see verses 1–9). How does Paul use that to lead into his request regarding Onesimus (see verses 10–14)?

5. What does it mean that God "has in these last days spoken to us by His Son" (Hebrews 1:2)? What does it mean that Christ has been appointed "heir of all things"?

6. To what does the author of Hebrews compare God's Word? What role does the Word of God play in the life of the believer and the unbeliever (see Hebrews 3:12–13)?

7. Why is Jesus able to sympathize with our weaknesses? In light of what He has done for us as our great high priest, how are we encouraged to approach God (see Hebrews 4:14–16)?

8. What does it mean that some of the recipients of the epistle of Hebrews were dull of hearing? What were the symptoms of this condition (see Hebrews 5:9–14)?

WEEK 48

BELIEVERS PERSEVERE THROUGH TRIALS

HEBREWS 7-13

READING PLAN:	**330** | Hebrews 7	**331** | Hebrews 8	**332** | Hebrews 9
333 | Hebrews 10	**334** | Hebrews 11	**335** | Hebrews 12	**336** | Hebrews 13

In Hebrews 7, the author comes to the focal point of his book. This chapter concerns the most significant part of Judaism—the priesthood. Without the priests, no sacrifices could be made, and without the sacrifices, no forgiveness of sins could be obtained. Obedience to the law was important, but the offering of sacrifices was even more essential—and only the priesthood could offer them. No wonder the priesthood was exalted in Judaism!

The author makes his argument by mentioning a mysterious person who appears briefly in the Old Testament: "Melchizedek, king of Salem, priest of the Most High God" (Hebrews 7:1). There is much conjecture about the identity of this person, but it is best to view him as an actual person whose priestly ministry was a "type" of Christ's later ministry. In other words, Melchizedek was an ancient man whom God intended to serve as a picture of Jesus. His life and ministry served as a limited analogy of what Christ would do much later during His earthly ministry. In the same way that Melchizedek's priesthood was superior to the Levitical-Aaronic priesthood, so Christ's ministry is superior to that of Melchizedek.

Overall, the epistle of Hebrews is a study in contrast between the imperfect and incomplete provisions of the Old Covenant and the infinitely better provisions of the New Covenant offered by Jesus, the perfect high priest. Included in the "better" provisions are a better hope, testament, promise, sacrifice, substance, country, and resurrection. Those who belong to the New Covenant dwell in a heavenly atmosphere, worship a heavenly Savior, have a heavenly calling, receive a heavenly gift, are citizens of a heavenly country, look forward to a heavenly Jerusalem, and have their names written in heaven.

An obstacle in the way of the Hebrews' faith was their failure to see that everything connected with the Old Testament ceremonial law was preparatory and transient. So the writer pursues a clear explanation of the better character of the New Covenant. His point in doing this is not to demean the old way of relating to God but rather to show its shadowy incompleteness. The author of Hebrews says that Christ—whose perfect and complete ministry far surpassed the ministry of ancient priests—now dwells in a new sanctuary. Christ's place of ministry under this new arrangement is not an earthly tabernacle but a heavenly one. There He continues to minister on behalf of His people, bringing their heartfelt gifts (such as their worship, repentance, and thanksgiving) to the Father.

Jesus' superior position, and His superior sanctuary, provide clear evidence of His superior ministry. The old priesthood and sacrificial system were only shadows of the real thing—real forgiveness and real reconciliation with God through Christ. "He has made the first obsolete. Now what is becoming obsolete and growing old is ready to vanish away" (Hebrews 8:13).

Christ's death had long been a stumbling block to the Jews—a dying Messiah contradicted their theological presuppositions. Aware of this theological blind spot, the writer of Hebrews proceeds to demonstrate the necessity of the Messiah's sacrifice and reveal the character of that sacrifice. In this record of Jesus' death, from the theological rather than the historical standpoint, the Hebrews were being reminded of the ineffectiveness of the old sacrifices and shown the meaning and depth of Jesus' death. Christ was the perfect and one-time-only sacrifice for sin—for all humanity, for all time.

What follows is a comprehensive study of faith: what it is and what it looks like in a life. Hebrews 11, sometimes called the "Saints' Hall of Fame," forms an honor roll of the Old Testament figures who lived and died by faith. The names of the men and women would have been familiar to the author's audience: Abel, Noah, Abraham, Sarah, Jacob, Joseph, Moses, Gideon, Sampson, David . . . to name a few. Also included, perhaps surprisingly, is "the harlot Rahab," who due to her faith in the God of Israel "did not perish with those who did not believe" when the walls of Jericho came down. The author makes it clear through this that from the time of Adam on, God has honored *faith*—not works.

Hebrews was written in a climate of persecution. The Jewish Christians had turned their backs on the religious traditions in which they had been raised. The persecution from their Jewish friends came mainly in the form of social and economic pressure, though some believers had been imprisoned. So the author encourages these weary believers to run the race of the Christian life with endurance, reminding them that God uses hardships as a means of training His children. He then ends his epistle with a practical chapter presenting some of the essential ethics of Christian behavior that will portray the true gospel to the world, encourage people to trust in Christ, and bring glory to God.

REFLECTIONS

Jesus was the only sinless human. Jesus was undefiled by any moral or spiritual blemish. For thirty-three years, He was mingling continually with sinners and constantly being tempted by Satan. Yet Jesus never contracted the least taint of sin or defilement! Just as the rays of the sun can shine into the foulest stagnant pond and not lose their radiance and purity, so Jesus lived His life in the sinful, defiled world without losing the least of His beauty and purity. He moved through the world and remained untouched by any of its blemishes. He came into the most direct and personal contact with Satan, yet left as spotless as before they met. There never was a priest who was undefiled—until Jesus.

The Old Covenant had a purpose. The Old Covenant symbol is not bad and never was bad. It had a God-given purpose. It pointed to the Son, represented the Son, and foreshadowed the Son before He came to earth. But now that the Son had come, the symbol had no further purpose. The old sacrificial system actually was over when the veil was split in two and Jesus' sacrifice was complete (see Matthew 27:50–51). At that time, Christ's unique, never-to-be-repeated sacrifice was finished with the result that all in Christ had direct access to God (see 1 Timothy 2:3–6). The destruction of the temple completed the closing of the Old Covenant—by removing the place of sacrifice that no longer served a purpose. The age of the Mosaic law and the Levitical priests was over. The age of the Son was here forever.

Jesus' sacrifice was once-and-for-all. In the Lord's Supper, we remember Christ's sacrificial death, as He commanded us to do. But He is not re-sacrificed. The Lord told His disciples to remember His death, not to try to redo it. The work of sacrifice is done, there will be no more, and forgiveness is provided for those who trust in this perfect sacrifice. "This Man, after He had offered one sacrifice for sins forever, sat down at the right hand of God" (Hebrews 10:12). Salvation—glorious and perfect salvation—is promised in the Old Covenant and purchased in the New.

> By one OFFERING He has perfected FOREVER those who are being sanctified.
>
> HEBREWS 10:14

The Christian life is a marathon, not a sprint. Endurance is a steady determination to keep pressing ahead. It means continuing even when everything in you wants to give up. When you are running a hundred-yard dash, speed is important, because the race is over quickly. But when you are running a half-mile event, it is endurance that counts. The Christian life is more like a half-mile race than it is a hundred-yard dash. Many well-intentioned Christians start out fast, but as the race goes on, they slow down, give up, or just collapse. The church has always had many short-spurt Christians, but the Lord wants those who will "make the distance." There will be obstacles, and there will be weariness and exhaustion, but each of us must endure if we are to win. God is concerned with our steadfastness. "Therefore strengthen the hands which hang down, and the feeble knees, and make straight paths for your feet, so that what is lame may not be dislocated, but rather be healed" (Hebrews 12:12–13).

STUDY QUESTIONS

1. In what ways does the author of Hebrews portray Jesus' priesthood as superior to that of the Old Covenant (see Hebrews 7:11–22)?

2. According to Hebrews 8:1–13, what is the superiority of the New Covenant over the Old Covenant? Give some specific examples.

3. How do the earthly temple and tabernacle the author of Hebrews describes contrast with the heavenly sanctuary in which Christ is now serving (see Hebrews 9:1–5)?

4. In Hebrews 10:19–25, the author lists some "marks" that will be evident in the lives of those who respond positively to the gospel. What are those marks?

5. What is faith according to how it is described and pictured in Hebrews 11:1–29? Which of the Old Testament characters the author mentions are familiar to you?

6. Why is running a footrace a good metaphor for the Christian life (see Hebrews 12:1–2)? What other analogies can you recall that are used in the New Testament?

7. Review the teaching about divine chastening given in Hebrews 12:3–11. What do you learn about its purposes, prevention, and perils? Why should it not be despised?

8. How would you describe what is meant by the "sacrifice of praise" in Hebrews 13:15? What other kinds of sacrifices are pleasing to God?

WEEK 49

BELIEVERS HAVE AN ETERNAL INHERITANCE

JAMES 1–2 PETER 3

READING PLAN: **337** | James 1–3 **338** | James 4–5 **339** | 1 Peter 1–2 **340** | 1 Peter 3 **341** | 1 Peter 4–5 **342** | 2 Peter 1–2 **343** | 2 Peter 3

James is believed to be the earliest written book of the New Testament. It was authored by the oldest half brother of Christ and brother of Jude. James had at first rejected Jesus as the Messiah, but later he believed and became leader of the Jerusalem church. His book is reminiscent of the book of Proverbs. James passionately desires for his readers to be uncompromisingly obedient to the Word of God. He complements Paul's emphasis on justification by faith with his own emphasis on spiritual fruitfulness that demonstrates true faith.

James wrote primarily to Christian Jews who had been scattered abroad because of persecution. Given this situation of his audience, his primary emphasis in the opening section of his epistle is that if a person's faith is genuine, it will prove itself during times of trouble. James states that a faith that is not *acted out* is really no faith at all. By this, James is not stating that a person is saved by works—in fact, he asserts that salvation is a gracious gift from God. Rather, James is emphasizing that the genuineness of one's profession of faith in Christ is evidenced more by what a person does than by what he or she claims.

James supplements his argument with two illustrations: Abraham and Rahab. Each person was justified not by their words or religious activity but by their actions—putting everything that was dear to them on the line and entrusting it to the Lord without reservation. It is in the vortex of the great plans, decisions, trials, and crossroads of life that true faith unfailingly reveals itself.

James notes a person's speech can be a test of his or her living faith: "Out of the same mouth proceed blessing and cursing. My brethren, these things ought not to be so" (James 3:10). Likewise, wisdom is a test of a person's faith. Those who possess the wisdom of man—wisdom from below—will demonstrate by their lives that they have no saving relationship with Christ. However, those who possess genuine saving faith will manifest the wisdom from above . . . which is the wisdom of God.

Next, James addresses a person's attitude toward the world. James argues that faithful Christian living involves separating oneself from the world and all of its contaminations and drawing near to God. Doing the will of God is yet another test of genuine faith. A constant disregard of God's will marks the presence of pride—and God resists the proud but gives grace to the humble.

Building on Jesus' teachings, James next presents a denunciation of those who profess to worship God but in fact worship money. He instructs those who are suffering at the hands of the rich and powerful to be patient and keep perspective. And to the Jewish believers, he commands them not to swear oaths but be distinctive in speaking the truth. Finally, James upholds a commitment to prayer as a prerequisite to enduring affliction. His exhortation embraces the entire church: individual believers are called to pray as well as the congregation. His main focus is on the casualties of the spiritual battle—the persecuted, weak, defeated believers in need of spiritual healing through prayer.

Peter also wrote his first epistle to followers of Jesus who were scattered across the Roman Empire due to escalating persecution. This targeting of believers likely began in the wake of Emperor Nero's burning of Rome, an act that he blamed on Christians. As the preeminent apostle of the time, Peter recognized the need to help his maligned brothers and sisters live victoriously. So, taking pen in hand, his goal is to remind them of the future inheritance that is waiting for them.

Peter urges a lifestyle rooted in hope, void of bitterness, and focused on the second coming of the Lord. In addition—displaying Christ as the paragon of a triumphant attitude in the midst of hostility—he calls these beleaguered sufferers to live honorably and humbly in front of unbelievers as well as other believers. He notes that a watchful attitude creates a "pilgrim mentality." It reminds believers they are citizens of heaven who are only sojourning on earth. It should also remind them that they will face the record of their service to God and be rewarded for what stands the test at the judgment seat of Christ.

In the final portion of his letter, Peter addresses church leaders. Times of suffering and persecution call for the noblest leadership. Those who shepherd God's flock have responsibilities that should never be taken lightly. Peter concludes by impressing on his readers that by their humility and submission, their love for one another, and by patient endurance of suffering, they can bring glory to God and evangelize a hostile world. And God will—through it all—perfect, establish, and strengthen them.

While 1 Peter was written to help suffering Christians, 2 Peter was written to expose, thwart, and defeat false teachers. The difference in themes explains certain emphases, such as why one letter teaches the second coming of Christ is near and one deals with its delay. First Peter focuses on the immanency of Christ as a means of encouraging persecuted believers. Second Peter, dealing with scoffers, emphasizes the reasons why that imminent return of Christ had not yet occurred.

More than just a complaint against wolflike teachers, Peter's message is that the best way to defend against spiritual error is to know the *truth.* Peter emphasizes having a thorough and intimate knowledge of Christ. Christianity is based on objective, historical, revealed, rational truth from God and is intended to be understood and believed. How does one differentiate between varying truth claims? By knowing the divinely inspired, completely authoritative, and trustworthy Scriptures. Peter also wanted believers to be able to discern the deceivers themselves, so he describes the characteristics of these false teachers—exposing their immoral character as well as their destructive doctrines.

Peter closes with the end times and the judgment to come. He desires for his persecuted brethren to know that even though the false teachers were scoffing, the Day of the Lord was sure. In light of the certainty of these events, he calls for the sanctification of God's people. With so many souls hanging in the balance, they needed to live exemplary lives and use their time to tell others the way to be saved.

REFLECTIONS

Good works are evidence of faith. No one can be saved by works. Salvation is entirely "by grace . . . through faith" (Ephesians 2:8). Yet it is also true that "faith by itself, if it does not have works, is dead" (James 2:17). Genuine faith not only should, but *will*, produce genuine good works, notably repentance and submission to Christ's lordship. This is the expression of the new nature, created in the new birth (see 2 Corinthians 5:17). It will not be perfect obedience and repentance, but good works will be present. We might say that it costs us nothing to become a Christian but everything to live fully as one.

God is worthy of our praise. In our humanly oriented society, God's desire for exclusive credit can seem inappropriate—but only because people have no concept of His greatness, holiness, and glory. What views they may have of Him are merely projections of themselves. The praise that people so desire is undeserved, and their motives for wanting it are sinful. But God seeks glory for the right reason—because He alone is deserving of it. His seeking glory is a holy desire, for He is supremely worthy.

We cannot be passive in calling out evil. Peter writes, "There will be false teachers among you, who will secretly bring in destructive heresies . . . and bring on themselves swift destruction" (2 Peter 2:1). When people's eternal souls are at stake, the church cannot be passive. Nor can it hide behind false humility that fears being judgmental—or behind false love that fears offending other people. Jesus was supremely humble, yet He never called evil anything but what it was: *evil.* Christ was supremely loving, yet He never withheld a warning that might save His hearers from hell. And He had nothing but intense anger for those who, by their false teachings, led people away from God and directly toward hell.

STUDY QUESTIONS

1. What do you learn about the reward God promises for enduring trials and temptation (see James 1:2–15)? How do trials act as an equalizer to the rich and the poor?

2. What two examples does James cite to show the futility of faith without works (see James 2:14–24)? How are these good examples of dead faith?

3. According to James, where does the root of the problem of evil speech lie? What types of evils are caused by the tongue (see James 3:1–12)?

4. What is significant about Peter calling believers "pilgrims" (see 1 Peter 1:1–12)? What does this term suggest for us as modern-day believers?

5. What kind of radically different conduct and lifestyle does Peter say is expected of all followers of Christ (see 1 Peter 2:11–12)? What are "fleshly lusts"?

6. What does Peter urge believers to do in the face of suffering (see 1 Peter 3:13–22)? What does this mean? How does one do this?

7. Peter speaks about the power of Christ in 2 Peter 1:1–11. Why is this an important starting point? What does Christ's power do for believers?

8. Peter was keenly aware that his days on earth were numbered. In light of his impending death, what was his great concern (see 2 Peter 1:12–15)?

WEEK 50

BELIEVERS LOVE ONE ANOTHER

1 JOHN 1–JUDE 1

READING PLAN:	**344** | 1 John 1–2	**345** | 1 John 3	**346** | 1 John 4
347 | 1 John 5	**348** | 2 John 1	**349** | 3 John 1	**350** | Jude 1

Although it is believed the "beloved" disciple John was advanced in age when he wrote the three general epistles that bear his name, he was still actively ministering to churches near the end of the first century. As the last remaining apostle, his testimony was highly authoritative among the churches. Many believers in Christ eagerly sought to hear the one who had firsthand experience with the Lord Jesus throughout His earthly ministry.

John, like others in the early church, was concerned about the plethora of false teachers and their destructive messages. He speaks of these teachers—which he uniquely calls "antichrists"—as those who depart from the true Christian fellowship, deny the Christian faith, and deceive the Christian faithful. The apostle did not specify the nature of their heresy (it was probably an early form of Gnosticism) but instead, in his brilliant first letter, combated the heretics by positively summarizing the fundamentals of the Christian faith.

Specifically, John gives his readers a litmus test for determining the genuineness of a teacher, message, or person's claim of salvation. True believers will pass the *doctrinal* test:

they will subscribe to orthodox views of Christ and the reality of sin. They will pass the *moral* test: obeying Jesus and loving the brethren. No one can claim to belong to God or be commissioned by God unless his or her life is marked by sound faith, obedience, and love operating in concert together.

> Let us LOVE one another, for LOVE is of God ... everyone who LOVES is born of God and knows God.
>
> 1 JOHN 4:7

As the elder statesman of the church, John was beloved for his devotion to Christ and love for the saints. This is what earned him the epithet "apostle of love." So it is no surprise when he states, midway through his letter, that genuine Christians will love in radical ways. First John 4 constitutes a long unit describing what love is, its availability to all, and five reasons why Christians must live by it. John's zeal for the truth also shaped his letter. He presents the fundamentals of Christianity in absolute terms—often through stark contrasts such as light versus darkness or children of God versus children of the devil. Those who claim to be Christians must display the characteristics of genuine Christians. Those who do not display these characteristics were never truly born again.

The apostle repeatedly spirals back through these truths, examining them from various angles to drive them home in the minds and hearts of his readers. In his last "spiral," John emphasizes the victorious nature of the believer. This is one of his fundamental tests for genuine fellowship. Although the Bible uses many different terms to describe Christians, John highlights one particular term: *overcomer*. The believer has continual victory over the world.

John concludes with a presentation of the witness, or testimony, of God and the Spirit to confirm the truth of the deity of Christ. He also presents five Christian certainties: the assurance of eternal life, the promise of answered prayer, the guarantee of victory over sin and Satan, the pledge that Christians belong to God, and the certainty that Jesus is the true God. The greatest certainty of all, the Incarnation, guarantees the certainty of the rest—a doctrinal foundation on which they could build their lives.

Second John also deals with the problem of false teachers in the church, but this time the apostle's focus is on hospitality. In John's day, hospitality included opening one's home and caring for needy Christians, including traveling preachers. Among the congregations John oversaw, itinerant false teachers were taking advantage of Christian hospitality to advance their cause. The woman and her family addressed in the greeting of this letter may have shown these false prophets hospitality, or John may have feared that the false teachers would attempt to take advantage of her kindness.

The apostle sternly warns his readers against showing hospitality to such deceivers. The gracious hospitality commanded of Christians must be discriminating; their kindness must be focused on those who adhere to the fundamentals of the faith. Sound doctrine must serve as the test of fellowship. Truth is the necessary condition of unity and the basis of hospitality.

Third John records the apostle's tribute to the practice of hospitality. In the most personal of his three letters, John commends a man named Gaius—the sole recipient of the letter—for the support that he had demonstrated to some faithful ministers. Meanwhile, John speaks against Diotrephes, who had refused to welcome visiting teachers in a manner worthy of God.

Jude is the last general epistle in the New Testament and is named after its author, who was a half brother of Christ. Like his brother James, Jude became a leader in the church at Jerusalem. At the time of his writing, all the apostles had been martyred except for John. With Christians under severe political attack from Rome and the aggressive spiritual infiltration from Gnostic-like apostates, Christianity was thought to be extremely vulnerable. So Jude calls believers to contend for the faith and calls the church to rigorously defend biblical truth in the midst of intense spiritual warfare.

Jude's epistle is devoted exclusively to confronting *apostasy*—defection from the biblical faith. He vividly describes the apostates in terms of their character and unconscionable activities. They were false teachers pretending to be true whose intentions were to lead God's people astray. The apostates were Satan's counterfeits whose stealth made them dangerous but whose degenerate personal lives and fruitless ministries betrayed their deception. Jude concludes by bolstering the courage of believers in Christ's power. He proclaims Jesus as the one who is able to keep them from stumbling. No matter what their enemies might throw against them, the power of Christ will sustain them from apostasy.

REFLECTIONS

There are no gray areas when it comes to obeying Christ. John is often black-and-white in his thinking. There are not many gray areas in his teaching because he tends to state things in unqualified and antithetical language. He tells us that we are either walking in the light or dwelling in darkness. If we are born of God, we do not sin—indeed, we cannot sin. We are either "of God" or "of the world" (1 John 4:4–5). If we love, we are born of God; and if we don't love, we are not born of God. John says all these things without qualification and without any softening of the hard lines.

We are to practice hospitality. Christians should not only meet the needs of believers and unbelievers whom they encounter but also look for opportunities to help those they do not know. This is the scriptural definition of hospitality. As Hebrews 13:2 instructs, "Do not forget to entertain strangers, for by so doing some have unwittingly entertained angels." We should view any opportunity to demonstrate hospitality as a privilege, not a drudging duty. Gaius undoubtedly had that sort of attitude in his hospitality toward itinerant teachers, because he received John's commendation (see 3 John 1:5).

Jesus protects us from evil. Jude warns against false prophets. He wrote his letter about apostasy—a departure from the faith. But in the midst of that apostasy, there was a group of true believers. They saw false teaching and corruption coming into the church, and also the values of society going down the drain. Undoubtedly, they were apprehensive about being swept away by all that wickedness. But Jude wrote there was no reason for them to fear, because true believers are "called, sanctified by God the Father, and preserved in Jesus Christ" (1:1). The Greek term stresses a watchful care to guard something as cherished as a priceless treasure. What was Jude saying? That Christ guards us from all evil.

STUDY QUESTIONS

1. In 1 John 1:1–4, the apostle reveals his overall purpose for writing this epistle. What was that purpose? How does John describe his experience with Christ?

2. What is John's strong warning to his readers when it comes to loving the world (see 1 John 2:15–17)? What are the consequences of dismissing this command?

3. What does John mean when he urges his readers to "test the spirits"? What is the first test of a true teacher of God (see 1 John 4:1–6)?

4. How does John describe the Holy Spirit in 1 John 5:6–12? What three witnesses does John cite as being in agreement about the Son of God?

5. What positive counsel about Christian relationships does John offer in 2 John 1:1–13? How does John emphasize the importance of truth?

6. For what specific actions and traits does John commend Gaius? What does John say in this epistle about "missionaries" (see 3 John 1:1–12)?

7. On what figures and events from biblical history does Jude base his warnings? How does he describe the false teachers in the church (see Jude 1:5–15)?

8. What aspects of our relationship with God through Christ are lifted up in the doxology of Jude 1:24–25? What is Christ able to do for us?

WEEK 51

BELIEVERS LOOK TO JESUS' RETURN

REVELATION 1–11

READING PLAN:	**351** | Revelation 1	**352** | Revelation 2	**353** | Revelation 3
354 | Revelation 4–5	**355** | Revelation 6–7	**356** | Revelation 8–9	**357** | Revelation 10–11

By the time John penned the book of Revelation, he was an old man living in exile for his faithful preaching of the gospel. When John was arrested, he was ministering in Ephesus and the surrounding cities. The Roman authorities banished him to the small, barren island of Patmos. From this remote location in the Aegean Sea southwest of Ephesus, John wrote to strengthen the congregations that he could no longer minister to in person.

John records the details of a set of visions he was given unveiling the future of the world. He describes key people and events to come, including the political setup of the end times, the last battle of human history (Armageddon), the career and defeat of the Antichrist, the events surrounding the second coming of Christ, Jesus' thousand-year earthly kingdom (called the Millennium), the glories of heaven, and the final state of the wicked and the righteous. Yet Revelation is primarily "the Revelation of Jesus Christ" (1:1) in His glory.

John's opening vision of Christ reveals Him to be the glorified Lord of the church. For persecuted believers at the end of the first century, this reminder of Christ's present ministry surely provided great hope and comfort. The congregations to whom John had ministered were beginning to feel the effects of persecution. At least one man—probably a pastor—had already been martyred, and John himself had been exiled. But the storm of persecution was about to break into full fury on these churches that were so near to the apostle's heart.

The seven churches John mentions in Revelation 2–3 are not metaphorical; they were existing churches in the Roman province of Asia Minor (modern-day Turkey). Jesus rebuked five of the seven for tolerating sin, ranging in severity from waning love at Ephesus to apostasy at Laodicea. Two of the churches, Smyrna and Philadelphia, were commended for their faithfulness and perseverance. They stand as either grim warnings or good models for all other churches.

John also had the privilege of visiting heaven. This was his second vision, and it begins with the apostle's attempt to describe the indescribable majesty of God's throne room. With flashes of lightning and peals of thunder proceeding from the throne, the cherubim and elders (representing the redeemed

of the church) sing hymns of praise to God. As they celebrate Him as the Creator and Redeemer, God the Father gives Christ a scroll—the title deed to the universe—sealed with seven seals.

Jesus sequentially breaks the seven seals, with each seal unleashing a demonstration of God's judgment on the earth during the seven years to come. This "Great Tribulation" period fulfills Daniel's prophecies, and as John the apostle foretells, it will be a time of evil from false christs and false prophets, with natural disasters occurring across the globe.

John reveals the world is headed toward a cataclysmic final battle called Armageddon. Up until that climactic holocaust, wars on earth will increase, crime will escalate, there will be economic upheavals, and the world will experience unprecedented natural calamities that mark the outpouring of God's wrath. The second half of the Great Tribulation will feature the Day of the Lord, in which God unleashes vengeance on the earth in intensifying waves. Though it is a time of unparalleled judgment for the sinfulness of mankind, it will also be a time of unparalleled grace in salvation.

The first four seals unleash riders on different colored horses that represent the false peace (white), war (red), famine (black), and death (pale) that will fall on the earth. The fifth seal describes the force of the saints' prayers for God's vengeance. The opening of the sixth seal marks the beginning of the Day of the Lord. So terrifying will these judgments be that people will be forced to finally acknowledge God as the source of the calamities that have come to the earth. The Day of the Lord will be one of wrath and holy vengeance—of distress, devastation, desolation, darkness, and doom. It involves a complete renovation of the universe and the earth by judgment and restoration in two parts that are 1,000 years apart: the end of the seven-year Tribulation period and the end of the Millennium.

When the Lamb opens the seventh and final seal, the judgments of the Day of the Lord will worsen and expand. This final seal contains the trumpet and bowl judgments. In Revelation, trumpets primarily announce impending judgment. The first four trumpets signal the divine destruction of earth's ecology, while the final three involve demonic devastation of earth's inhabitants.

After the judgment of the sixth trumpet comes an interlude, during which time God comforts His people with the assurance that they will ultimately be victorious. Two witnesses then appear (several biblical observations suggest they might be Moses and Elijah) who are granted power and authority by God to preach a message of judgment and salvation during the second half of the Tribulation. These two prophets will represent the culmination of God's testimony to Israel: a two-pronged message of His judgment and His gracious offer of the gospel to all who will repent and believe.

The sounding of the seventh trumpet marks the end of this interlude. It will unleash the seven bowl judgments and herald the imminent return of Christ, which will usher in the long-anticipated day when all the purposes of God concerning humankind and the world will be consummated. The wicked will be punished, the righteous will be glorified, and sin's dominion will be broken.

The message of the seventh trumpet is that Jesus—King of kings and Lord of lords—is about to take the rule of the earth away from the usurper, Satan, and from earth's petty human rulers. As John relates, "Then the temple of God was opened in heaven, and the ark of His covenant was seen in His temple. And there were lightnings, noises, thunderings, an earthquake, and great hail" (Revelation 11:19).

REFLECTIONS

Be ready for the King's return. Jesus came the first time in humiliation; He will return in exaltation. He came the first time to die; He will return to judge His enemies. He came the first time to serve; He will return to be served. He came the first time as the suffering servant; He will return as the conquering king. The challenge the book of Revelation makes to every person is to be ready for His return.

Worldliness is a serious sin. For many in today's church, the term *worldliness* has an old-fashioned ring to it. They associate it with prohibitions against things like dancing, going to the movies, or playing cards. Today's user-friendly, seeker-oriented, market-driven church doesn't preach much against worldliness. To do so might make unbelievers (not to mention many believers) uncomfortable, and is therefore avoided as poor marketing strategy. But unlike much of the contemporary church, the Bible does not hesitate to condemn worldliness for the serious sin that it is. Worldliness is any preoccupation with or interest in the temporal system of life that places anything perishable before that which is eternal.

God will take back what is rightfully His. The events in Revelation 4–5 anticipate the divine judgment that will be poured out on the sinful, rebellious, cursed earth in Revelation 6–19. Awestruck by the indescribable majesty of God's throne, and the flashes of lightning and peals of thunder that proceed from it, the cherubim and elders begin a series of hymns of praise to God. These hymns celebrate God as Creator and Redeemer, rejoicing that He is about to take back what is rightfully His. This is the moment that all Christians—and the entire creation (see Romans 8:22)—long to see realized.

God will enact judgment. While the Bible reveals that God is loving, merciful, and gracious—the Savior of sinners—one other truth it reveals about Him, which is decidedly unpopular today, is that He is a God of vengeance against those who reject both Him and salvation in His Son. God's vengeance is not to be equated with petty human vindictiveness and bitter desire for revenge. Rather, God's holiness, righteousness, and justice demand that He take vengeance on unrepentant sinners. Vengeance belongs to God alone because all sin is ultimately against Him and an offense to Him.

The Day of the Lord is coming. There is a sense in culture today in which the present age is deemed to belong to humans; they are free to do whatever they want within certain limitations. In reality, it is *Satan's* day, during which the "god of this age" (2 Corinthians 4:4) has been granted certain liberties within the parameters of God's sovereign tolerance. However, the Lord will not permit the present state of affairs to continue forever. He will end "humanity's day," overthrow Satan, destroy the present evil world system, and establish the earthly kingdom of the Lord Jesus Christ. This future time of judgment is known, appropriately, as the Day of the Lord. It is a day that involves a complete renovation of the universe and the earth by judgment and restoration. The prophet Joel wrote of this time, "Alas for the day! For the day of the LORD is at hand; it shall come as destruction from the Almighty" (Joel 1:15).

THE TRIBULATION (REVELATION 6-19)

Jesus said to the church in Philadelphia, "Because you have kept My command to persevere, I also will keep you from the hour of trial which shall come upon the whole world, to test those who dwell on the earth" (Revelation 3:10).

Christ's mention of the "hour of trial"—an event still future that for a time severely tests the world—must refer to the Tribulation. This seven-year period occurs before Jesus' earthly kingdom is consummated (the Millennium) and features the unleashing of divine wrath in a series of judgments expressed as seals, trumpets, and bowls.

The seven seals include: (1) the Antichrist's reign [6:1-2], (2) human conflict on earth [6:3-4], (3) famine [6:5-6], (4) death [6:7-8], (5) persecution [6:9-11], (6) mega-natural disasters [6:12-17], and (7) unleashing the seven trumpets [8:1-5].

The seven trumpets include: (1) fires [8:7], (2) pollution of the seas [8:8-9], (3) contamination of fresh water [8:10-11], (4) celestial disruption [8:12-13], (5) demonic invasion [9:1-12], (6) demonic war [9:13-21], and (7) unleashing the seven bowls [11:15-19].

The seven bowls include: (1) incurable skin sores [16:2], (2) death of all sea creatures [16:3], (3) fresh water turning to blood [16:4-7], (4) humans scorched with great heat [16:8-9], (5) worldwide darkness [16:10-11], (6) anticipation of Armageddon [16:12-16], and (7) the Day of the Lord [16:17-21].

The two witnesses serve a purpose. Fulfilling the Old Testament requirement of two or more witnesses to confirm testimony (see Deuteronomy 19:15), the two prophets of Revelation 11:1–14 represent the culmination of God's testimony to Israel: a two-pronged message of His judgment and gracious offer of the gospel to all who repent and believe. While it is impossible to know the identity of these witnesses, several observations suggest they might be Moses and Elijah. First, like Moses, they strike the earth with plagues, and like Elijah, they have the power to keep it from raining. Second, both Moses and Elijah were present at the Transfiguration, the preview of Jesus' return to this world. Third, both Moses and Elijah used supernatural means to provoke repentance. Fourth, Elijah was taken up alive into heaven, and God buried Moses' body where it would never be found. Finally, fifth, the length of the drought that the two witnesses bring (three-and-one-half years) is the same as that brought by Elijah.

We are to warn the world. John, being an exile on Patmos, had no opportunity to preach to all nations. However, he could still record these prophecies to warn sinners that, while judgment is presently restrained, a day is coming when the seventh angel will sound his trumpet and sin's dominion will be broken. In that day the freedom of Satan and his demons will end, godless men will be judged, and believers will be glorified. Revelation 10–11 presents a brief interlude of hope tinged with bitterness that reminds true followers of Jesus of their evangelistic responsibilities to warn the world of that day.

STUDY QUESTIONS

1. Consider the amazing appearance of the Son of Man in John's first vision (see Revelation 1:13–18). What do these images convey about Christ?

2. Note the varied descriptions that Jesus gives about Himself in Revelation 2:1, 8, 12, 18. What do these descriptions reveal about Christ?

3. According to Revelation 3:1–22, what was true about the church at Philadelphia? What is the significance of the crown mentioned in verse 11?

4. What is the identity and significance of the Lamb in Revelation 5:1–7 whom John saw standing? Why was the Lamb worthy to take the scroll?

5. Who does John see worshiping in heaven together (see Revelation 7:9–17)? According to the elder in John's vision, what is the identity of these individuals?

6. Some have described the result of the sounding of the fifth trumpet in Revelation 9:1–12 as "hell on earth." What will happen when this event unfolds?

7. In Revelation 10:1–7, John sees an angel come down from heaven. What happens next? What did the angel do and what was John commanded to do?

8. What power is given to the two witnesses in John's vision? What happens to them when they finish their testimony (see Revelation 11:1–14)?

WEEK 52

BELIEVERS OBTAIN AN ETERNAL REWARD

REVELATION 12–22

358 | Revelation 12
359 | Revelation 13
360 | Revelation 14
361 | Revelation 15–16
362 | Revelation 17–18
363 | Revelation 19
364 | Revelation 20
365 | Revelation 21–22

In God's story of redemption, Satan and his demonic hosts have attacked the human race, turning the earth into the battleground in their war against God, His angels, and the elect. In the future, Satan will launch another deadly assault against humanity. This attack will take place during the Great Tribulation. He and his forces will unsuccessfully battle Michael and the heavenly host (that is, the holy angels of God). As a result of their defeat, the devil and his demons will be permanently cast down to the earth. With his theater of operations restricted and his time running out, Satan will then marshal all of his fallen angels in an all-out attempt to deceive and destroy the souls of humankind.

This is what comes next in John's vision. Revelation 12–13 is actually a digression, taking the reader back through the Tribulation from Satan's perspective. We discover there are three terrible enemies to come: Satan (the dragon), the Antichrist (the first beast), and the false prophet (the second beast). The beasts represent the final Antichrist, whose career spans the same time period as the seal and trumpet judgments. As his title indicates, the

Antichrist will set himself up against Christ and the people of God. Paul called him the "lawless one" (2 Thessalonians 2:8). This man is not Satan, though Satan is the force behind him.

The Antichrist (the first beast) will be primarily a political and military leader, but the false prophet (second beast) will be a religious leader. In the last days before the second coming of Christ, the false prophet will exalt himself, declaring himself to be God and demanding the world's worship. Politics and religion will unite in a worldwide religion.

John's divine vision next previews the end of the Great Tribulation. He is shown the triumph and vindication of the 144,000 faithful Israelites redeemed by the blood of the Lamb, the destruction of the Satanic world system, and a summary view of the battle of Armageddon, the great and terrible "winepress of the wrath of God" (Revelation 14:19).

The apostle John glimpses the Tribulation saints who have overcome the beast. They are singing songs of praise like one gigantic choir, rejoicing over the accomplishment of God's entire redemptive work prior to Christ's return. John also introduces the seven angels tasked with pouring out the seven bowls of wrath—God's final Tribulation-period judgments.

The bowl judgments are described in rapid-fire fashion, each one stronger in fury and intensity than the last. Collectively, they depict the fall of the worldwide political, economic, and religious kingdom of the Antichrist and his loyalists. These golden bowls, which John's readers would have associated with functions of temple worship, are shallow. Their flatness pictures how the judgments will be emptied instantly rather than slowly poured, drowning those who refuse to drink the cup of salvation.

Revelation reminds us that in the cosmic battle going on now and continuing into the future, no one can be neutral. Every human being is either part of the domain of darkness or part of the kingdom of God. In the last days, God will still offer people the life-giving gospel of the Lord Jesus Christ. However, a day is coming when the siren call of hell will be so loud as to be all but irresistible.

John pictures the kingdom of the Antichrist, symbolically called Babylon (named after the original birthplace of idolatry), intoxicating the world and drawing it into an orgy of rebellion, hatred, and idolatry. People will ignore the preaching of the gospel and the warnings conveyed by God's judgments and will stubbornly cling to their sin. At their rejection of all God's offers of grace and mercy, death will come upon humankind on an unprecedented scale. But even then, people will not repent. In fact, they will make the irrevocable choice to side with the forces of hell and curse God.

As the destiny of this satanic kingdom unfolds and the beast's worldwide systems are destroyed, we are shown how the world will end: with the Battle of Armageddon and Christ's second coming—events that mark the close of the Tribulation. Then we see the binding of Satan, Christ's 1,000-year reign over the earth (the Millennium), Satan's final rebellion, and the Great White Throne Judgment.

When the smoke clears following God's final punishment of the wicked, the earth as we know it will be no more. John records the revelation of the city of God and the beginning of the eternal state. Clearly, paradise lost in the garden of Eden will be paradise regained! Satan, the beast, and false prophet will be thrown into the lake of fire. God will create a new universe, a new heaven and a new earth, to be the eternal dwelling place of the redeemed. Christ the Bridegroom will marry His bride, the church, in the final ceremony of redemptive history. The citizens of heaven—Old Testament saints, Tribulation saints, and all those converted during the millennial kingdom—will dwell in its capital city, the New Jerusalem. It will be a place of perfect holiness marked by the awesome glory and presence of God.

The book of Revelation begins with the words of Jesus to the seven churches. It concludes with the penetrating words of Christ, the Alpha and Omega, the Morning Star. The Lord of life and King of eternity is coming soon! May our earnest and sincere prayer be the same as that of John: "Amen. Even so, come, Lord Jesus!" (Revelation 22:20).

REFLECTIONS

Jesus is the sovereign King. The message of Revelation is that Jesus is the sovereign King of kings and Lord of lords. History is moving toward its culmination in His earthly reign. When He returns, He will bring covenant blessings to the redeemed and eternal judgment to those who reject Him. In the light of that sobering truth, Peter exclaims, "What manner of persons ought you to be in holy conduct and godliness, looking for and hastening the coming of the day of God?" (2 Peter 3:11–12).

Some will love the darkness rather than the light. The scene depicted in Revelation 17–18 reveals that in spite of God's terrifying judgments, many will still refuse to believe. It seems incredible that, having experienced the fury of God's judgment and having heard the message of salvation, these people will cling to their sin. But the sad truth is that "the light has come into the world, and men loved darkness rather than light" (John 3:19). The unbelieving world rejected Jesus when He came, it rejects the life-giving message of the gospel now, and it will continue to reject the truth during the future outpouring of God's wrath and judgment. Having gone on sinning willfully after receiving the knowledge of the truth, these people have nothing to look forward to except a terrifying expectation of judgment (see Hebrews 10:26–27).

> The LIGHT shines in the darkness, and the darkness did not COMPREHEND it.
>
> JOHN 1:5

God wants us to know that He wins. The book of Revelation reveals the end of human history, including the final political setup of the world, the career of the Antichrist, and the climactic Battle of Armageddon. It reveals the coming glory of Jesus' earthly reign during the millennial kingdom, describes the Great White Throne Judgment, and depicts the eternal bliss of the new heaven and the new earth. It reveals the ultimate victory of Jesus Christ over all human and demonic opposition. The book of Revelation also describes the ultimate defeat of Satan and sin, the final state of the wicked (eternal torment in hell), and the final state of the righteous (eternal joy in heaven). In short, the book of Revelation is the front-page story of the future of the world written by someone who has seen it all. "He who testifies to these things says, 'Surely I am coming quickly'" (22:20).

STUDY QUESTIONS

1. The main characters described by John in Revelation 12:1–17 are a woman, a male child, and a dragon. Who or what is signified by each of these characters?

2. What is the "image" made by the beast? Why is the mark of the beast significant during the end times (see Revelation 13:14–16)?

3. The bowl judgments form the content of Revelation 16. What is the nature of each of these catastrophes? What was the response of the inhabitants on earth following them?

4. How are the 144,000 described in Revelation 14:1–13? What are they doing? John saw several different angels in this vision. What were they each doing?

5. The scene in Revelation 17 opens with the image of a harlot. What is spiritual adultery? What title did John see written on the harlot's forehead—and what does it mean?

6. How do the kings and merchants respond when they hear the news of Babylon's destruction in Revelation 18:9–20? In what did they have their security?

7. What does John state in Revelation 20:1–3 will be the judgment of Satan? What will be the reward of the faithful witnesses during the millennial kingdom (see verses 4–6)?

8. What similarities do you see between the garden of Eden and the new city of God in Revelation 22? What consequences of the Fall will be reversed in God's new kingdom?

ABOUT THE AUTHOR

John MacArthur is the pastor-teacher of Grace Community Church in Sun Valley, California, as well as an author, conference speaker, chancellor of The Master's University and Seminary, and featured teacher with the Grace to You media ministry. After graduating from Talbot Theological Seminary, John came to Grace Community Church in 1969. Today, several thousand members participate every week at Grace Community Church in dozens of fellowship groups and training programs, most led by lay leaders and each dedicated to equipping members for ministry on local, national, and international levels.

In 1985, John became president of The Master's College (formerly Los Angeles Baptist College; since 2016, The Master's University). Located in Santa Clarita, California, it is a distinctly Christian, accredited, liberal arts institution offering undergraduate and graduate degree programs. In 1986, John founded The Master's Seminary, a graduate school dedicated to training men for full-time pastoral and missionary work.

John is also chairman and featured teacher with Grace to You. Founded in 1969, Grace to You is the nonprofit organization responsible for developing, producing, and distributing John's books, audio resources, and the *Grace to You* radio and television programs. *Grace to You* radio airs more than 1,000 times daily throughout the English-speaking world, reaching population centers with biblical truth. It also airs over 1,000 times a day in Spanish, reaching twenty-seven countries across Europe and Latin America.

John has written hundreds of study guides and books, including *The Gospel According to Jesus, Our Sufficiency in Christ, Strange Fire, Ashamed of the Gospel, The Murder of Jesus, The Prodigal Son, Twelve Ordinary Men, Twelve Extraordinary Women, The Truth War, The Jesus You Can't Ignore, Slave, One Perfect Life, The Gospel According to Paul, Parables*, and *One Faithful Life*. John's books have been translated into more than two dozen languages. *The MacArthur Study Bible*, the cornerstone resource of his ministry, is available in English (NKJV, NASB, and ESV), Spanish, Russian, German, French, Portuguese, Italian, Arabic, and Chinese.

John and his wife, Patricia, live in Southern California and have four married children: Matt, Marcy, Mark, and Melinda. They also enjoy the enthusiastic company of their fifteen grandchildren.

JOHN MACARTHUR
MATTHEW
THE COMING OF THE KING
MACARTHUR BIBLE STUDY SERIES
OVER 2 MILLION SOLD

JOHN MACARTHUR
JOHN
JESUS—THE WORD, THE MESSIAH, THE SON OF GOD
MACARTHUR BIBLE STUDY SERIES
OVER 2 MILLION SOLD

JOHN MACARTHUR
ACTS
THE SPREAD OF THE GOSPEL
MACARTHUR BIBLE STUDY SERIES
OVER 2 MILLION SOLD

JOHN MACARTHUR
ROMANS
GRACE, TRUTH, AND REDEMPTION
MACARTHUR BIBLE STUDY SERIES
OVER 2 MILLION SOLD

JOHN MACARTHUR
PHILIPPIANS
CHRIST, THE SOURCE OF JOY AND STRENGTH
MACARTHUR BIBLE STUDY SERIES
OVER 2 MILLION SOLD

JOHN MACARTHUR
1 & 2 TIMOTHY
ENCOURAGEMENT FOR CHURCH LEADERS
MACARTHUR BIBLE STUDY SERIES
OVER 2 MILLION SOLD

JOHN MACARTHUR
HEBREWS
CHRIST—PERFECT SACRIFICE, PERFECT PRIEST
MACARTHUR BIBLE STUDY SERIES
OVER 2 MILLION SOLD

JOHN MACARTHUR
JAMES
GUIDELINES FOR A HAPPY CHRISTIAN LIFE
MACARTHUR BIBLE STUDY SERIES
OVER 2 MILLION SOLD

JOHN MACARTHUR
REVELATION
THE CHRISTIAN'S ULTIMATE VICTORY
MACARTHUR BIBLE STUDY SERIES
OVER 2 MILLION SOLD